PAWS

TO

PROTECT

ALSO BY THE AUTHOR

Alyson Books:
Paws & Effect: The Healing Power of Dogs
Paws and Reflect: The Special Bond Between Man and Dog

Barron's Educational:
Brussels Griffons: A Complete Owners Manual

PAWS

TO

PROTECT

DOGS SAVING LIVES
and RESTORING HOPE

SHARON SAKSON

FOREWORD BY KEN FOSTER, AUTHOR OF
The Dogs Who Found Me AND *Dogs I Have Met*

alyson books
NEW YORK

MANUFACTURED IN THE UNITED STATES OF AMERICA

Published by:
ALYSON BOOKS
245 WEST 17TH STREET
NEW YORK, NY 10011

Distribution in the United Kingdom by:
TURNAROUND PUBLISHER SERVICES LTD.
UNIT 3, OLYMPIA TRADING ESTATE
COBURG ROAD, WOOD GREEN
LONDON N22 6TZ ENGLAND

First Edition: DECEMBER 2008

08 09 10 11 12 13 14 15 16 17 [a] 10 9 8 7 6 5 4 3 2 1

ISBN-10: 1-59350-094-7
ISBN-13: 978-1-59350-094-8

LIBRARY OF CONGRESS CATALOGING-IN-PUBLICATION DATA ARE ON FILE.

COVER DESIGN BY VICTOR MINGOVITS
BOOK DESIGN BY VICTOR MINGOVITS

THESE PAGES ARE DEDICATED TO ALL MILITARY, POLICE, AND SEARCH AND
RESCUE DOGS AND THEIR HANDLERS, PAST, PRESENT, AND FUTURE. YOUR
DEEDS AND SACRIFICES ARE BRAVE AND HONORABLE AND WILL ALWAYS
BE REMEMBERED BY DOG LOVERS LIKE ME.

CONTENTS

FOREWORD
On Dog Heroes and the Meaning
of Being "Rescued"

BY KEN FOSTER

THE WORD "RESCUE" pops up frequently around dogs. After I adopted Brando—my crazy, enormous, brindle soul mate—from BARC (Brooklyn Animal Resource Coalition) in New York City, people on the street asked if I had rescued him. "I got him from a shelter," I explained, somewhat haltingly, unsure if this is what they meant. Eight months later, he was with me in the park on 9/11 when one of the planes flew overhead. On the news, we watched the search and rescue dogs as they did their work through the rubble of the towers. There were so few survivors, they began hiding live bodies for the dogs to "save," in order to give the dogs hope.

I remember one officer being interviewed just after the incident; he had responded to the scene with his K-9 partner who was killed when the buildings came down. He blamed himself, because he had left the bomb-sniffing Labrador Retriever, Sirius, in his basement office when he went to see what happened. Sirius was the only K-9 to die on 9/11. Prior to what many of us still refer to as "the incident," the dog owners of my East Village neighborhood had been planning an emergency fundraiser to complete repairs to the dog run in Tompkins Square. I suggested we give the money to NASAR, the National Association of Search and Rescue Dogs, and everyone agreed. A few weeks later, as the crowd gathered in a small club on Avenue B and waited for raffle prizes to be drawn, we were surprised by a group of guests on a break from Ground Zero: several officers with two exhausted dogs. While music blared and appetizers were passed around the room, these two dogs slept soundly for an hour while the guests stared at them, in awe of all the work they had done.

Occasionally, I hear from people who are a bit confused about the fact that animals and people coexist in the same world. For these folks, any sacrifice made for a dog is a misappropriation of resources that would be better spent on a person—as though it wouldn't be possible to do both. It is this same kind of person who sometimes doubts some of the stories I tell about my own dogs. These people might enjoy the episode in which my Rottweiler, Zephyr, sits on my chest to wake me after half my heart has stopped pumping, and they are intrigued when I claim that she pressed her ear to my chest to check the beat when I returned from the hospital with a pacemaker installed. But they don't actually believe it could be true. They can think what they like—Zephyr and I know the truth.

Sula, the youngest dog in my house, is also the one true rescue. An American Pit Bull Terrier, Sula was running loose on the street, her eye ripped open, and no shelter would take her in because of her breed. These animal people obviously didn't know the story of Sergeant Stubby, the decorated war hero whose honors included a Purple Heart. Stubby was a pit bull too, and it was quite a thrill to see him included with all of the other heroes in this book.

When I visit inner-city schools, where kids' associations with dogs are frequently negative, stories like these are essential. You can imagine the conversations we have about Stubby, and their surprise to learn that pit bull heroes aren't limited to legends from the past, they exist today too. Diane Jessup runs a program in Washington State (www.lawdogsusa.org) that trains pit bulls for work in law enforcement, applying their intelligence and tenacity to search for drugs, explosives, cadavers, and more. Many of these dogs come from dogfighting busts or from areas in which the breed has been banned due to misguided stereotypes.

—

WE LIVE WITH OUR DOGS in a world that seems increasingly two-dimensional, with expectations for ourselves and our dogs reduced to the level of cartoons. This is where the work of real heroes comes in: they teach us, again, that there is a value in selflessness, loyalty, and community. If these dogs have unlimited heroic potential, just imagine what we can do, too.

ACKNOWLEDGMENTS

MANY THANKS to those who were generous with their time as I researched this book: Kathleen Golden, Associate Curator of the National Museum of American History; U.S. Border Patrol, Brent Barber in San Diego and Bonnie Myers in Washington, DC; Lisa Wright, aide to Congressman Roscoe Bartlett (R-Maryland); Dawn Fones, director of the State Farm Arson Dog Program; Steven Gallagher, Assistant Fire Chief, Chillicothe, Ohio; Lt. John Kerwick of the Metropolitan Transit Authority of New York City; Sgt. Craig Bunting of the Mercer County, New Jersey, Sheriff's Office; World War II veteran William Wynne; Vietnam War veterans and Military War Dog handlers Ron Aiello and Greg Dunlap; and Military Working Dog handlers Staff Sgt. Jerrod Gaertner and Staff Sgt. Robert Black.

From the Department of Agriculture, Janet Rapaport in New York; Lisa Beckett, trainer in Orlando; Sherrie Keblish, of the Beagle Brigade in Miami; and Rick Engeman, National Wildlife Research Center in Fort Collins, Colorado; Denise Grimm and Donna Hreniuk, Laura LoPresti, Jennifer Michelson and Gylla MacGregor of the New Jersey Rescue and Recovery K-9 Unit.

And my friends and assistants Gini Sikes, Patti Fitzgerald, and Shannon Talley.

INTRODUCTION

DOGS HAVE NEVER BEEN so widely used to protect human society as they are today. They work in immigration, customs, fire departments, and even for the Internal Revenue Service. They are bomb sniffers, guardians, sentries, and arson detectors. They track live people and uncover dead bodies. At border crossings and airports, they sniff for drugs, bombs, and contraband. They act as scouts, trackers, messengers, minefield clearers, booby trap locators, tunnelers, water patrol, lifeguards, Search and Rescue, and explosive detectors. The President of the United States does not go anywhere until the Secret Service has had dogs probe the area. They're tireless and faithful workers. They ask little in return.

Dogs have always helped humans. Thousands of years ago, when the first canines showed up at the campfires of our early ancestors, they showed they could perform amazing services. Instead of eating the game they hunted, they brought it back for their human friends. They barked a warning when warriors from a marauding tribe approached the camp. They chased hungry wolves from flocks of sheep.

They became renowned as fierce guardians. There is something about a ferocious dog that elicits an instinctive fear in humans.

That's one reason why they are so effective in capturing escaped convicts and interrogating prisoners. A guard dog is ready to bite you as soon as you break the rules and there's nothing you can do about it. You might be able to outrun or outsmart a fellow human. But a dog is working on a different level, one you don't understand.

The world we live in today might have been a very different place if it hadn't been for dogs. One legend is that Napoleon, who hated dogs because Josephine's lap dogs constantly bit him, fell into the icy water around Elba in 1815. He would have drowned except for a Newfoundland who plunged into the water and rescued him. He recovered to regain his throne in France, eventually leading his army into the suicidal battle at Waterloo.

Every land mine found by every dedicated dog is a vessel of demolition meant to destroy human lives. Many of the soldiers who slogged through Vietnam, tramped through Kosovo, and now trek through the alluvial plains of Iraq would not be here except for dogs who alerted them to trip wires and IEDs. Bomb-sniffing Military Working Dogs removed death from their path.

Police dogs are in ever-wider use. The K-9 Unit has become a popular career path as the K-9 assignment crosses many of the traditional lines that separate each department. Officers work with Robbery, Narcotics, Patrol, Transit, Crowd Control, Protection, Housing, Detectives, Domestic Disturbance, Crime Scene Investigators, School Education, and Lost Persons. They don't have to limit themselves to just one of those areas. In addition to protecting officers from harm and searching for illegal drugs, dogs find pirated CDs, stacks of cash, nitrogen, guns, and cadavers. They reassure children who are victims of abuse. They scan our luggage for bombs, keep uninspected meat and produce from entering our borders, find lost children, look under collapsed buildings for people alive and dead, and spend hours comforting the survivors of tragedy. They are rehabilitating prisoners. They are doing jobs no one ever thought to ask them about before.

At the same time, they never stop doing their basic job of providing love and support. We go to war, pollute our environment, and invent better and more efficient ways to kill each other, but our dogs stick with us, always faithful, loyal, and ready to serve.

We are entering a new era with our dogs, because our species is learning to listen. Our ancestors trained dogs to do physical tasks; hunting, carting, guarding, and herding. In this century, humans are learning how to teach dogs to use their more refined skills, such as their sense of smell, but also to use their minds. Police, military, and Search and Rescue dogs sometimes work out complex problems and pick the right solution. Dogs sniffing for bombs and explosives have to ignore myriad distractions of the environment to find the culprits. Think about that Labrador Retriever sorting through the luggage before your flight. He has to smell underwear, toothbrushes, tee-shirts, Chanel No. 5, Prell, Crabtree & Evelyn hand lotion, unwashed socks, dry-cleaned shirts, Valium, headscarves, allergy medication, museum guides, bikinis, men's cologne, sleeping bags, backpacks, hiking boots, Kaopectate, house keys, paperback and hard cover books, tennis rackets, baseball gloves, old leather purses, suntan spray, Nikes, umbrellas, full sets of golf clubs; disposable ponchos, souvenir Statues of Liberty, pashmina shawls, bottles of hot sauce and cheese cracker snacks. The list of smells is endless. And yet, if there's a bullet or gunpowder or dynamite present, he finds it. The agent apprehends the culprit and you are safe to fly another day.

The dog, for his part, is happy to do the job, partly because of his generous nature and partly because time spent with his handler is an important priority in a dog's world.

Among handlers, I found a surprisingly wide range of interests. Very few said they grew up as devoted dog lovers who were determined to spend a career with canines. They were sports fans and romantics, diehard Republicans and confirmed Democrats, former teachers, babysitters, accountants, students with a high school degree and some with Masters Degrees in Science. There were salesmen, psychologists, chaplains, engineers, chefs, waitresses, seamstress, nurses, dental assistants, veterinary technicians, insurance agents, claims specialists, ballerinas, one research chemist, a restorer of broken ceramic pottery, bookkeepers, grocery store clerks, photographers, native Americans and recent emigres, contractors, carpenters, farmers, and one pit boss. There was no end to the various professions in the backgrounds of dog handlers.

Each had seen some special magic in the idea of including a dog in their work. All of them were able to build a relationship that grew over time in familiarity and ease, in the comfortable way partners work together.

The same was true for their personalities. There was no one type of person who chose this path. There were extroverts and introverts, Leos and Pisces, individuals with a great deal of ambition and ones who were perfectly happy with their little corner of the world as it was. But there were three things they had in common. First, I found far more upbeat characters than negative ones. For that, probably some of the credit goes to the dogs, who are always happy about every minute they get to spend with you and never predict a dire outcome to the day. Second, they were always people who loved their jobs. They were willing to work long hours, travel great distances, and go to great lengths to fulfill the K-9 unit's task. They were admirable in that regard. Third, they were people who took seriously their responsibility to guard and ensure the safety of their fellow citizens. Handlers allowed the canine to become part of their life, not an unusual or outlandish part, but a harmonious individual in the person's landscape.

This book is about dogs with difficult real world jobs, jobs as policemen and customs agents and sailors and Marines. And yet through all the physical work they do, these dogs love their owners unconditionally. They provide a shoulder to lean on and company for a walk. The right dog with the right handler creates a wonderful partnership.

That's what these dogs have in common with our own dogs; they are loyal friends and companions. That's why there are an estimated 65 million pet dogs in the United States. They make up a significant part of many families, usually a steadfast, reliable, loyal part. Dogs continually demonstrate loyalty, honesty, trust, and unconditional love in a way which humans have never been able to match.

They are friends who sometimes inadvertently bring out the best in us. They continue to admire us in spite of our flaws. This book taps into the spiritual nature and intuitive sense and amazing intelligence of dogs. Maybe, as some handlers claimed, they are really earth-sent angels and therefore divine. But maybe being canine is just as good.

THE FIRMEST FRIEND: MILITARY WORKING DOGS

In life the firmest friend,
The first to welcome, foremost to defend,
Whose honest heart is still his master's own
Who labors, fights, lives, breathes for him alone.

—from "Inscription on the Monument of a Newfoundland Dog,"
Lord Byron, Newstead Abbey, October 30, 1808

DOGS HAVE BEEN our companions in war since the day one man beat another to death with a stick. Their roles constantly evolve, not because dogs' abilities change, but because with each passing war, trainers gain greater understanding of what their dogs can do. When I first started to research the use of military war dogs, I believed that the skill of the dog was largely a matter of training. The better a dog was trained, I thought, the more attentive he would be to the pungent smell of nitroglycerin, ballistite, and dynamite. The dog with the most training would be the one you would want to lead your platoon patrol, as he would be more likely to spot snipers or warn of trip bombs. But that wasn't the case. Instead, the proficiency of the dog turned out to be a direct correlation to the strength of the bond formed with the handler. Incredibly strong bonds form between war dogs and their masters as they work together in dangerous situations. These dogs are special in their training but just like everybody else's dog in their desire to please and love their handler. At the heart of the skilled bomb detecting team is the same ancient dog-human relationship experienced by all of us who own dogs.

We know from ancient writings and drawings that dogs have always served alongside man, protecting him and joining him in battle. In some of these stories, dogs have been injured. Some have given what Abraham Lincoln called, "The last full measure of devotion." They died on the battlefield while protecting their masters:

The greatest of early warriors, Alexander the Great, in 350 B.C., had a large Greyhound named Peritas.[1] Ptolemy wrote that when Alexander faced Darius of Persia on the plains at Guagamela, Darius was believed to have the upper hand because of his much-feared weapons of mass destruction, fifteen war elephants. But when one of these beasts charged Alexander, Peritas leapt forward to protect his master and bit the elephant's lip, hanging on and causing the animal so much pain that it retreated. Alexander the Great lived to go on to other battles, eventually conquering all of the known world. Peritas did not. He was trampled beneath the elephant's feet.

Alexander led a royal funeral procession through the streets and erected a monument in the dog's honor. He named a city after him, and ordered residents to hold a celebration in Peritas' memory every year.

---

[1] His breed is a matter of dispute. Greyhounds were documented as the primary breed in the Middle East at that time. Other historians make this dog a Molosser, a mastiff-type dog found in Asia. The breed hailed from Tibet and had recently been carried out from that country by traders and warriors.

Attila the Hun used giant Molossers and Talbot Hounds, ancestors of the bloodhound, in his successful campaign to consolidate power in the fifth century throughout Europe and Asia. Sketches from the Middle Ages show dogs dressed in coats of mail fighting alongside their knights. Prior to the invention of gunpowder, a strong, aggressive dog who could attack the enemy would have been extremely valuable.

When Columbus sailed to the New World, his ships' manifests show that he took with him two hundred foot soldiers, twenty cavalrymen, and twenty dogs.

The man regarded as the father of the United States, General George Washington, was well known for his love of dogs. While he did not have working military dogs in his troops, he is famous for an incident after the Battle of Germantown, when he discovered a stray Fox Terrier wearing a beautiful, inscribed collar. The inscriptions identified him as the property of British General William Howe, Washington's adversary who had just defeated him in this battle. Washington was a well-bred gentleman of his era. He did the proper thing: he returned the dog, with a polite note.[2]

Benjamin Franklin was a brilliant politician and scientist and also a dog lover. He saw the possibility of using dogs in the military, and recommended in 1755 that dogs should be trained to work as sentries and attack dogs. He predicted that dogs could be used to help soldiers by detecting Indians. But no one else was interested in the idea. It was not put into practice.

As Americans traveled widely throughout the world, and participated in other countries' battles, they came to know that many dogs were being utilized by foreign armies, just not by Americans. In the Napoleonic Wars of the early nineteenth century, one former soldier wrote about the dogs of a Prussian Jaeger

---

[2] After the war, Washington had an extensive breeding program at Mount Vernon. He developed the first American breed, the American Foxhound.

regiment. "In finding the missing and wounded with which the millet field were strewn, nothing even approached our pack of seven English dogs. In our last engagement, fifty-three men were found more or less badly wounded in utterly unsuspected places, where the stretcher bearers and the surgeons would never have even dreamed of looking." He wrote, "The performance of the ambulance dogs was beyond all expectation."

The first official use of hounds by the U.S. military came during the 1835 Seminole War. Dogs were taught to track Indians and runaway slaves. Having dogs track them for the white man was a huge betrayal to North American native Indians. Their culture made extensive use of dog power. Some paintings from the period show medium-sized dogs that resemble Australian Shepherds[3] pulling the Indians' sledges or following at the feet of their horses.

Stories of several dogs survive from the Civil War. They were not trained military dogs, but mascots who went to war with their owners and found ways to be useful. A black and white Bull Terrier named Jack served with the Pennsylvania 102nd Infantry. He stayed on the battlefield after fighting was over, comforting wounded soldiers, a kind of self-taught therapy dog for the troops.

The Germans established the first school for training war dogs at a town near Berlin in 1885. The first known training manual for war dogs was written there.

In 1898, during the Spanish-American War, Teddy Roosevelt's Roughriders took dogs along as scouts in the fields of Cuba.

Among the thousands of books about dogs in the Madison Avenue library of the American Kennel Club, there is an article in *Scribner's* magazine dated 1905 by Lieutenant Charles Norton Barney, Medical Dept. U.S. Army. He writes that he thinks it would be a good idea to train dogs to seek out wounded soldiers on the

---

[3] Despite the name, an entirely American breed.

battlefield. Since those that can move are likely to be hiding, a dog with his powerful nose would be a better searcher than a man. He writes that he can find no information on this in American or English literature but it seems a good idea. "There is no novelty about the use of dogs in war as messengers, sentinels, scouts, and even as combatants," Lt. Barney writes. "The prowess of the war dogs of the ancients is celebrated in fable, in history, and in sculpture. The Greek heroic poets and early historical writings relate that war dogs were used by Aeneas during the siege of Troy and by Cambyses during the Persian conquest of Egypt. Plutarch relates that Agesilaus, King of Sparta, used dogs against the Thebans at the siege of Mantinea, and that Philip of Macedonia kept a troop of large hounds to guard his camp. Ancient Roman historians state that the Cimbri and Teutons had war dogs protected by mail and spiked collars and that the Gauls used war dogs which were much feared by the Roman legionaires. Bituitus, chief of the Arverni, sent a messenger into one of the Roman camps to protest against the advance of the Romans into Gaul. A tall man with a bard beside him singing the praises of his clan, and after him, a pack of immense hounds pacing in ranks like soldiers."

But Lt. Barney's good idea was never translated into a training program.

By the early part of the twentieth century, dogs were being utilized throughout Europe for military and police work. During World War I, all combatants except Americans employed military dogs. The British taught them to be messengers by teaching the dog to love two handlers. One put reconnaissance notes in a pouch in the collar and commanded them to find their way back to their other master. The dogs always found them, no matter how far he'd been taken. Many of their notes summoned reinforcements, which often saved the lives of a small troop. The French and Belgian Armies employed dogs for messenger, ambulance, and draft work.

In Italy, during World War I, dogs delivered food to troops in hard to reach, mountainous regions. In 1915, the German Army had six thousand war dogs; they rescued more than four thousand wounded men. The Russian army employed hundreds of specially trained Scotch Collies and Airedales. A surgeon from Philadelphia, Malcolm C. Grow, was surprised to find that his Russian orderlies on the German front were lacking in many essential medical supplies, but were equipped with Airedales, who were put out on the field after the fighting to find wounded men. When the first dog returned, "In the light of my electric torch I saw that he held in his mouth a crumpled, blood-stained cap. His master took the cap in his hand, snapped the leash on the dog's collar, lifted him up on the parapet, and crawled up after him, followed by two stretcher-bearers."

Grow followed them, crawling through the icy field, and noticed that they passed several cold and lifeless bodies on the way to the wounded man.

"Do the dogs ever take you to dead bodies?" I asked the orderly.

"No, Excellency, never," he replied. "They sometimes lead us to bodies which we think have no life in them, but when we bring them back the doctors, by careful examination, always find a spark though often very feeble. It is purely a matter of instinct, which, in this instance, is far more effective than man's reasoning powers."

The Collies were a different matter altogether. They had been trained as combatants. Their job was to carry explosives that were supposed to detonate beneath the German tanks, techniques used in later years by kamikaze pilots and suicide bombers. Towards that end, the Russians trained the dogs to associate only good things with tanks. Their meals were fed to them only under the tanks, so they would run there when they were hungry. When the trainers felt the dogs were ready, they took them to the front, as close to the German tanks as they dared, and released the dogs. They were shocked when the dogs ignored the German tanks and eagerly turned around and found their way back to Russian tanks, the ones used to train them. Some Russian tanks were destroyed. The Collie experiment was ended immediately

One interesting discovery: ambulance dogs should never be used as messengers. Once they encountered a wounded man, they either stayed with him to comfort him, or returned back to their unit to summon help, and forgot all about delivering the message. The Europeans noted they were unsuccessful in retraining medic dogs to ignore the wounded. They never forgot their original training.

From 1914 to 1918, during all the Great War battles, one historical estimate claims that more than seven thousand military working dogs were killed in action.

In the spring of 1918, U.S. captains and lieutenants who were observing the work of European war dogs on the battlefield recommended that the Americans procure five hundred dogs from French training centers to work as sentries, messengers, and to accompany troops on special missions. From what is now known about the use of military working dogs, these dogs would have proved highly effective protectors and motivators for the troops. However, the project was disliked back in Washington, so the matter was dropped. It makes me want to leap back in time and shake the shoulders of those Department of Defense officials and ask them, "What were you thinking?" The contribution of dogs has proven so valuable it's hard to imagine refusing such a simple, effective, and inexpensive tool to your troops.

But there were no American war dogs back then. Unless you consider the case of Stubby.

STUBBY, THE MOST DECORATED CANINE WAR HERO

IN THE ENTRANCE to the Carroll Administration building at Georgetown University, someone hung an elegantly framed old photograph of a heavyset, brindle and white dog, whose breed, to my eyes, was American Staffordshire Terrier. That's the American Kennel Club's official moniker for the breed. In the United Kennel Club's registry, they call this breed the American Pit Bull Terrier.

At any rate, he looked like a friendly dog. He was alert and curious, and seemed proud to display a big, official medal on a ribbon around his neck. The inscription announced that this dog was Georgetown's football team's[1] mascot from 1920 to 1922. Since my interest in dogs at that time did not extend to the bull breeds, I always dashed past on my way to class.

If I'd known then that this was Stubby, the Most Decorated Canine War Hero in United States history, I'd like to think I would have taken time to learn about him, or at least saluted as I hurried by. His contribution to the welfare of American soldiers was in many ways unique. Back in 1918, the United States had

---

[1] The team name is the Hoyas. The current mascot is a white Bulldog.

no war dog program, and no plans to implement one, despite constant recommendations from both dog handlers and soldiers. Those who had fought overseas had seen firsthand the utility of the Europeans' war dogs and wanted that extra protection for U.S. soldiers. But the officers at the top of the command chain disparaged the idea. The Quartermaster General's Office of the Army already had plenty of animals under their control. Horses and mules were declining in use, but were still needed to pull tanks and ambulances out of the mud. They had enough to do.

Stubby was a stray who turned up one day in the summer of 1917 at the Yale Bowl in Connecticut. The young soldiers of the 102nd Infantry, part of the Army's 26th Yankee Division, were drilling on the field, and during their rest break, several tossed crackers to Stubby as he made his way down the line. Corporal J. Robert Conroy patted the friendly dog and asked, "How are you today?"

Stubby decided he'd made a friend. He showed up the next day, and the next, and pretty soon every day the new soldiers drilled. He took to following Conroy back to his dorm, and Conroy repaid the friendship by letting him sleep under his bed and feeding him from the college dining room.

Stubby was very intelligent, so Conroy taught him to shake hands, a trick that was in great favor with the troops. Then he realized he could teach him to raise his paw up just a little farther towards his brow when he was given the order to, "Salute!" Stubby learned it quickly. From then on, whenever he saw Conroy salute, he saluted, too. The men thought it was hilarious. They made poor Stubby do it over and over, which he did, without complaint.

When the Yankee Division traveled to Newport News, Conroy hid Stubby in with the equipment on the railroad car. The night before they sailed for France, Conroy went down to the ship, the U.S.S. Minnesota, and introduced Stubby to the military police officer who was guarding it. According to Conroy, the officer was charmed by Stubby's military salute, enough to let Conroy sneak him on board the next day, under his overcoat. He stashed Stubby in the coal bin until the ship was two days out at sea, and then brought him up on deck. The men were glad to see him. Somehow having a dog along made the voyage a little easier. He was a reminder of home and normal life and of all the things they were fighting for. Dogs were forbidden, but the officers made a point of looking in the other direction when Stubby was around.

That's how Stubby the Pit Bull got to the war. They landed in St. Nazaire in January of 1918, and quickly moved to battle at the front lines at Chemin des Dames, northwest of Soissons. Stubby was not a trained war dog. He was the unit's mascot. He cheered everyone up with his unflagging friendliness.

Conroy said that Stubby noticed the first night that when the soldiers heard the whine of an incoming rocket, they dove for cover in the trenches. He went with them, and a frightening explosion followed.

The second night, as they sat shivering around a fire, "Stubby suddenly stood up and looked into the distance, his ears alert. He whined and ran to the foxhole."

Conroy and the men didn't hesitate. They ran for cover, even before they heard the unpleasant sound. The rocket came in, eerily close to its mark. It hit so close to the camp that Conroy and the others would have been killed or wounded by shrapnel if they hadn't moved out of the way. Stubby's warning had saved their lives. His hearing was far more acute than theirs. He could hear that high-pitched whine from a great distance.

Conroy's unit took part in seventeen battles in France. Stubby did, too. He stuck with the men, no matter where they went: Chateau-Thierry, the Marne, Saint-Mihiel, and the big and final battle of the Great War, Meuse-Argonne. During one of the battles of the Marne, the Germans suddenly ceased fire. The Americans knew that they had not retreated, but they were glad to let their guns go silent for the night. As the men slept exhausted in the trenches, the Germans quietly rolled in chlorine gas bombs, placed so that the wind would carry the fumes directly onto the sleeping men. World War I was a dirty war, and chlorine gas was one of its particularly awful weapons. It is a toxic, irritant, pale green gas. It is added to water supplies as a disinfectant. But in full strength, it attacks the lungs and starts destroying the membrane instantly, until the victim cannot breathe. If you've ever leaned too close to an uncapped bottle of chlorine bleach in your laundry room, you know what this smell is like.

Only Stubby was awakened by the terrible smell. He started barking. Conroy rose, understood the danger, and put on his gas mask. He roused the other men. All were able to get their gas masks on in time to save their lives. World War I gas masks were manufactured at great expense. They were unwieldy but they worked. Soldiers who lost or dropped their gas mask might not survive a gas attack. Only one soldier was injured, the one who had no gas mask because no mask would fit him, the soldier who had given the warning: Stubby. Conroy tried in vain to get a gas mask around Stubby's head, but it didn't fit. No seal was established to keep the gas out. As the gas crept in, Conroy watched helplessly as valiant Stubby stumbled, and then toppled over. His lungs were closing. Without air, he would soon die.

Conroy took Stubby in his arms and left the front. He walked for miles, to a temporary Red Cross field hospital set up well behind the front lines. He laid Stubby's body on a stretcher, gasping as he explained how the dog had saved his men's lives. Conroy was ready to fight if any doctor dared to suggest that a dog did not deserve medical treatment in a man's hospital. But Stubby's reputation preceded him. The staff had already heard about the brave dog of the 126th. They gave Stubby lifesaving oxygen and let Conroy sit with him in a corner of the tent, talking softly to the dog and stroking his body. If these were Stubby's final moments on earth, Conroy wanted to be with him.

Exhausted, Conroy dropped off to sleep. When he woke the next morning, the heavy brindle and white body was lying motionless on the cot. He stared, willing the dog to be alive. But he did not see the chest rise and fall. He leaned towards the cot and whispered, "Stubby?"

The heavy tail beat a rat-tat-tat on the bed. Stubby was alive.

Conroy had to return to his unit. But the hospital staff promised to take care of Stubby, and they did. When Conroy came to pick Stubby up, the nurses pleaded with him to leave Stubby with them. It seemed that now that Stubby felt better, he would wander among the beds of the wounded, looking for a pat and a rub. He seemed to know when a patient was in pain, and he'd stick by the man's side, pressing up against him. The nurses didn't want to lose their new assistant.

But Stubby's regiment missed him. He had to go back. The unit credited him with saving their lives the night of the gas attack, and again and again over the next eleven months. Once Stubby was back with his unit, a rocket never directly hit them. Stubby gave them enough warning that they could run for cover. No enemy breached their camp. Stubby's barks got the soldiers ready to shoot and convinced the enemy to hasten away.

In April 1918, the 102nd took part in a raid on a small town held by the Germans, Seicheprey. There was lots of artillery. Stubby showed no fear of all the loud noise. The Germans were surprised at the Allies' presence and unprepared to fight. As the French and Americans pressed forward, the Germans began to withdraw. Stubby was in the front line with the soldiers who were forcing the Germans back. One German soldier threw a hand grenade that blew very close to him. He was wounded in the forechest.

Once again, Conroy was able to get prompt medical attention for the dog.

After they pushed the Germans out of the next town in the battle of Chateau Thierry, the women of Domremy made Stubby a chamois coat, embroidered with the flags of the Allies. After seeing action in Neufchateau, the unit awarded Stubby a medal, which was sewn onto his coat. He wore it proudly.

One night in the Argonne, Stubby woke up next to Conroy, sniffed the air, and growled. Conroy was instantly alert. He recognized that this was not Stubby's rocket alarm. Instead of running back and forth, barking furiously, and taking cover, Stubby was quiet, but tense as a coiled wire. Then he sprang up and ran into the darkness. Conroy grabbed his rifle and followed him. Up ahead he heard the sounds of a scuffle, and a man's voice shrieked in pain.

Conroy caught up and found Stubby behind some bushes, holding on to a man by the seat of his pants. His teeth were firmly locked in the man's flesh. When Conroy bent to examine the man, Stubby bit harder, enough so that Conroy had no trouble taking the man's pack and a map and notepad from his pockets. What he found stunned him; the man was a German spy, drawing a diagram of American trenches. He was carrying an Iron Cross; an award bestowed on those whose work most greatly benefited Kaiser Wilhelm II and the German Army. Conroy decided the medal should be Stubby's, in honor of his deed. That, too, was sewn onto his coat. The story of how Stubby captured the German spy made the rounds throughout the American Expeditionary Forces. For his effort, he was awarded the honorary rank of Sergeant, which made him the highest-ranking dog to ever serve in the Army. Sergeant Stubby continued to serve until November 11, 1918, the day the war ended.

Stubby's story made the press, inspiring others with his loyalty and courage. The French acknowledged his help, awarding him the French Medal Commemorating the battle of Verdun, the St. Mihiel Campaign Medal, the Chateau Thierry Campaign Medal, and the Grande War Medal of the Republic of France. All went onto his coat, eventually joined by three service stripes, the Yankee Division YD Patch, two American Legion Medals in honor of his attendance at two of their annual conventions, the New Haven World War I Veterans Medal, and in honor of his war injuries, the Purple Heart. General John "Black Jack" Pershing awarded him a special Gold Medal, and declared him a "hero of the highest caliber." Stubby returned the honor with his trademark salute. By the end of the war, Stubby was known not only to every regiment, division, and army, but also to the whole AEF.

When he returned to the U.S. after the Armistice, a wildly enthusiastic American public greeted Stubby. He was named a lifetime Honorary Member of the Red Cross and the American Legion. The YMCA issued him a lifetime membership card good for "three bones a day and a place to sleep." He met three presidents, Woodrow Wilson, who he met and saluted while still in France, Warren G. Harding, and Calvin Coolidge. He led more U.S. military parades than any other dog in history.

Conroy had decided to enroll in Georgetown Law School, so he was in Washington from 1921. He accompanied Stubby to the White House three times. According to Georgetown University records, Stubby "served several terms as mascot to the football team." He also provided the halftime entertainment by running out onto the field and pushing the football around with his head. Some accounts credit Stubby with inventing halftime entertainment.

On one trip from Connecticut to Washington, Conroy stopped at the Majestic Hotel in New York City. As he signed the guest book, the clerk peered over the desk and coldly informed him "Dogs are not allowed in this hotel."

Conroy drew himself up into his military bearing and sternly informed the man, "This is not a dog. This is a war hero."

The situation was brought to the attention of the hotel's

owner, Copeland Townsend, who had read about Stubby and allowed him to stay, as long as he signed the guest book. Stubby did so with his paw. Townsend decided to give Stubby the kind of attention usually reserved only for movie stars. He assigned him a special room and appointed one of his chefs to cook exclusively for him.

Complications from his war injuries and old age separated Stubby from his master on April 4, 1926. The *New York Times* devoted a half page, three-column obituary to the dog, more than many of the human war heroes received. With so many fans, Conroy was persuaded to take a rather unusual step. Instead of burying him, he had Stubby mounted. A plaster cast was made of his body, and his skin stretched over it. Stubby was donated to the Smithsonian Institution. He can be viewed at the National Museum of American History in Washington. Scholars can research his hundred-page scrapbook in the archives. I'm told Stubby is one of the favorite exhibits of the curators. He's lent out to other museums, when requested. He recently spent three years on display at the Hartford Armory as part of an exhibit of that state's military history. It was Stubby's return to his old home state.

Stubby did a lot to publicize his breed, generally acknowledged to be a Pit Bull, which is one of the few breeds who claim their origination in the United States. Because of his example, the breed was used in posters and paintings of the times to signify sturdiness, dependability, and loyalty. It was adopted as a mascot by RCA and Buster Brown shoes, and a Pit Bull named Petey was prominently featured in the *Our Gang* series of short comedy movies produced by Hal Roach starting in 1922.

Stubby was more than a dog. He was an ambassador for the United States, a symbol to the French of the sincerity and strength of resolve of the U.S. soldiers to drive the Germans from their country.

Stubby's Medals:

Three Service Stripes
Yankee Division YD Patch
French Medal Battle of Verdun
First Annual American Legion Convention Medal
    Minneapolis, Minnesota, November 1919
New Haven World War I Veterans Medal
Republic of France Grande War Medal
Saint Mihiel Campaign Medal
Purple Heart
Chateau Thierry Campaign Medal
Sixth Annual American Legion Convention Medal

Pit Bulls were used in dog fighting and another popular sport of the nineteenth century, "ratting," in which a dog was dropped into a pit full of rats. The dog who killed the most rats won. The dogs' ears were cropped so their opponent or the rats could not gain an advantage by biting the ears during the competition. Stubby appears to have had his ears cropped in the fashion of the day.

As for his tail, Pit Bulls commonly had their tails docked close to the back, again so that there was nothing for the opponent or the rats to grab on to. In Stubby's case, just the last quarter was docked. Whether it was the result of a puppy injury or done intentionally, there is no way to know. At any rate, it was his tail that gave him his name. It was stubby.

LET SLIP
THE DOGS OF WAR[1]

SOLDIERS WHO came back from World War I brought with them hard-working new breeds who seemed ideally suited for guard duty: German Shepherds and Doberman Pinschers.

Even with strong recommendations to acquire working dogs, between the wars, the only dogs working for the U.S. military were sled dogs. Fifty huskies and Malamutes were assigned to military stations in Alaska. The sled dogs brought food, supplies, and mail when snow made the roads impassable. Forty sled dogs accompanied Richard Evelyn Byrd on the first scientific expedition to the South Pole in 1933. On their return, they were conscripted by the Air Force and used to rescue airmen who crashed in desolate, snowbound parts of Newfoundland, Greenland, and Iceland.

There is a pattern, beginning more than a century ago, of military officials in Washington insisting that dogs are not necessary in the modern army. Maybe they thought the constant requests for sentry dogs and search dogs were just thinly veiled attempts to secure a place for a canine mascot. If so, they were

---

[1] A phrase from Julius Caesar, 3.1.270, "Cry 'Havoc!' and let slip the dogs of war."

wrong. Or were these officials simply men who did not like dogs? They were either unaware of canine capabilities, or very shortsighted.

Then, on June 13, 1942, Seaman Second Class John C. Cullen strolled out of the Coast Guard Station in Amagansett on Long Island for his nightly beach patrol duty. He was twenty-one, but looked much younger. Cullen stumbled upon four men landing a dinghy on the beach. One was dressed in a suit, the others wore bathing suits. Cullen called out, "Who are you?"

The man in the suit replied, "A couple of fishermen from Southampton who have run aground."

Cullen spoke up, "What's in the bag?"

"Clams."

As a Long Island native, Cullen knew there were no clams for miles around. That meant that these men were not fishermen. German submarines and U-boats had recently been seen frequently in the Atlantic Ocean just off the U.S. coast. Could these men be German spies? Cullen was scared, but didn't show it. He pretended to accept the stranger's answer.

In a friendly voice, the stranger said, "Why don't you forget the whole thing? Here is some money. One hundred dollars."

Cullen said, "I don't want it."

The man took more bills out of his wallet. "Then take three hundred."

Cullen thought fast. He realized that a casual citizen out for a night walk would probably take the money. So he answered, "O.K."

The stranger gave him the money, saying, "Go home because I don't want to have to kill you."

Cullen went straight to the Coast Guard, who alerted the Navy and Army. The agents were captured a few days later; on the same day another Nazi landing from the Atlantic took place, this time on Ponte Vedra Beach near Jacksonville, Florida. The enemy agents were carrying maps and plans for a two-year program designed to destroy war plants, railways, water works, and bridges in the United States.

Several well-known dog breeders pointed out that enemy spies would not be able to land on beaches patrolled by dogs without being spotted. With their sharp hearing and excellent night vision, dogs would exponentially increase the effectiveness of one man keeping watch on the beach. When the Department of Defense declined, the breeders got together with the American Kennel Club and started the Dogs for Defense program.

They asked U.S. citizens to donate their pet dogs to be trained for the military. The request spread like wildfire throughout the country. An amazing eighteen thousand pets were donated over the course of two years. Owners knew from the outset that their dog might be shipped off to battle. They might never see them again. Even so, dog lovers sent the military their best and beloved canines. Only half proved aggressive enough to be useful during the war. The others had to be disqualified for being undersized, disease, temperamental defects, inferior scenting powers, or extreme excitability under gunfire. Those went back to their families.

Dogs for Defense was eventually absorbed into the Office of the Quartermaster General. That agency made the most sense for the organization of an animal program, since they had been responsible up until recently for maintaining the military's horses and mules.

After the German spy incident on the beach, military interest in developing the potential of war dogs began to grow. The Army Ground Forces requested one hundred messenger and scout dogs and one hundred sled dogs, trained for message carrying and cable laying, first aid, and scout work. Dogs for Defense was able to provide the dogs, but up to this point, they were mostly unable to train them. They had recruited volunteer trainers from among the general civilian population. These were people who taught dogs to sit, stand, and stay, bring in the newspaper, and accompany their owner quietly on walks. They had no experience in training war dogs and not much idea of how to do it. The idea was just too new. After three months of training, there were still no dogs that could perform satisfactorily.

On July 16, 1942, the Secretary of War directed the Army Ground Forces and Army Air Force to get involved in the training of the dogs. This was a great boon to the program. The volunteer trainers could devote only a day or two a week, so the trainers of the dogs sometimes changed every day. That often meant that the training techniques changed every day. The dogs were confused. When Army personnel took over, handlers were assigned who could devote full-time to it. The dogs learned their new jobs quickly in that situation.

The program started with the assumption that dogs would be employed in small numbers for sentry duty. But requests from units in the field came in rapidly and soon far outstripped the number of trained dogs. Officers now realized that in addition to carrying messages, patrolling camps, and raising morale, the canine nose could detect hidden mines. A training program for that skill was set up in Maryland. Another innovation was putting a handler together with a dog and training them together, then keeping them together. Partners trained this way were highly effective. Dogs were trained for five jobs: as sentry, sled and pack, messenger, mine detector, and scout dogs.

There was a widespread but incorrect belief that dogs could not be used in the Pacific Theater because they were not useful in the heat of the jungle. The War Department sent six scout and two messenger dogs to operate with troops in the Pacific in the spring of 1943 to assess their abilities. It was an experiment that proved highly useful. There was not a single instance when a patrol led by a war dog was fired upon first or suffered casualties. In contrast, dogless patrols were ambushed constantly and suffered many casualties. During this period, the patrols led by dogs were officially credited with 180 Japanese casualties and taking twenty Japanese prisoners.

The observer with the dogs in New Guinea reported that the dogs could quickly detect the enemy, even at a great distance or disguised in the underbrush. The dogs had no fear of water or travel by small boats. Messenger dogs covered great distances with great speed over any kind of terrain. Also, the presence of dogs greatly boosted the morale of the soldiers. Patrols with alert dogs operated more efficiently and covered greater distances.

A number of war dogs established outstanding records. A Shepherd-Collie mix named Chips was on sentry duty with his handler in Sicily when he suddenly broke away and charged down the beach and seemed to leap into a sand dune. The soldiers who came running up behind him found Chips holding a German pillbox machine gunner on the ground by his throat. Five other Nazis had dropped their guns and raised their arms in the air, surrendering to the dog and hoping not to be next on his hit list. The commander in the field awarded Chips the Silver Star and the Purple Heart. Both were later revoked as contrary to Army policy, which prohibits commendations for animals.

In the South Pacific, another Shepherd, Sandy, was trained to carry messages between his two handlers, Sgt. Guy C. Sheldon and Sgt. Menzo J, Brown. During the Cape Gloucester Campaign, the advance units were held up by Japanese machine-gun fire from pillboxes and fortifications. The walkie-talkies were temporarily out of commission, so the unit could not send for help. A message was dispatched with Sandy back to the Battalion Command Post. Sandy had to travel through tall Kunai grass, swim a river, and make his way beneath constant artillery fire, and finally jump a barbed wire fence that was protecting Sgt. Sheldon's unit. The location was a great distance from where Sandy had last seen Sgt.

Sheldon. But he tracked him down. As a result of this message, artillery fire was directed on the Japanese defenses. The American units were saved, and able to advance.

Another dog, Pal, blocked an explosive charge with his own body on April 23, 1945, at San Benedetto Po, Italy. He was killed instantly when his body absorbed most of the shrapnel, which prevented the wounding or death of the entire advance patrol of seven men.

At the end of World War II, the Quartermaster Corps with the help of the civilian "Dogs for Defense" organization gave the surviving dogs decompression training with the purpose of returning them to their original owners. During this rehabilitation period, handlers made a point of convincing the dog that every human being is a friend. The dog was given thorough obedience training of the kind civilians used, such as "sit," "heel," "lie down." When the dog was ready for civilian life, his owners were contacted to find out if they wanted him back. Almost all of them did. Three thousand dogs were returned to their families in this way. Most families were shocked at how well-behaved these ex-soldiers were.

The Army Quartermaster Museum in Fort Lee, Virginia, has letters from some of the owners:

> Dolf arrived yesterday afternoon in excellent condition
> and survived the long trip remarkably well. He knew each
> and all of us immediately and within a very short time had
> taken up where he left off two years ago. He is beautifully
> trained and his behavior is remarkable. He had not in the
> least forgotten many of the things we had taught him.
> John B. Osborn, New York

> Thank you for your good care and training of our dog Mike.
> He knew all of us and still remembers the tricks he knew

before he entered the service. My son, Edward, an Army officer, and all of us are proud of his honorable discharge and his deportment.

Mrs. Edward Jo Conally, Salt Lake City, Utah

I want to thank you for the wonderful dog you returned to us. Smarty is a perfect example of health and alertness and she was so eager to show us her obedience commands that we understood them even before the instructions arrived two days late. It was a genuine sacrifice for Herbie to donate his dog to the armed forces, but now he is receiving his reward by receiving a dog more beautiful and better trained than he ever thought possible.

Mrs. Herbert E. Allen, Washington, D.C.

As in all wars, soldiers sometimes picked up mascots in the field, often smuggling them into camps, onto ships, and back to the United States. Quite a few dogs, cats, and even a few monkeys became U.S. citizens in this manner. But perhaps the most unusual story to come out of World War II about a mascot concerned a four-pound Yorkshire Terrier, found deep in the jungles of New Guinea.

THE YORKIE
IN THE JUNGLE

ON A HOT MARCH DAY in New Guinea in 1944, young Pfc. Bill Wynne stood in the makeshift motor pool garage of the Navy's 5212th Photo Recon Wing and contemplated an excited, terribly groomed little dog who someone had tied to the wheel of a truck.

"Where'd that dog come from?" he asked.

A mechanic stuck his head out from under an engine and told him that another photog had found the elfin dog in a foxhole in the jungle, a story Wynne found hard to believe. It seemed bizarrely impossible, given that the tiny dog was obviously pedigreed and well-bred, and that this unit was located in sparsely-populated Nadzab, New Guinea, a village referred to by the commanding general as "the Japs' back door." The island was on the front line of the Pacific Theater and had already endured two years of battle. It was considered a crucial spot to break Japanese supply lines and keep them from overrunning Australia. It was not the kind of place where a cultured lady might purchase an elegant little lap dog. But the story turned out to be true.

Bill thought he was looking at a Poodle. In fact, he was looking at his future.

He offered two Australian pounds for the creature, but when the owner balked, he was too cautious to offer more. He didn't think the weak little dog would live much longer. She was small and underfed and frail. His G.I. boots were taller than she was. But when her owner was thrown out of a poker game, he accepted Wynne's offer, the equivalent of about six and a half bucks U.S., to buy his way back in.

He kept the name she'd been given, Smoky, a word which seemed to describe her light gray, silky coat. "She became my new best friend," Bill Wynne said.

New Guinea was the kind of place where a lonely, homesick young Ohio man needed a friend. For U.S. troops, New Guinea was not a nice place. They were surrounded by steamy, dank, dense, tangled jungle and steep mountains full of fast-flowing, ice-cold creeks. It was always rough going because of the jagged terrain. The rain was incessant, which meant that they were always wet.

Tropical storms could rage up out of nowhere and last an unpredictable amount of time. One particular day, a tropical storm destroyed twenty of the two hundred strong U.S. air fleet stationed in New Guinea. Tropical illnesses loved the place, and debilitated the men with malaria, dengue fever, dysentery, and scrub typhus. Large mangrove swamps slowed the overland movement of troops. There were no roads or railways. Supply lines were dirt trails that had been used by natives over the centuries. Rain constantly reduced these trails to muddy glue. It fragmented any deployment of a large operation.

Additionally, New Guinea is the most linguistically diverse area in the world, an island of seven million people who speak a total of 1,071 languages. Some of its provinces contain tribal groups who had never been contacted by outside civilization.[1]

The World War II campaign in New Guinea never took on the

---

[1] BBC documentary *First Contact* February 1, 2007.

cachet of the fighting to retake Europe. There was no glorious march into Paris. No kindly Italian farmers shared their tomatoes and bread. But the battle for New Guinea was absolutely essential in the fight to keep the Japanese from overrunning other island nations in the Pacific. New Guinea was the first stand in the U.S. force's drive across the Central Pacific. If the Japanese could hold New Guinea, they planned an onslaught to invade Australia, just one hundred miles away.

The men who were there understood the dangerous, tactical position they held. They were not about to let the Japanese have their way. They fought remorselessly along the New Guinea coastline, which meant the Japanese armies retreated into the jungles and mountains, where they were well hidden and could emerge to make strategic attacks against the Allies. That's where Bill Wynne and the Twenty-sixth Photo Recon were based, in the inland central island village of Nadzab.

The squadron's mission was aerial reconnaissance. That meant that cameras flew out every day on Lockheed P-38 propeller driven aircraft, deep into the enemy's territory, without guns or fighter protection, and shot thousands of photos of enemy strongholds and troop movements. They documented where Allied forces had been successful and destroyed ammo dumps or airfields. It was extremely perilous work.

The squadron set up a makeshift photo lab, with processors and printers and all the attendant chemicals: rinse fix and developer, bleach fix and replenisher, photo emulsion, silver nitrate, silver halide salts, toxic solvents, poly filters and rack rollers, plates and collators and decollators, cutters, trimmers, punches, assemblers, guillotines, printer ink, extra film and canisters, as well as the lenses necessary to magnify the photos enough that they would be useful to a general in need of information. There were so many battles going on in the winter of 1944 that Bill Wynne and his squad ran continuous twelve hour shifts, churning out stack after stack of aerial photos. It was hard work. But their commanding general, General George Churchill Kenney, had given them a motto when he said, "The side with the best photo reconnaissance wins the war."

Bill Wynne and the other photographers had decided that was going to be their side.

One week, a G.I. came running excitedly to Bill. "I know what kind of dog she is!" He was waving a *National Geographic* magazine in one hand. "She's a Yorkshire Terrier. Look, here's a picture!"

Bill was amazed to see that it was true. The issue was devoted to very rare breeds of dog and featured a big color photo of a Yorkie who could have been Smoky's double, although a very well-bathed and groomed one—same silky hair, same intense black eyes, same tiny weight class. That was one mystery solved.

The Japanese were making their final stand in the northern island city of Hollandia. From there, they were still able to send bombers to attack U.S. and Australian airfields and troop headquarters. And they still controlled small pockets of Japanese soldiers who were hidden in the hills. Without Hollandia, Japan would have no communication with any of their soldiers left on the island. If they could be defeated in Hollandia, they lost New Guinea.

Photos taken by Wynne's squad showed three hundred and fifty enemy planes on three Hollandia airstrips. With that intelligence, the Fifth Air Force bombed and strafed the fields. Fifty of the enemy pilots fought back in the sky, and all fifty were shot down. After three days, aerial recon showed that all three hundred and fifty planes had been destroyed. The Japanese air force was severely depleted. They retreated north to Biak Island, just off the coast.

During this hectic time, Bill says, "Smoky became a tremendous morale booster." He and the tiny dog bonded. Bill fed her bully beef, "a kind of canned hash we got from the Australians," and anything she could eat from his kit which contained mainly dehydrated potatoes, powdered milk and eggs, coffee, canned fruit, and citric acid. Smoky was happy with mutton, which came in jars. There was no fresh meat available. Bill said, "That diet would have killed the modern Yorkie in three months." But Smoky continued to thrive.

Taking good care of your dog in New Guinea was an altogether different matter from taking care of your dog in Cleveland. Bill kept her tied to his cot when he slept. If she snuck out into the jungle, there were pythons capable of swallowing whole pigs. Although Smoky loved chasing butterflies, ticks inhabiting flowers carried scrub typhus, a disease that at the time killed nine out of ten of its victims. He decided to bathe her every day. "Her tub was my helmet," Bill said. "It was also my wash basin and shaving sink." There was also danger from the native tribes, who might not appreciate Smoky. Bill learned during a pre-flight briefing that three crewmen who had survived the crash of their plane had been eaten by one of the inner island tribes.

He'd always had dogs. He'd grown up with dogs. He'd even been taking his latest mutt, Toby, to obedience classes in Cleveland when the Army came along and drafted him. So he started Smoky on some basic commands; "Sit," "Stay," "Heel," and "Come." She was clever and learned quickly. Bill says the two formed a strong bond and could almost unerringly read each other's clues. Smoky trusted Bill so much she would play "dead dog," pretending to fall dead when he shot her, and not moving even when he poured her four-pound body from hand to hand.

Many nights passed this way; either training Smoky or entertaining the other guys with things he'd taught her. "Smoky became a tremendous morale booster," Bill remembered. He taught her to sing, "Owoowoowoowoo," when he played the harmonica, but had to stop when one of his tentmates said ominously, "When a dog cries, someone is going to die."

Yank Down Under magazine, published by the U.S. military in Australia, ran a contest seeking the "Best Mascot of the Southwest Pacific." There were four hundred candidates for the title. Most units had picked up a native mutt. Some had strange mascots, like the vicious monkey, Turbo. After he bit too many men, the unit drove him out to the jungle and tried to lose him. But his homing skills turned out to be excellent, and he kept finding his way back, where he'd pillage the men's tents for cookies, candy bars, or cigarettes.

The Twenty-sixth Photo Recon decided to enter Smoky in the contest on the grounds that she was cuter than any other dog. Bill snapped the official photo: little four-pound Smoky sitting in his helmet. Bill's helmet is battered and scratched, but Smoky peers happily at the photographer, her black eyes alert.

Several weeks later, Bill found himself in the hospital with dengue fever, a debilitating virus transmitted by mosquitoes. The symptoms are high fever and sudden, intense pain in the joints. Bill's fever went to 103 before he recovered, and as he did, some of the squadron visited, bringing Smoky, who restored his spirits. They also brought his mail, which contained several copies of *Yank Down Under*. A letter from Sgt. Don Brewer notified him that Smoky had won!

They were thrilled. While the nurses carried Smoky around the hospital to visit other patients, Bill flipped through the copies of *Yank Down Under* he'd been sent. On one, handsome field artillery Captain Heidenreich was wedding WAC lieutenant Grace Guderian beneath an archway of swords held by friends in Manila. Their faces were lit up with the happiness of new love. The picture made Bill miss his own sweetheart, Margie, back in Cleveland. If he ever got out of this place, he was planning to go home and marry her.

The nurses interrupted his reverie by plopping Smoky back

down on his lap. They told him they were amazed at how much little Smoky cheered the patients. Even a man lying with his face to the wall, who hadn't spoken to anyone since arriving at the hospital with multiple fractures, had turned around and smiled at her and said hello. Smoky covered his face with kisses. A television network that had not yet been invented, called Animal Planet, would eventually note this date, July 14, 1944, and this hospital as the first known attempt at therapy dog visits.

After the victory at Hollandia, the Twenty-sixth Photo Recon unit was ordered forward along with General Kenney's Fifth Air Force. Next, they moved forward another step, this time to the northern island of Biak, a necessary military goal because of its three excellent runways built on hard coral. At Hollandia, aircraft touched down on soft soil, and large, heavy planes couldn't land there.

Bill Wynne was asked to shoot pictures with a crew of the Third Emergency Rescue Squadron on a mission to search for a pilot who had been shot down over enemy lines. There were still five thousand Japanese troops on Biak. If the pilot had survived the crash, an infantry patrol would go out to rescue him. Bill loaded the K24 aerial camera with film and equipped himself with his .45 caliber automatic, an extra clip of bullets, and his Bowie knife. He left Smoky in the care of one of his tentmates. They flew into territory where "enemy fire is probable and expected." Bill clicked photos of the crashed P38. The cockpit was mangled. "The poor guy hadn't had a chance," Bill recalled sadly.

They got back to Sorido airstrip with thirty-five minutes of combat time logged. Men who logged three hundred hours could go home. Bill offered to keep on flying. It meant getting home sooner, and it also put him behind a camera again, a position he preferred to the exhausting hours in the developing darkroom. It also put him in the enemy's gunsights, but he preferred not to dwell on that.

When he got back from that first trip, one of his tent neighbors asked, "Hey, Wynne, if you get knocked off, can I have Smoky?"

This was followed by a chorus of other men, asking him to leave Smoky to them. Bill was disgusted. "From now on, she goes with me," he told them. "If I go down, we go down together!"

He taught Smoky to lie quietly in his musette bag, a small canvas knapsack, during the flight. The crew of seven consisted of the pilot, co-pilot, navigator, engine mechanic, radio operator, and two medics who doubled as gunners. The medics were amused to find Smoky on board, and hung her bag over a stretcher. Bill had already worked out her escape plan. If they went down, he was going to strap her bag to his chest before leaping out and parachuting. He rehearsed the maneuver, but happily never had to use it.

In all, Smoky was credited with twelve combat missions. She was awarded eight battle stars.

They survived the battle for Biak but any celebrations were short lived. Their next orders were for an island much closer to Japan, the Philippine Island of Luzon. Bill and his friends broke down their photo lab and got it aboard LST 970 for the trip. At the last minute, Bill and forty-nine others were ordered to change to another ship, LST 706. The Photo Recon unit was considered vital to front-line operations. The general had ordered the team split so that in case one unit went down with the ship, there would still be a small cadre to rebuild the unit and get to work.

On the voyage to Luzon, Bill's unit was part of the greatest naval fleet that had ever been assembled on the planet. One hundred seventy-five thousand men were aboard one thousand battleships, destroyers, aircraft carriers, cruisers, and transporters. They were still in the tropics, but if you were out on deck, the hot, humid air was relieved somewhat by sea breezes. Bill kept his cot next to a Jeep that was strapped to the deck.

Word filtered back to the men that the first part of the convoy, two days ahead, had been heavily hit by kamikaze pilots. On the fourth day, general quarters sounded, and for the first time, it was not a drill. Bill saw twelve dots in the sky headed towards the ship, and had time only to grab Smoky and roll under the Jeep before shrapnel started to rain down on the deck. The gunners on the 706 blasted 40mm Twin Bofors at the fighter planes. One plane turned back; the other started to fume black smoke and then twisted in the air, spiraling into a nosedive into the sea.

Bill leapt out to join in the victory celebration; the ship had not been heavily hit, and they'd downed one plane. As he stood, he noticed a path of shrapnel that came across his area of the deck and slammed into the Jeep. If he hadn't rolled Smoky under the Jeep, that shell would have cut a path through him.

"She saved my life," Bill remembers years later. "If I'd remained standing, or if I'd have hesitated another minute, I'd be gone."

General quarters sounded again. This time the men could see two more Japanese planes headed their way. Bill watched as the gunners blackened the air. One plane kept on coming straight at them. Just fifteen hundred feet away, the gunners managed a direct hit. The suicide plane, heavily loaded with explosives, plopped uselessly into the sea. The second plane picked a target ship just behind them. These gunners were not so lucky. The plane crashed directly amidships. The sky lit up with fire and smoke. Bill and his crew watched helplessly, each thanking their lucky stars that the direct hit had not been on them.

Before the voyage was over, twenty-four ships were sunk and sixty-seven heavily damaged. By the luck of the draw, Bill's was not one of them. They landed on Luzon with little resistance because General Yamashita hadn't expected the Americans on that beach. His troops were miles away, defending an empty beach, while the Americans sprinted onshore.

Now Bill's unit was attached to the Sixth Army and their commander was General Krueger. He ordered the unit to set up fast. The vast majority of the American fleet was now in the Philippines and had begun the work of forcing the Japanese out and back to their own country. Aerial reconnaissance continued to be one of the most important strategic assets, so Bill and the men worked night and day to get the photos to General MacArthur, Admiral Nimitz, and the Navy battle planners.

On a sunny afternoon, Bill was lounging near the photo lab when a sergeant from the Communications section showed up and asked to see Smoky. Bill recognized that Sgt. Bob Gapp was measuring her with his eyes. But he didn't know why.

"Say, Bill," the sergeant said nervously, "we've got a problem down at the airfield. I wonder if Smoky could help us out."

The problem turned out to be that the Communications section was unable to get cable and wire from one side of the airport to the other, for vital communications. A seventy-foot wide taxiway lay in the way, and it was being heavily used by F5s and P51 and P61 bombers on their way to battle. In order to dig a ditch in which to place the cable, the runway would have to be shut down for at least three days, which would double up traffic on the other runway and force dozens of planes to gather together in one spot, a parking technique the Americans always avoided because it was an easy target for enemy bombers. Japanese pilots looked for such groupings in order to take out several planes with one shell.

Not only that, but also 250 men from three squadrons working day and night along the runway made another tantalizing target. They would be out in the open and unprotected.

Sgt. Gapp showed Bill a pipe that already ran under the taxiway. It had a circumference of eight inches. "Could Smoky pull a wire through this pipe?"

Bill lay flat and peered through. He could see daylight at the other end, but just barely. The joints had started to give way so there was a pile of dirt every five feet where sand had started to leak through.

"We'll try it on one condition," Bill said. "If she gets stuck, your boys dig right down and get her out."

"Agreed," the sergeant said with relief. They had to wait over an hour until the air traffic slowed down and the taxiway was clear. Sgt. Gapp pushed Smoky into one end. Seventy feet away, Bill ordered, "Smoky, come!" He could see her hesitate. An intelligent dog with an instinct for its own survival is not going to enter a dark, dirty, seventy-foot pipe under any circumstances. But Smoky had been trained to follow Bill's commands. Events had already proven that she trusted Bill with her life. So at his urging, she hunkered down and began the trip.

Smoky was seven inches high. The pipe was eight inches, but since much of it was filled with sand, Smoky often had to get down and crawl her way through. But she did it. She got caught once, but when Bill called out, "Stand! Stay!" she stayed quietly where she was while Sgt. Gapp worked the string loose. As she crawled, she kicked up dirt into brown clouds that totally blocked Bill's view. Suddenly, he saw two dark eyes right in front of his face, and Smoky flew out of the tunnel and into his arms. "Atta girl, atta girl," he said.

Sgt. Gapp promised her a huge steak.

Moments later, air traffic on the taxiway resumed. But Communications had already started to pull a wire through the pipe, and followed that with a heavy cable. It wasn't long before vital lines of communication had been established.

Word of Smoky's exploit spread quickly, and everywhere she was greeted with applause and cheers. Bill said, "When she climbed through that tunnel, her status changed from mascot to war dog. She was a soldier now. She had helped to win the war."

Maybe that sounds like an exaggeration. She crawled her way

through that seventy-foot pipe because her owner, Bill, told her to, and she trusted him. It took her two minutes. But consider this. Smoky's deed meant that Sgt. Bob Gapp was not digging on the runway when a Japanese fighter pilot swooped in. He lived to return to Montana and marry Estelle Sweeney and produce four children. Each of those children now has children of their own, and Bob is their smiling, good-natured grandfather.

It meant that Norma Gambone got to see her fighter pilot son, Chad, return to Chesapeake City, Maryland, after the war, because he had not been forced by the digging project to park his plane in the midst of eleven others on the crowded airfield when a Japanese bomber wrecked eight planes with one well-placed bomb. Twenty years later, as a Pan Am pilot, Chad's quick thinking saved a plane loaded with passengers from crashing in the Florida Everglades when it developed engine trouble. He landed 120 people safely at Fort Lauderdale International, because he hadn't died that day in Luzon.

It was one little act by one little dog. But everyone knew that the ripples of effect from that mission spread out over dozens and potentially hundreds of lives. Many small acts by many people had the same reverberations every day, and no one stopped to notice. But the selfless courage of one four-pound dog was inspiring to everyone who heard about it. Everyone wanted to congratulate Smoky. Unexpected honors started to come their way. *Yank Down Under* and the Ninety-first Photo Wing newsletter, *WingDing*, wrote feature stories about her, and Bill and Sgt. Gapp recreated the scene at the entrance to the pipe for the photographer. Bill had a Philippine seamstress sew a little coat for Smoky out of felt. He pinned her medals and stripes on it. She wore it proudly.

While they waited for the war to end, Bill taught Smoky to slip down a sliding board, roll a barrel with her feet, weave through Bill's legs as he walked, climb ladders, balance and walk blindfolded on high wires, and ride a specially made scooter. They were a featured act in makeshift talent shows on the base. They visited hospitals and lightened the spirits of sick and dying soldiers. They performed for any group of soldiers anywhere they could. Their success was partly due to Bill's relentlessly genial personality. He had already formed the habit of greeting every stranger as a friend, with a smile and handshake that emanated good cheer. It was partly due to his amazing success at dog training. He was making it up as he went along, but Smoky always seemed to understand him. She pushed every trick to the limit. She was a natural born performer who worked for the applause of the crowd. Bill liked standing in her shadow and watching how the crowd focused on her, totally absorbed and impressed with everything she did.

The war finally ended. Bill Wynne went home and married Margie and applied for a photography job at NACA, the National Advisory Committee for Aeronautics. in Cleveland, the precursor of the current day National Aeronautic and Space Administration, better known as NASA. It was an important job that would pay well. Margie advised him, "This time, keep your application serious. Don't put in all that stuff about the dog."

Bill agreed that was a good plan. He wanted the job. He needed to buy a house with several bedrooms, not only for the children they planned to have, but to keep Smoky and Margie apart. The two hated each other on first sight. Both wanted to be first in Bill's affections.

When he turned in the application, the personnel manager said, "You didn't put anything under 'Hobbies.' Don't you have any hobbies?"

Bill sheepishly answered that his hobby was training his dog. The Cleveland Press had done a feature story on Smoky, the War Hero, and her fame had spread through the city. Famed dog writer Maxwell Riddle called Smoky, "The best trained dog I've ever seen." His words meant something because in his line of work, he'd seen thousands of them. They had been performing again, this time at nightclubs and city park events. Bill wrote all this up in the "Hobbies" section of the form. But no job offer was forthcoming.

Bill jumped at the chance to take Smoky to Hollywood. He thought she could be a star as great as Lassie or Rin Tin Tin. He and Margie enjoyed their weeklong drive across the country, with one of Bill's buddies along to share the driving. In Hollywood, Bill threw himself into training dogs for Rennie Renfro. He had genuine talent at the work. Dogs adored him and followed his directions.

But Marge was unhappy. She didn't like California. She missed home and her mother. Bill was gone for long hours every day, and without a job, she had nothing to do. She hadn't felt right physically, either, since she'd set foot in this state. They agreed she would return to Cleveland while Bill pursued landing a steady dog-training job. If he did, she'd come back and set up house.

But that never happened. In her doctor's office in Cleveland, Margie learned she was pregnant. She didn't want to be on the other side of the country from her mother for the big event. Bill longed to stay in Hollywood, but an official looking envelope arrived that changed all that. It was an offer from NACA. They wanted him to fly as photographer on de-icing missions, documenting the effects of various de-icing systems their scientists invented. Bill and Smoky drove home.

Once ensconced in NACA, flying constantly in dangerous cold and storms, he felt part of a big and important mission. So he was surprised when the head of his department called him in and asked him to bring Smoky to perform at a talent show for children on the weekend.

Bill said, "We'd be happy to come."

"That's good," said his boss. "Did you know the reason I hired you was to get that dog in the show?"

Even when Bill was pursuing his career, Smoky turned out to have influence on his life.

He and Smoky took a Sunday morning job at Channel 3 entertaining children on the *Castles in the Air* show. Bill said proudly, "We went forty-two weeks without repeating a trick." All of it was live. There were no shows on tape. That was in 1950. In 1954, Channel 3 brought Bill and Smoky back for a thirty week series called, *How to Train Your Dog with Bill Wynne and Smoky*.

Smoky was a performer and trooper by Bill's side for twelve years, which took her through the birth of six of his nine children, and a switch in careers from aeronautical photographer to photojournalist at the *Cleveland Plain Dealer*. On February 21, 1957, Bill came home from work to find the elderly Smoky asleep in her room. She never woke up. The little soldier who had stuck so loyally at his side for so many years was gone.

Once again, newspapers featured her story. The death of the little war dog made news across the country. Smoky's existence was brought to the attention of an ever-widening circle of admirers. The Yorkshire Terrier Club of America credited Smoky for the breed's nascent popularity. The peppy little tykes made wonderful house pets. More and more people wanted to take one home.

Shortly after Smoky died, Margie picked up the ringing phone to hear the voice of a polite, obviously educated woman. "I'm Grace Heidenreich," the caller said, "and I've just read in the newspaper about your Yorkie. I had a Yorkie once, years ago. I lost her on the island of New Guinea."

Marge knew what to say. "Hang on," she sighed. "I'll get Bill."

Grace Heidenreich explained her story. She'd been a nurse in the South Pacific, engaged to Captain Heidenreich, assigned to field artillery. On leave to Brisbane, he'd impulsively bought her a Yorkshire Terrier puppy. Grace took the puppy with her to the field hospital where she was stationed in Dobadura, New Guinea. Her friends were as delighted with it as she was. She named the puppy, "Christmas," in honor of the season. One evening, she took Christmas with her to the traveling variety show put on by Bob Hope and other celebrities from the States. The puppy was loose, scurrying between Grace and her many friends. When the show was over, Christmas was gone. Grace searched and searched but no one could find her. She was heartbroken over the loss. They knew that someone must have picked the little dog up and carried her away. She never saw or heard of Christmas again.

But this morning, she picked up a newspaper and read that the little war dog hero was a Yorkshire Terrier who'd been found on New Guinea. Was there any chance it could be the same dog?

Bill assured her that it was. This was the missing piece of the puzzle he'd wondered about for years. How did a purebred little dog get so far from civilization on the jungle island? Now he knew.

He told her about Smoky's long and glorious life. They enjoyed speaking so much that they hatched a plan to meet up and drink a few toasts to the wonderful Christmas/Smoky.

That's when they discovered they lived two blocks apart.

The little purebred dog who had enriched the lives of two owners in the South Pacific had belonged to two different people who lived in the same small suburban Cleveland neighborhood.

Not only was that a wild coincidence, but when Grace told him about wedding her husband while on leave to Manila, Bill remembered the cover of the *Yank Down Under* magazine he'd received when Smoky won "Best Mascot." It had featured a happy military couple tying the knot. He'd been looking right at Smoky's owner then, and hadn't known it.

There is a bronze life-size sculpture of Smoky sitting in Bill's helmet in Cleveland Metroparks Rocky River reservation. A story recognizing Smoky was aired during the broadcast of the Westminster Dog Show in February 2008. She is one war dog who has never been forgotten.

THE TOUGHEST DOG
IN DA NANG

IN THE 1950S, an Army base in Colorado was being decommissioned. Publicity stated that the K-9 Corps was being disbanded. It wasn't true. The dog unit was simply moved to another base. But the public reaction was immediate and loud. Letters poured in to the Secretary of Defense.

> I strongly request you to reconsider demobilizing the K-9 Corps. These dogs performed a very useful service during the war as I can personally attest to; I owe my life to one of these dogs. While fighting in Korea I was attacked and one of these dogs took over my attacker and I was able to recover my footing and escaped. Please reconsider.
>
> Frank Conanno, West Babylon, N.Y.

> I have read in various periodicals your intention of disbanding the K-9 Corps. I am taking this means of voicing my objection to such a move. As a Gold Star Mother, I believe I understand the meaning of losing someone close. Various reports coming back from the battlefields in World War II and the Korean Conflict have given detailed

descriptions of how these wonderful dogs saved many American lives. Please, before you abandon this work, attempt to economize somewhere else and keep these wonderful animals on the job.

Mrs. H. Distel, Garden, Cal.

I am in the Army and was put into the scout dog platoon and trained dogs for nine months in the States and have had the same dog all the time. This dog, Star, has saved my life and about twelve other men's lives. I would like to know if there is any way that I could have him discharged the same time that I am. I would gladly pay the government for the dog and take all the responsibility for him."

Corporal Max Meyers, Twenty-Sixth Infantry, Scout Dog Platoon, APO #60 San Francisco, Cal.

I am writing to protest against the effort to dispose of the Army's dogs. Dogs are indispensable in our Army. I know many other persons who feel this way. A dog has nature's own radar; his nose. He can notice things even in the dark. He is courageous, noble, trustworthy, and honest. His ears are keener than human ears. He is a swift messenger; there isn't a thing on this old Mother Earth that is so faithful, so loyal, so willing to give his life for his master than a dog. Disposing of the dogs would be the greatest mistake that the Army could make.

Wendy Bogue, Eau Claire, Wis.

The Army hastened to respond to the letter writers that they agreed with them about the usefulness of the dogs. They had no intention of disbanding the K-9 Corps.

During the long years of the Cold War, the Air Force started its Sentry Dog School at Lackland Air Force Base in Texas. Today, all military working dogs and their handlers are trained there for all the services; this has increased continuity. The dogs are far more effective than they've ever been for American soldiers. They have skills that have saved many American lives.

In 1965, as part of the attempt to build up the South Vietnamese Army, the United States began to supply them with military working dogs and trainers. They attempted to teach the Vietnamese soldiers how to work with the dogs as sentries and patrol dogs. The program was a huge failure. The Buddhist Vietnamese didn't want dogs, and the handlers did not grow attached to them. Their culture despised dogs. It cost more to feed the dogs than a handler. The large shepherds often weighed as much as the small framed Vietnamese handlers did. Dogs and handlers were not able to form effective teams. The Vietnamese looked on the dogs not as guardians or pets, but as a potential source of food. Since the dogs weren't working out, they ate them.

In the same year, after an attack on the U.S. Air Base at Da Nang, the military sent over twenty dog teams as an experiment, to see if they'd be useful. Apparently, no one remembered the great work of the dogs in tracking Japanese during World War II. The handlers and dogs were trained together, so they formed a unified team who understood each other's signals and worked effectively. This experiment was a huge success. U.S. bases that had been attacked repeatedly by ground enemies in the past were not attacked at all once the dogs were in place at the perimeter. When dogs went out on patrols, the order was, "Dogman, take the point."

With the dogs leading them, no one snuck up on the small units. With the dogs on the alert for enemy soldiers, the units never walked into an ambush. Captured Viet Cong confirmed their fear of the dogs. The bounty placed on the head of a war dog was said to be the equivalent of ten thousand dollars, double the bounty for killing an American soldier.

Greg Dunlap says he waited twenty years before he started to write the story of Blackie, his Military Working Dog in Vietnam.

"I wasn't mature enough back then to put it all together," he reflects. Returning from Vietnam was a nightmare. "People threw things at you, spit on you, yelled at you on the street. It was terrible."

But now, through the prism of distance and adulthood, he can reminisce about the dog he says saved his life many times. Blackie's story starts the day twenty-year-old Sgt. Dunlap arrived at the kennels in Da Nang. The kennel master, Staff Sergeant Wolfe, told him there was only one unassigned dog, so it was his.

Walking down the row of kennel runs, he saw a big, handsome German Shepherd sleeping in the back of his cage. When Dunlap stopped to look at him, "He uncoiled and hit the gate full force! The day worker said, 'He's the nastiest dog here.'"

Blackie was a patrol dog, selected for this work because he was aggressive. He didn't do the detection work that relied on his nose. His job was to keep strangers out of the Americans' compound. At the moment, Dunlap was a stranger to him. It took two days of sitting in front of his kennel talking to the monster in a soothing voice, to get him to calm down enough so Dunlap could get him out.

"The day I went in, they had a man standing by with an M-16. If he nailed me, they were going to shoot him before they went in to get me." Dunlap found out later there were bets going in the hooch that favored him getting nailed before he managed to touch the dog.

"He chased me out four times before he let me in. Opening that door a fifth time, letting him sniff up and down my legs was an experience I have never forgotten. I just stood there, scared, my testicles trying to climb back up inside my body. The whole time I was telling him that we were going to be good friends, if he didn't bite me."

He was supposed to wear a muzzle, but when Dunlap went to put it on, Blackie growled. "Okay, no muzzle," he agreed.

The pair spent two days training together, and then was pressed into patrol duty. It was an auspicious night. January 31, 1968, the start of what came to be known as the Tet Offensive. The Viet Cong had begun a massive, countrywide attack on one hundred towns and villages with eighty thousand troops. It was the kind of organized and efficient battle that generals had been assuring the politicians and the American public that the Viet Cong were not capable of mounting. Their intelligence was wrong.

That night, an experienced handler accompanied Dunlap to show him the ropes. The man had only a few days left before he could go back to the States, and he was apprehensive that their position was going to be hit. "At midnight, Chuck made me muzzle Blackie and get into the bunker. I thought he was being overly cautious. Sure enough, midnight came and all around us outside the fence, the Vietnamese were celebrating Tet. Guns going off all over the place. At one time the sky was full of tracers everywhere you looked."

Blackie was going crazy, constantly barking and lunging for the fence. Dunlap tried to hold him down. He thought all the rockets were scaring him.

There was a loud whooshing, whistling sound, and two rockets exploded one hundred yards away. That night, 125 rockets hit the Da Nang base. "It was quite a first night," Dunlap says. He found out later that a Viet Cong unit was set to attack at his location, but got bogged down and couldn't make it to the fence before the sun came up. Blackie had been trying to tell Dunlap—There's someone out there! But Dunlap hadn't learned how to listen to him yet.

Thus began the interminable year of night after night patrols of the perimeter. On a good night, the temperature dropped as low as eighty-five. But most nights were as hot, sweaty and insufferable as the days. "In that entire year, I got five nights off," Dunlap remembers.

Being Blackie's handler brought a certain amount of respect. He'd already had three handlers, so the Marines had seen him enough times to be frightened of him. He was always ready to charge. He threatened to bite anyone who displeased him. They didn't mind having Blackie out on sentry duty, but nobody wanted Blackie to come anywhere near them.

One Marine annoyed Dunlap by telling him to wake him up at one a.m. ("What am I, an alarm clock?") So Dunlap cooperated by going to the man's bunk at one and placing Blackie over his sleeping body. As the man slowly woke up, he realized Blackie was on top of him. His panic and attempt to get away, caused Blackie to go after him and try to keep him right there. He never asked for a wake-up call again.

They had been on the job several weeks when the sergeant announced at guardmount—the roll call and assigning of tasks at the beginning of a shift—that a Second Lieutenant who had just come in from the States was going to be checking up on every station, making sure the guards knew their instructions and passwords. "We're sending him to you first," the sergeant told him. He didn't say why, but he gave Dunlap a meaningful look that was easy to interpret.

That night, Dunlap kept Blackie charged up by having him keep alerting to the Marines. When anyone walked by, Blackie would barrel out to the end of his lead, barking and terrorizing them. Blackie was so threatening that the Marines never got used to him. When Dunlap knew the lieutenant was approaching and only twenty feet away, he let Blackie alert on him.

"Halt! Who goes there?" he called.

The lieutenant and a sergeant gave their names.

"Advance and be recognized!" Dunlap said, all according to regulations. They advanced, and Dunlap reported his post secure, and the men stood talking. He could see the lieutenant was getting angry, but he didn't know why.

"Airman, aren't you supposed to salute when you report your post as secure?"

"No, sir," Dunlap replied. "Regulations state that I am not supposed to salute you because my dog may interpret that as a signal to attack, sir!"

"REGULATIONS? WHAT REGULATIONS? I HAVE NEVER HEARD OF ANY REGULATION STATING THAT, AIRMAN!"

The lieutenant felt he had caught a terrible error in Dunlap's routine. He proceeded to chastise him for it.

"AIRMAN, I HAVE NEVER HEARD OF ANY SUCH REGULATION. I'M AN OFFICER AND YOU WILL SALUTE ME WHEN YOU REPORT YOUR POST TO ME, GOT IT?"

His fate was now sealed. Dunlap had been surreptitiously letting out a little of Blackie's leash as each word of the abuse went on. Now only slack lead lay at his side. Blackie had plenty of room. The lieutenant was five feet away. Dunlap figured Blackie had about three and a half feet of leash.

Dunlap snapped to attention, raised his hand to salute, (and secretly gave Blackie a kick) "YES, SIR!"

Blackie shot out like a black and tan rocket leaving the tube, displaying his ferocious teeth. Dunlap said, "He lunged with a fury I hadn't seen since the first time he chased me out of his kennel."

The lieutenant's face went white, but he stood there, with Blackie's nails raking his chest and his saliva splattering over his uniform. Dunlap said, "Just how scared he got, only his laundry lady knew for sure."

The officer sputtered and walked away, flinching every time he heard Blackie bark. When they got off duty and walked back to the kennel, other handlers told Dunlap the lieutenant's next visits had been uneventful. He stayed well away from them. He didn't ask anyone to salute.

Every night, Dunlap and Blackie patrolled the perimeter while the Marines slept. On nights when he was unbearably sleepy, he'd set an alarm for half an hour and order Blackie to stay on watch. "I knew that I could safely snooze and that he'd stay up watching for me. I'd wake up, stretch, and tell him to lie down. Those were the only times he would ever sleep on the job, when I told him to. You should have heard him snore! He watched for me, I'd watch for him. He understood our arrangement."

Once, Dunlap tripped coming back from patrol and his helmet fell off. Blackie picked it up and kept on going, so they went to the kennel like that, the dog carrying the three-pound metal helmet in his mouth. It amused Dunlap. What he didn't realize was that Blackie now considered the helmet *his*. If he put it on the ground, Blackie took it, and when he did, there was no getting it back from him. Dunlap recalled a scene when incoming rockets were about to land, and he wanted the helmet on his head. Blackie said no. The two of them rolled around on the ground, fighting for control of the helmet, while the Marines hooted.

"That made me mad," Dunlap said. "I said, 'Dammit, this isn't funny!' And the chorus came back, 'Yes, it is.'"

Blackie won the helmet that day. "He could crush cannonballs with his jaws," Dunlap says. "He became very attached to me, but I never forgot that." He says he still bears a long scar on his ring finger from the one time Blackie nailed him.

The Marines hated him; the people in the kennel hated him. Greg Dunlap was his only friend. But Blackie was a dog who was very, very good at his job. Dunlap recalled a day they were posted near Marine Bravo Company on the south side of the camp. They were close to the bunker of the CQ, so there wouldn't be any joking around with Marines that night.

Dunlap wanted to maintain a low profile while they were within sight of an officer. But almost as soon as they got there, Blackie snapped to alert to something beyond the fence.

If the enemy was approaching, Dunlap had to let the Marines know, now. But if he notified them, and Blackie was wrong and there was no enemy, he'd be in a lot of trouble, not to mention it would bring more hatred down on Blackie than he already had. "And just then—another one!" Dunlap said. "Ears straight up and focused, nose and eyes going back and forth searching, but ears fixed in front. There was something there."

Dunlap asked the Marines if any of their people were out beyond the fence, and got the question, "Why?"

"My dog is hearing something out there." The Marine got on the radio and told the CQ. "He calls down to me that the Captain is coming and wants to talk to me. I'm thinking, 'Oh, great. I hope I didn't put my foot in my mouth.'" He looked down at his dog. Blackie was still staring into the distance. "Blackie was never wrong," he thought. "He never gave a false alert. Never."

The Captain approached and asked, "What's going on, K-9?"

"Sir, my dog is hearing some noise out there ahead of our position. From the way he's acting, I'd say it's more than a little ways off. I was asking the guys in the bunker if you had anyone out in the bush in front of us poking around tonight."

"We have an LP out about a half to one klick or so. But they're not supposed to be making any noise. That dog of yours able to hear that far out?"

"He's hearing something out that way," Dunlap replied.

The Captain contacted the listening post by radio. When he turned back, he told them that one guy had been playing with his Zippo lighter, but stopped. That couldn't be it, could it?

Dunlap had the solution. "Tell you what. Ask him to count to ten and do it again." Dunlap had no idea if Blackie could hear a Zippo lighter that was one kilometer away. All the men were mentally counting down, four, three, two, one—pause and— Blackie snapped his head around, ears up, hair bristling across his back and a low growl emanating from his chest. "A perfect textbook alert," Dunlap said. "You'd have to be blind to miss it."

As he moved away from the group, he heard the Captain, "in full officer fury, chewing out some poor Marine about how if my dog can hear him screwing up all the way back here, Charlie only has to be in the same country to do the same."

The Captain called out, "Good job, K-9!"

Dunlap thought to himself, "One thing for sure, next time anyone on K-9 says his dog is alerting, this company of Marines is going to pay real close attention."

There were outings to China Beach in the summer, a romp in the saltwater that was supposed to wash off the ever-present fleas and ticks. And there were lots of tricks to play; he was once walking with one of the other dogs; a gentle Shepherd named Cinder, and lifted her into the back of a Jeep. When the driver and passenger turned around, they both leapt out of vehicle so fast they fell. They thought Blackie was sitting behind them.

Somehow, the year in hell passed. Dunlap found himself nearing the day he could leave Vietnam, a joyful moment except for one thing. Even when he wrote about it, Dunlap put his feelings in the second person, an attempt to keep the pain of these words away:

"At the end of that six-foot leash was another individual, and they weren't going home with you. As far as they were concerned, they were home. And you being there with them was all they ever asked for. You were leaving, and they were staying behind. How could you explain that? You had told them every story about your life you could remember, and not just once. All your dark secrets, regrets, triumphs, and embarrassments. Everything! And through it all, they had just sat there, and acting like it was the first time they had heard it. They had enjoyed every word out of your mouth, and had thanked you afterwards for the tale.

"They watched your back, acted as your muscle and your counsel. You poured out your heart to them, and they gave back all their love, devotion, and respect. Now you were leaving, and they were staying behind. How do you explain that and feel good afterwards?

"Every one of us acted the same on that last day. We'd joke around the hut with everyone. The usual banter. Then you realize the full impact of the day. You were leaving, and they were staying behind. We had shared a bond, a trust, and it was ending. In one respect you felt such joy at leaving. Yet in another, such sadness at what you were leaving behind.

"Goodbye, Blackie. Believe me, I'll never forget you."

—

DUNLAP KEPT his promise. He says not a day has gone by that he hasn't thought about his dog. Forty years later, his e-mail address bears Blackie's name. "He was the ideal animal for the situation I was in," he says sadly. "This was truly a unique animal. He affected everyone that he touched or came into contact with through his presence. There are six handlers, whom we know of, who were deeply touched by him."

I asked if he thought that Blackie had saved American lives. "Without a doubt," he instantly replied. "Before the K-9s, that base was attacked and infiltrated. After the dogs got there, it was never infiltrated. No base guarded by sentry dogs in Vietnam was infiltrated. The Viet Cong had a price on every soldier's head. But the price on a dog's head was twice as much."

THE DALMATIAN WHO WENT HOME FROM THE WAR

KEVIN DOYLE and Margaret Emmerly met at an anti-Vietnam War rally in Washington, D.C. Dancing on the green lawn of the National Mall, they yelled, "End the War Now!" and "Bring Home the Baby Killers!" and sang along with antiwar songs by Bob Dylan and Joan Baez. They rode back to Washington on the bus for all the marches against the Vietnam War, and were in the crowd that cheered John Kerry and eight hundred other antiwar veterans when they tossed their medals and ribbons over a fence at the front steps of the United States Capitol Building.

In between protests, back in Margaret's small hometown in Oklahoma, they married and gave birth to a son, James, named after their favorite singer, James Taylor. They inculcated little Jimmy with their own peace, love, and antiwar values. So they were shocked to their boot soles when Jimmy, at age eighteen, announced he had joined the Navy.

Once enlisted, Jim decided to take on the eleven months of extra training that would qualify him as a Navy SEAL, the elite Special Operations Forces who specialize in unconventional warfare, guerrilla warfare, foreign internal defense missions, counter-terrorism, and special reconnaissance operations. The physical training is extremely rigorous. Men can't pass unless they can do forty-two push-ups in less than two minutes, at least fifty sit-ups in two minutes, six pull-ups from a dead hang, and run 1.5 miles in under eleven minutes. In high school, Jim had already begun training himself as a marathon runner. The physical tasks were not a problem.

That's how young Navy Lieutenant Doyle found himself in Croatia in 1995, doing reconnaissance work with a SEAL Special Warfare Unit along the Dalmatian coast. The world had not yet heard the name Slobodan Milosevic, the country's president who would eventually stand trial for war crimes. But there were deadly battles going on around the tourist towns of Dubrovnik and Split Croatia, as Milosevic's Serbian Nationalists attacked the minority Albanians, attempting to completely eliminate them.

There was an important policy issue at stake. President Clinton wanted to intervene to stop "ethnic cleansing," the name given to what was going on in the former Yugoslav Republic because the United Nations had voted that it was not genocide. But it didn't matter what you called it. As Doyle and his unit tramped through the small villages and towns, what they saw was mass murder. Their job was to document and provide indisputable evidence of what was going on. It was hard work, and very wearing on the men, both physically and emotionally.

These civil wars were turning out to be the bloodiest conflicts on European soil since World War II. Hundreds of thousands of people were compelled to leave their homes and many thousands more lost their lives, often in atrocities such as the Srebrenica and Bratunac massacres. The people had been reduced to poverty. Ethnic hostility ran high. Doyle and his unit were constantly reminded of the importance of their work, which was to document enough of what was going on that forces from other countries would be compelled to step in to stop the violence. They saw dead bodies every day.

Doyle sometimes saw military working dogs with their handlers, checking buildings for explosives and searching cars for bombs. He'd had dogs as a child, "little white balls of mutt," he called them. But the military working dogs never struck him as pets. "Those dogs are serious animals," Doyle said. "I look at working dogs as tools. When I'm with a dog like that on the field, that dog was bred specifically to insure my safety and the accomplishment of the mission. If I were to develop attachment it would make my job that much harder. It's better in that kind of environment to not develop that. It's a coping mechanism."

Then came a day the platoon was sent out on a non-routine patrol. They were walking through country that had just been hit by armed men, following a path of ruination. Everything had been destroyed: homes, cars, trucks, stores, even the wooden carts the farmers used to sell vegetables in the street. They witnessed the destruction and documented it. It was like walking on the moon; there were no other people to be found, anywhere, only dead bodies.

In the farming land along their path, they came upon a house that had been burned down the night before. Two stone chimneys stood shakily at either end, but there was very little of the house left in between. In these cases, they always looked for survivors. They found none. A father, mother, and three children had been lined up and shot in the head, execution-style. In order to cope with the horror, Doyle and the men had a way of not taking it all in. They didn't want to stop and think about the normal human lives that had been destroyed here.

These houses always had a big basement, useful to the farmers for storing grain and other crops. Doyle and six other men made their way gingerly down the staircase, rifles pointing in every direction. You never knew if one of the insurgents had been left behind, specifically to shoot anyone who came to aid the victims. "Our adrenalin was pumping. We were all looking over our shoulders."

One man heard a stirring underneath the rubble. With the tip of his rifle, he pushed away debris and uncovered a trunk. When he lifted the cover, he called out, "Hey, look at this!"

In the box was a litter of white puppies, seven in all. Doyle picked them up and was amazed to see that two were still alive. A male and female, only a few weeks old, had obviously been stashed in the trunk for safekeeping by a caring owner. Now, the family members were dead. The puppies had survived, even while the family was losing their lives.

Doyle said, "They weren't getting enough oxygen. Had we been an hour later they would have died, too."

Doyle held the female, and a shipmate held the male. They were at a loss about what to do. Both puppies were in bad condition. They were close to death. The medical corpsman pointed out that both were grossly dehydrated. That was a condition the man had been trained for, and he knew what to do. So, with the agreement of the group, he took out his medical supplies and gave them both an IV of life-saving liquids. As the liquids reached their systems, something amazing happened. The two puppies began to squirm and move their legs. They started to revive. Their lives had not yet been lost.

Doyle says that while some men were touched by the puppies' plight, others "were sickened by it." They had just humped through miles of destruction in which they'd found no living humans. Coming upon these struggling puppies was a shock. What to do? The group could not agree. Some felt they should put the puppies down and get on with their mission. Others were adamant that they could not leave these little lives here alone. Doyle said, "It's like when a ship is at sea, you have to go to help that ship that is in distress. That's how this was."

They decided to call tactical operations center and report. Doyle said, "When we did that, we were shifting the responsibility off our own shoulders and onto theirs." While they waited for an answer, they began documenting the scene, using a procedure for collection that could be utilized by the U.N. if evidence was ever needed in the case. To their surprise, the answer came back that they were to proceed to the refugee camp, about ten clicks away, and find any neighbors of the family. The puppies could be turned over to them.

Lt. Doyle still shakes his head in wonder at that order. "They could have told us to leave them there and get on with our mission, and that would have been a completely legal order. I've always thought there must have been a P.R. person hanging around that day who said, 'Hey, returning puppies would be good publicity.' Or something like that."

They plotted out a route to the refugee camp. Doyle says there was little grumbling. Everyone in the platoon agreed this was important. But it meant abandoning their original mission. "It was a mission we had trained hard for and traveled a great distance to do. And we didn't get to do it because of this dog. You got a bunch of warriors who want to go do something, hoo-rah! And now all of a sudden, 'We got to carry a dog?' But we fulfilled that mission with the same vigor we would have used if we went to fulfill the other one."

They humped for three hours to reach the refugee camp. Doyle says, "Humping is hiking without the fun." There was a sad moment when the male puppy, which had been pressed against a corpsman's chest, died. The men stopped to bury it; then they continued. Doyle remembers, "I had the female puppy in the crook of my left arm. The puppy got really heavy so I made a sling out of a bungee strap because my arm started getting cramped. It worked fine. The important thing was I could have dropped the puppy and pulled my gun or my knife if I had to." But after a while, even the sling arrangement became painful. But pain is something a SEAL knows. "You have to grin and bear it and just think about how you can stretch when you get wherever it is that you're going."

A refugee center is one of humanity's self-made wonders. This one contained twenty-five thousand people. Hundreds of military tents were lined up in neat rows, each one enclosing a family group who had lost their home, land, jobs, means of support, and many loved ones. A chain link fence enclosed its many acres of suffering and loss, a barricade against the further harm of these disrupted lives. A constantly changing guard of United Nations forces patrolled it. Lt. Doyle remembers that as they approached, they saw a group of about twenty Polish soldiers on one side and ten Turkish soldiers guarding another approach. It was a bit amusing because Doyle noticed, "There was no way these two groups could talk to each other. They didn't understand a thing the other group said."

The platoon was asked to leave their weapons outside the fence, which meant unstrapping and unbuckling numerous rifles, pistols, grenades, and knives. Everything was coated with mud. Doyle remembered, "It was a cold, nasty, wet, misty kind of weather that day."

Inside, they were taken to a tent that was a kind of office, where all the thousands of people and their stories were locked on to computers. "They had laptops and files and everything in this place was organized. They knew where everybody was." Refugee camp officials had already located the dead family's closest neighbors and summoned them, but hadn't told them why.

As the neighbors approached, Doyle could see that they were terrified. "To them, a uniform represented a death sentence. Their experience was that people in uniforms did one thing; they killed you." Accordingly, the parents were in front, sheltering their children and elderly behind them. Doyle says it was hard to see exactly how many of the surrounding crowd were family members. "They have no TV, no games, nothing. We were the entertainment for the day. Guys in uniform looking dirty and ragged. With grease on our faces. Warriors. Unlike the clean-shaven nicely dressed people guarding the place. "The interpreter introduced a man in his forties. The Slavic names were difficult for the Americans to grasp. "It was Vag-lock, or something like that," Doyle said. His family was grouped tight behind him.

The SEALS felt uncomfortable. Standing next to Doyle was a very senior, very high-ranking Navy SEAL. Doyle says, "This guy was a diehard warrior. He thought this mission was completely frivolous. He was tired of carting around the fricking puppy." The men began to shuffle, wanting to deliver the puppy and get out of there.

The translator began to explain. Doyle saw that the family was still frightened. They simply couldn't believe they could be called in front of uniformed men without something terrible happening. For a moment, there seemed to be a misunderstanding in which the family thought that these Navy SEALs were actually the killers. Doyle says, "That's when I pulled out the puppy."

The adults seemed frozen, trying to take in this sudden shift. But a pretty young girl about ten years old pushed to the front of the crowd and reached out for the puppy. As she cuddled it in her arms, the men didn't need the translator to know that she knew this puppy. It belonged to her friends.

The translator was explaining that this was all that was left of their neighbors. He was saying in Slavic, "These men are not the ones who committed the atrocities. They are here to give you what's left of them. They are here to offer you their sympathy over the family that passed away."

They all started crying, all at the same time. They hadn't known the family was dead. They had lived next to these people for generations. These people had worked hard and lived well for most of their lives. It was just in this recent time that killing began, making all of their familiar country unsafe.

The little girl was absolutely in shock. Doyle recalled, "I thought this child was going to cry but I don't think she could. She'd seen so much, so many horrific things. The atrocities were unbelievable. They would hack people's arms off and leave them. I know she saw that stuff. There's no doubt. I don't think she could cry. These kids would grasp on any little bit of goodness and humanity they could get, just to soak it up and stay alive that much longer."

Doyle said, "I remember them looking around and looking at their tent. Saying something to each other that I would interpret as, 'Where the hell are we going to keep this dog?' The father and mother spoke with the girl, and she said something back." Then, the girl stepped forward and pushed the puppy back to Doyle. She said, "Will you take care of this dog for me? Take her with you and give her a home. Give her to your child."

She nodded at Doyle, smiling, saying, "Take this dog with you. Take it back. You raise it."

The translator introduced the girl as, "Emira." She continued to press the puppy back into Doyle's arms. He said, "It makes me weep even today to recall the look on her face when she realized that we were not the enemy and that we were truly empathetic to their plight. She hugged me for a long time."

The rest of the family was overwhelmed by the humanity being demonstrated towards them. Emira said through the interpreter that her family would not be able to take care of the puppy. She said that the remaining days or weeks of her own life would probably be here in this god-forsaken place. She didn't think she would ever go home. There was no place for a puppy.

Doyle didn't know what to do. He turned to the CO, a man he calls, "the toughest, meanest, strongest man I had ever known in my life." There were tears in his eyes. Doyle said, "This guy understood a lot of the local language. He may have heard a lot more from them than I did from the translator." Doyle asked him what they should do. He knew regulations well, and they weren't allowed to accept gifts, much less take a dog. "The CO looked at the little girl and me and then he just nodded his head. He said, 'Yes.'"

Doyle thought that getting a dog from this country back to the United States would prove too difficult. But he was working with Navy SEAL psychology when he held up the puppy and said to the older officer, "We can't take this dog! How in the hell would we get this dog home? We can't do it. There's no way we can get a dog to the States." When presented with a challenge, a Navy SEAL steps up. By stating the problem the way he did, Doyle said, "It was like I dare, I double dare, I triple dog dare you. He took it as his challenge to get the dog home."

A truck was summoned to transport the SEALs back to their base of operations. They were just halfway through a ten-week deployment, so the first problem was going to be how to care for this puppy while still in country. Luckily, the puppy became extremely fond of MREs, "meals ready to eat." The platoon had plenty of those. There were different main courses every day, tuna salad, corn dogs, or ham. Doyle noticed, "She loved ham slices and scrambled eggs. Peanut butter and crackers. All government issued food. That was one thing we had, plenty of food."

Along the way, they learned that the all-white puppy was actually a Dalmatian, a namesake breed of the land. If you looked closely, you could see pale black splotches in her skin. She would eventually develop the unique black spots of the breed. With that in mind, Doyle named her, "Pebbles." He said, "Some guys had other names for her, some I can't mention, particularly after she'd chewed up some of their stuff."

Doyle and the puppy bonded quickly. Doyle didn't have a leash, but he found he didn't need one. When he took her for walks, the puppy stuck close to his side. Doyle said, "She was looking for comfort, and she was getting it, not just from me, but from all the men. Instant trust developed between her and me."

When the men went out on missions, Pebbles stayed in one

of their rooms. Doyle says, "We would swap out whose room she stayed in and whose stuff got to get chewed up. When she would chew things up, the guy would show up at my door with this mangled tee shirt and say, 'Okay, it's hers now.'" After the loss of multiple boots and tee shirts, they made a cage out of wood for the teething puppy. Then one day, traveling along a city street, a corpsman spied a plastic dog cage among the many things being offered for sale. Doyle said, "People were all over the side of the road selling everything they owned because they needed money." The platoon halted and bought it from him.

But even with the plastic cage, Doyle still had a problem controlling what the puppy ate. She was the pet and mascot of the whole group, so SEALs who cuddled her on their lap would share their hamburger, Twinkies, candy bar, or potato chips. Doyle said, "That poor dog got so sick. Even after I yelled at them the guys would still walk by her cage and stuff candy in. They thought, 'Hey, I eat it.'" Doyle spent a lot of time cleaning up after Pebbles vomited.

During this time, he noticed a metamorphosis among the seasoned warriors who made up the squad. "The meanest, toughest guys I've ever seen simply turned into giggling school boys around the puppy." Doyle felt that holding and caring for the puppy was a way "to connect with home, with kindness, and with their humility." It was a moment of relief for the men, but Doyle worried, "Having that puppy around made them lower their guard."

When the ten-week mission came to an end, sure enough, the Navy SEAL captain stepped up to help Doyle get her home. Doyle doesn't want to give too many details of the trip, because Navy and military regulations were broken to get the dog exfilled (military slang for go home) onto various planes, and he doesn't want anyone to face a court martial over it, even today, when he's retired from the service.

Once he reached his home on the West Coast, Doyle introduced Pebbles to his wife. The two quickly bonded. Pebbles had a bad case of worms, but once the veterinarian cured that, she experienced a growth spurt. At maturity, she was a normal sized, fifty-pound Dalmatian. Photos of her show a healthy, athletic dog with intense black eyes. Pebbles turned out to be an outstanding example of her breed. Dalmatian breeders admired her structure and good health.

Pebbles turned out to be a sweet and sensitive member of the family, and, as she grew, Pebbles also appointed herself guardian over their infant daughter, Bethany Ann. But she still retained some of the Dalmatian's nutty traits. For instance, Doyle remembers that the families on his block liked to close the street and have barbecues. "This Dalmatian would be running at top speed, going as fast as she could go, around everybody in a big circle for an hour. Everybody was looking at her like she was crazy. She wasn't interested in chasing something. She just wanted to run." Dalmatians are extremely sensitive, although not the easiest dogs to train. Doyle and his family never did get the Dalmatian properly leash trained. He shakes his head. "Even Cesar Milan would have had a tough time training with that dog."

Doyle began to notice something odd. Everyone who came around the house, family friends and babysitters and workmen, all fell in love with their dog, yet Pebbles was not one to greet people enthusiastically. She kept a distance. But once she accepted a person, she seemed to exert an almost magical hold on their heart. Doyle found he had no trouble finding dogsitters, even when he was away for a long stretch.

Sometimes he wondered how it was that he ended up with the dog. "Maybe because nobody else rogered up and said, 'I'll take it.' I just did it. I was the lucky one, I guess." If he hadn't come forward, or another platoon had found the puppies, he believes that someone else would have done the same thing.

"There are bad things that happen in the fog of war but overall the majority of people are good. Plato used to talk about that. It's an old concept. It still rings true. Regardless of the fear or personal sacrifice, everybody that I've ever served with would have done the same thing."

Pebbles remained a loving and healthy member of Doyle's family until she passed away at fourteen from age-related ailments. Doyle was devastated. The Dalmatian had held a large place in his life. He still sometimes sat up from a deep sleep, awakened by visions of the blood and mangled bodies the platoon had encountered on that mission in Dalmatia. He understood now that Pebbles had been "a candle of light in the middle of darkness. She helped all of us realize the value of life and humility."

Losing a beloved dog is a lonely sort of grief. Some of the platoon members had kept in touch over the years, and Doyle reached out to let a few of them know that Pebbles had passed. He was stunned by their reaction. "I received no less than a card and phone call from every single man that was on patrol with me, less the four of them who had lost their lives in service of their country." An even greater shock arrived several days later; a card of condolence from the tough Navy SEAL captain whose intervention had saved Pebbles' life. Doyle wiped away a tear as he said, "I could tell his wife had filled out the card and signed his name. But if he had told his wife about that mission and everything that happened with the puppy there, then it is obvious that it touched him a great deal more than I ever would have imagined." A year later, Doyle said he still misses her. "She taught me how to love unconditionally, because that's what she did."

Doyle sometimes wonders what kind of adult Emira turned out to be. He is haunted by the memory of her little face, pleading with them to take the dog. He tried to find out what had happened to her. He received word years later that the family had immigrated to The Netherlands.

"I was never able to confirm this as fact, but I hope that this story is published somewhere and that little girl, now fully grown, reads it and knows what she did for all of us. If you are reading this, Emira, thank you. We made sure the puppy had the wonderful life you wanted for her. I hope you have the wonderful life that you wanted for yourself."

SEVENTEEN POUNDS
OF EXPLOSIVES AND
THE DALAI LAMA

STAFF SERGEANT ROBERT J. BLACK was born and raised in southern California. He loved the sunny weather and easygoing lifestyle of Orange County, where a cool winter day is when the temperature ducks down into the sixties. He liked outdoor concerts and lying in the sand on Huntington Beach or Sunset Beach or visiting Disneyland, just thirty minutes away.

After high school, he got one of the prime jobs for a young Californian: disc jockey at a local radio station. In addition to all the other agreeable things life held, now he played his favorite music for everyone and got to talk about it while he was at work.

It was a comfortable life for a young man. But when he fell in love and wanted to get married, he started to see that he wanted more. He started thinking about the opportunities offered by the military. He talked it over with his dad, who had retired from the Navy. Then he signed up for the Air Force. From the beginning, he had his eye on becoming a Military Working Dog handler.

"The instructors would come to the Law Enforcement classes to enroll volunteers. But it was hit and miss about which class they would go to. So I went down to the kennel and met the noncommissioned officer in charge and told him how interested I was. He made sure to come to my class."

It was 1995. The United States military had just completed Operation Desert Storm. The Middle East was still an active area. Black was sent out on his first Temporary Duty assignment. to Qatar, then Al-Jaber Air Base in Kuwait, then to Prince Sultan Air Base in Riyadh, Saudi Arabia. He was working with a German Shepherd named Pete. Two types of duty made up most of these assignments, searching vehicles at the gate and walking the perimeter alone.

"If I had to walk the perimeter by myself, I'd be a little scared. But having a dog with you gives you a lot of courage. He's going to notice anybody a lot quicker than you would."

One day, Sgt. Black and Pete arrived back at the gate to find an argument going on between the guard and several men who were demanding to be let in. They were getting very vocal, screaming and yelling. Pete pulled him toward the commotion. As soon as the outsiders saw Pete, they quieted down and went away.

"Dogs are great deterrents. We always say, you can talk to another cop and try to persuade him to go your way. But you can't talk to a dog. A dog has one thing on his mind—he wants to bite you. They end up quieting down because they don't want to get bit."

Next was a yearlong assignment to Korea, difficult duty because soldiers have to leave their families for a year. But the next assignment was a good one, at Ramstein Air Base in Germany. Now he was living in Europe, enjoying a life that was very different from the one he'd lived in California. Then it was a Permanent Change of Station to Kirtland Air Base in Albuquerque, New Mexico.

He was partnered with an older dog named Zorro. Every day, as he took Zorro in and out of his kennel, a high-strung dog named Aron, who lived across the aisle, would go crazy, barking at them. "It was really annoying. I thought, 'I feel sorry who ever has to work with that dog.'"

Then Zorro retired. Much to his dismay, the high-strung barking dog became his new partner. "Aron was a straight bomb dog. He wasn't trained in patrol. So when I picked him up, he had a high drive and was harder to control than most dogs." It took a lot of training to get him patrol certified.

Aron was a Belgian Malinois, one who was on the small side for the breed. But Aron was a fast learner. It was a good thing, because in December of 2005, he accompanied Black on a six-month tour of Iraq. They found themselves attached to an army unit in Baquba, a city about thirty miles north of Baghdad, scene of some of the heaviest insurgent fighting. Baquba lies just outside the Sunni triangle of Samarra, Ramadi, and Falujah. The Army Third Infantry Division was finding it difficult to keep the insurgents from taking over. Dogs were at work every day. "We were attached to the Army because Army teams were getting over-tasked," Sgt. Black said. "So they started pulling from the Air Force, even though we aren't part of their service."

There was only one other team to handle the entire city and the whole Diyala province. Sgt. Black and Aron worked twelve-hour shifts with few breaks.

"We would go out with Special Forces or whoever was going out on missions. Whoever requested a dog for that day. The order would come down, 'You got a mission at three in the morning with the 1-68.' And they'd give you the best intel they could give you as far as what the mission is going to be."

Every mission had a name, such as Operation Fury, Operation Fort Defiance, Operation Moultrie II. Most missions were raids on small towns or villages where there was intel that somebody was selling arms or making explosive devices or harboring insurgents. On this day, at three-fifteen in the morning, Sgt. Black and Aron left FOB Warhorse with Alpha 1-68 on their way to the small town of Naqib.

The Army unit raided and secured the town. Then Sgt. Black and Aron were sent in to look for bombs or explosives. "We would essentially sweep their houses with our dogs. We would search farmers' fields and palm groves. We'd search anywhere they might be hiding explosives or caches."

Sgt. Black explained that the open field search was something many of the dogs were not prepared for. "We trained them to search vehicles and buildings. So when we took them to the field and told them to search, they would get confused. They'd look around for the vehicle, like they were saying, 'Where is it? What do you want me to do?'"

He'd given Aron some beginning training in an open field. So the dog understood what to do and worked the fields with his nose. Aron was quick to pick up the task.

At first, Aron and Sgt. Black weren't really welcome on missions because of one of Aron's bad habits. Sgt. Black said, "You put him in the Humvee and that dog barked from the time we left the base till we got to where we were going. Even if it took hours. Depending on how long the mission was, if he had any energy left at all, he would bark all the way back."

Aron's previous handler had liked this barking behavior and reinforced it. In the back of the Humvee, there was no way Sgt. Black could control Aron. They were both strapped into passenger seats with a wide space between them. Sgt. Black sat behind the driver. But whoever sat in the passenger seat had a terrible headache during the time Aron was with them. The dog was barking his head off just three inches from the man's ear. Sgt. Black sighed, "I got him to stop barking at signs and trees, but he would still bark at cars and people."

Sgt. Black found out that some commanders were requesting the other dog just because he was quiet. But that changed about five weeks into their tour.

"The Special Forces knocked on this farmer's door and interrogated him. We had intel that he was keeping arms for the insurgents. His neighbors said a lot of people were coming and going at odd hours. He denied everything, 'No, no fighters here, no weapons here.'"

Sgt. Black and Aron were sent out back to search his vineyard. It was a hilly place, with lots of irrigation ditches. There was a lot of foliage to climb through. Grapes were approaching full ripeness and would soon be harvested by packs of workers. There were date palms throughout the field and poplar trees waved overhead.

As they worked their way down one row, Aron's body suddenly went rigid and he pulled hard towards a nearby bush. He sniffed the lower branches and glanced back at Black. Then he sat down.

A squad of men who had been following them hurried over. "What's going on?"

Sgt. Black said tensely, "He found something." Then he stepped away to pat his dog and praise him for his good work. Both of them watched the squad work. What you are uncovering could be booby-trapped to go off in your face when you touch it. Even if it's not booby-trapped, it could be unstable. EOD men (Explosive Ordinance Disposal) work with their lives on the line.

But not this time. After not finding anything with the metal detector, and digging a fairly wide area, they turned to Sgt. Black skeptically. "Your dog didn't find anything," one soldier told him. "There's nothing here."

"Maybe he's just tired," another soldier suggested. "He's sick of searching. He just wants to sit down."

"I said, 'Give me a second. He's onto something. Let me expand my search area.'" Sgt. Black never doubted for a minute that Aron had made a find. "I'd been with him long enough to tell. A dog that's tired isn't going to pull hard and sit down and wag their tail. Aron wasn't tired. I could tell from his sniffing behavior, rapidly breathing in and out, that he had found something."

The ground was really hard. The farmer had raked up old shrubbery and had it piled nearby. There were lots of bushes everywhere. Sgt. Black walked behind the first bush and let Aron sniff back into the wind. Within seconds, the dog shot to the end of his leash and began rapidly sniffing another bush. He sat down and looked at his handler. His tail was wagging furiously.

The squad groaned. They knew they had to check every spot where the dog alerted. But if this was going to be another false alarm, they did not appreciate the extra work. They grumbled as they set about digging.

But when they brought over the metal detector, it signaled rapidly that there was metal in this ground. Now they believed something was there. But everyone was surprised at the size of the find. It was seventeen pounds of Czech-made C-4 explosive, detonation cord, and half a dozen instructional CDs.

Because of its stability and sheer destructive power, C-4 is the explosive of choice of terrorists in the Middle East. A small amount of C-4 can do a lot of damage. It's easier to smuggle past security forces than most explosives. But when ignited, C-4 explodes with a force wave of eighteen thousand miles-per-hour. That force turns the major organs of a human body into jelly. It is totally impossible to outrun an explosion occurring at eighteen thousand miles-per-hour even though Hollywood has their action heroes do it all the time. What really happens is nearly instantaneous. One second, everything's normal, and the next, it's totally destroyed. C-4 is a highly productive way to kill a lot of people in a hurry.[1]

---

[1] C-4 does not contain metal. But it is always buried in some kind of metal container, and that's what the metal detector picked up.

The troops took the C-4 back to the farmer, who feigned total surprise. "How did that get there?" he asked the translator. "I have no idea. A lot of people walk through my vineyard. I've never seen that before in my life."

Sure.

How many lives did Aron save? There is no way to know for certain. Insurgents had brought that C-4 into the interior of Iraq because they intended to use it. They planned to set up IEDs that could be detonated remotely with a cell phone. They planned to pack it in a car and have the driver crash into an American facility. They planned to let a suicide bomber carry it on his body as he walked through a crowded marketplace and blow himself up. However the explosive was to be used, Aron had prevented that from happening. That day, Aron saved a lot of lives. But only the small group of men surrounding him knew it.

The only paycheck Aron wanted for his service was his toy, a red rubber ball. He had worked long hours and made a hugely productive find, but he was happy because he had his ball to chew on. He bounced it up and down on the hard ground, growling at it and chasing it across the dirt.

Sgt. Black said, "After that, every time they went on a mission they requested my dog. The same unit kept requesting me again and again. They trusted my dog. They knew my dog could find stuff."

They decided to put up with Aron in spite of all that crazy barking. It was a good decision. A few weeks later, 168th Armored Division was sent on another targeted mission. They requested Aron and Sgt. Black. The unit had intel that a villager had been stockpiling weapons in his home. Aron, of course, barked all the way there. They weren't told the name of the small town. But a map shows Baquba is surrounded by, among others, Al Khalis, Balad, Cha Khanah, Rus, and Al Miqdadiyah.

The soldiers moved down the street in front of the man's

home while others patrolled streets nearby. They hadn't reached his home when the man, apparently aware he was about to be interrogated, burst out of his house and shot off rounds from his AK-47. The Americans hit the dirt and fired back, but he dashed behind the house and disappeared into a forest of palm trees.

The soldiers called for Aron to assist in the search. They had the area contained. They were sure the suspect was in the woods. But no one could find him. Sgt. Black gave Aron the order to find. Aron was happy to oblige. He pulled his handler into the forest and followed his nose through the trees.

The Iraqi had hunkered down in a hiding place behind a lot of old palm fronds and other discarded vegetation. He was well-hidden, and he knew it. He'd heard the soldiers tramp by him, back and forth, without discovering his hideout. He was planning to wait them out. Eventually, they'd go back to base and he'd sneak back into his home.

Suddenly, a roaring monster came at him, breaking through the palm fronds, barking loudly and angrily, scaring him so much that he popped out of the spot with his hands above his head, dropping the machine gun. Even though soldiers surrounded him with rifles pointed at him, his eyes were fastened on Aron. He was obviously in a state of complete terror. Sgt. Black said, "He was more afraid of the dog than he was of the guns." The soldiers led the insurgent away for interrogation. He seemed relieved to get out of range of Aron's teeth.

Aron helped the soldiers locate rocket launchers and rockets buried in his backyard. "He denied having them, though. When they questioned him, he pretended like he didn't know how they got there. 'I have no idea!' He played ignorant. 'Okay, whatever.'

"That's where our job ends. Once they interrogate him and load him up, our job is done. It's somebody else's job now."

In the six months Aron and Sgt. Black spent in Diyala province, they assisted in finding and detaining over 2,500 insurgents. Aron's work was incredibly effective. He got so good that instead of being happy to see the last of the noisy barking dog, the unit was sorry when the handler and his dog came to the end of their deployment.

"They gave me a certificate of thanks and appreciation and off we went. Another Air Force handler came in to replace me."

Sgt. Black says Aron wasn't necessarily better than other dogs. "He was a dog who did everything really well. He wasn't the greatest at everything. But Aron was a well-rounded dog. Each dog has their little quirks. Aron had his quirks with barking and being goofy at times."

I told Sgt. Black I considered Aron a hero.

"So do I. He's pretty darn cool."

When Sgt. Black and Aron got to Kirtland, the kennel master was there to meet them. He took the dog team back to the kennel so Aron could be put away for a good rest. There was none of the fanfare that greets the military units who ship out and come back in a group. But the lack of fanfare rankles a little with all of the Military Working Dog handlers. It's one reason why Sgt. Black agreed to tell this story. Aron doesn't ask for anything but his handler and his toy, he said. He works in anonymity, as hard and long as any soldier. He deserves a little recognition.

Sgt. Black went home to his wife, baby son, black Labrador Retriever, and Pomeranian. He was glad to be there in one piece, but a few months later, Sgt. Black and Aron were summoned from New Mexico by the Secret Service to Manhattan to provide protection for the United Nations General Assembly. Another event was taking place at the same time, the visit to Manhattan of the Tibetan religious leader, the Dalai Lama.

They arrived at a midtown hotel and met up with eleven other dog teams. All had been summoned to protect the dignitaries. They met with the Secret Service early in the morning and were given a list of tasks. Sgt. Black was told, "You have the most experience. We want you on the detail with the Dalai Lama for the next three days."

The first thing on the list: sweep fashion designer Donna Karan's studio at 711 Greenwich Street. She was holding a luncheon for the Dalai Lama. Sgt. Black put aside his usual casual sportswear and wore a suit for this assignment. They entered the ten-thousand-foot studio. Sgt. Black was impressed by the celebrities and fashions that surrounded them. But Aron didn't care. He ignored everyone and did his job, following the room with his nose, checking all the cupboards and closets and under the stage. Several people entered the room while they worked. When Black looked up, he recognized the actress Susan Sarandon and musician David Bowie watching them. When Black took Aron outside for a break, to let him romp around a little and relax, Susan Sarandon came out; she smiled and paused for Sgt. Black to snap her picture.

But there was no time to stop and talk; the Dalai Lama wanted to visit a museum that was having an exhibit of Tibetan art. Black and Aron rushed there to sweep it for bombs and explosives. Once again, Aron had his head to the ground, working hard, not caring that centuries of priceless paintings and gold-plated armor and Buddha statues surrounded him. The Secret Service agent ushered them out as the Dalai Lama and his entourage entered. Black says, "The Secret Service agents have a lot of respect for the dogs. But they want them out of the way when the event is going on. They don't want people looking at the dog and wondering why he's here and getting nervous."

On this trip, Aron's particular quirks were a little unnerving. There were lots of wealthy guests staying at the hotel, and quite a few of them had little lapdogs trotting at their heels. Once, the elevator door popped open and put Black and Aron face-to-face with a woman in high heels and diamonds and her five-pound white Poodle. Aron was a dog who had lived all his life in a military kennel. He was prepared to face invaders, armed men, hardened criminals, rebels, insurgents, and suicide bombers. But a tiny dog like that flustered him. He started barking and wanted to charge them, a move Sgt. Black blocked with his body while he dragged the seventy-eight-pound dog away.

Next it was back to the Dalai Lama's hotel, to check out his rooms before he retired for the night. The Tibetan entourage got back earlier than expected. Sgt. Black heard the ping of the elevator bell and saw the group starting down the hall. A Secret Service agent quickly moved them into an adjoining room. But the Dalai Lama had spotted them; he smiled and came towards the handler and dog with his hand out. Aron barked at him, as he was trained to do to discourage the approach of an unknown stranger. It scared the holy man.

"He didn't know he was the most peaceful man on earth," Sgt. Black said. "All he saw was someone coming at me. He's trained to protect me, and that's what he was going to do."

The Dalai Lama backed up and continued to his room.

Sgt. Black and Aron protected the man for three days. It was a busy time. The religious leader attended a debate about Tibet at Columbia University, picked up an honorary degree at Rutgers, and gave a talk to the assembled undergraduates on war, peace, and reconciliation. He granted an audience to the Tibetan, Mongolian, and Himalayan Buddhist citizens of New York at Madison Square Garden. He celebrated his seventieth birthday.

Before he left, the Secret Service agents in the detail asked if they could get their pictures taken with him. He graciously agreed. Sgt. Black and Aron got their picture taken, too.

Sgt. Black was still worried about Aron charging him the day before. He put on Aron's muzzle before they went in. "I told him,

'I'm sorry about my dog barking at you.' He said, 'That's okay, that's okay.' I said, 'That's why he has the muzzle on now, so you feel safe.'"

This time Aron sat next to the man, quietly.

With the Dalai Lama on his way to Buffalo, Sgt. Black and Aron were turned to the work of protecting the United Nations dignitaries while they attended the General Assembly. From sunup to sundown, the partners searched hotel rooms, meeting rooms, museums, vehicles, and theaters. They traveled from the Millennium Hotel to the Waldorf Astoria several times a day.

There was a lot of tension among the diplomats because the Democratic People's Republic of Korea announced that it had just conducted a successful nuclear weapons test. The UN consensus was that they should stop such work immediately and return to multilateral talks on the issue at UN Headquarters in New York. No one wanted nuclear war. No one wanted their country to be targeted.

When Sgt. Black looks back on that time, he says, "I have great history to tell my son. I protected the president and got to shake his hand. I protected the Dalai Lama and I have my picture with him to prove it. I traveled among all the world leaders." He laughs. "But you can't get a big head about it, because one minute, 'Hey, I'm with the Secret Service, I'm protecting the president,' and a month later you're in Iraq getting shot at. You get both ends of the spectrum."

"It's funny, because when I told my friends I was joining the Air Force, they said, 'What? The military? You've got to be kidding.' And now I go home and I'm telling them, 'I was hanging with the Dalai Lama in Manhattan. What have you been doing?' They're still hanging out in the same town, doing the same old job."

Sgt. Black considers his life as a dog handler so far. "I feel like I'm playing military," he laughs. "I haven't started working yet."

He thinks about how to explain the closeness he and Aron feel after a year of partnership. "I wrote a poem when I came back from Iraq. It's about how my dog got no fanfare when we came back. I went on leave, and when I came back, he got to play with his toy. That's all he cared about. He didn't care about Iraq and glory. He just cared about his handler and his toy."

ANOTHER FUN DAY
IN IRAQ

STAFF SERGEANT Jerrod Gaertner's partner is muscled, well-balanced, and stands alertly on his toes, leaning into the warm desert wind. He has an elegant appearance and proud carriage, as though he belongs in the palace that looms in the background, rather than the makeshift quarters of the working soldiers. He is strong, agile, alert, and full of life. His brown hair is neat and tinged with black. He resembles an extremely fit long distance runner or high jumper, except that he has four legs, rather than two.

What's odd about Sergeant Gaertner's Military Working Dog is his name: Oowen, pronounced "Owen" but spelled with two Os.

"All the dogs who come from the Air Force Puppy Program have two of the same first letters in their name," Sergeant Gaertner explained. Oowen was born at Lackland Air Force Base, the offspring of two Belgian Malinois Military Working Dogs. It's unusual for an MWD to be born in America. Most are purchased from European kennels. But about four years ago, the trainers and kennel master decided to try their hand at breeding a useful dog. If you judge by Oowen's litter, the program is a huge success. All six of the puppies are certified MWDs. Usually only a small percentage have the build, brains, athleticism, and cooperative nature it takes to make the grade.

"He's the biggest Belgian Malinois I've ever come across," says Gaertner about Oowen's one-hundred-pound frame. Most Mals hover around sixty-five pounds. When I present a photo of Oowen to a breeder of AKC purebred Belgian Malinois back in the States, his size annoys her. "The Europeans bred Malinois with Great Danes to increase the size," she sniffs. "They'll deny it, but it's true."

That's a violation of a purebred pedigree if you are registered with the American Kennel Club, but it doesn't matter at all to these partners in Iraq. Sgt. Gaertner is proud of his dog. He and Oowen have been in country only a month. They have earned a reputation as hard workers who are an asset to any unit. They have just come from a weeklong mission to a combat outpost in the middle of Sunni insurgent territory, back to their quarters at Camp Liberty.

Here's what happens when you ask questions of a soldier in the field. Where were you? "I can't answer that." What kind of mission were you on? "That would be something I am not a liberty to say." Can you tell me how Oowen worked with the unit on the mission? He considers the question. "I can't really talk about it," he finally says. He is exquisitely aware that he cannot divulge any details about U.S. operations. No enemy agent will ever pry loose an extra morsel of information from his lips.

What's important about Sgt. Gaertner and his partner is that when it's time to enter a building that might be rigged to explode, or cross a field that could conceal an Improvised Explosive Device, Oowen is at the front of the line, making sure it's safe for those who follow.

Camp Liberty, where Sgt. Gaertner and Oowen are billeted, was once Saddam Hussein's hunting grounds. Deer, fox, and ducks were plentiful here in the past, but now a glimpse of one is rare. Sgt. Gaertner can look out over the woods and wetlands and the artificial lake that Hussein had stocked with genetically-engineered, grossly overgrown carp. Hussein and his family enjoyed a huge palace with sixty-two rooms and twenty-nine bathrooms. Now, it's a tourist site for the military. Sgt. Gaertner and Oowen pose in front of the grandiose gold front door. The sign proclaims in Arabic that it was built in honor of the Iraqis who died fighting the Iranians in 1988 on the Al Faw Peninsula, a bloody siege that cost thousands of lives.

For the soldiers at Camp Liberty, there is a chapel, recreation building, PX, barbershop, Internet café, gym, basketball courts, and volleyball arenas. The Camp is occupied by around fourteen thousand troops living in what looks like an enormous trailer park, but is actually a small city of sturdy, wooden, air-conditioned bungalows called SEA (Southeast Asia) huts, replicas of those used by U.S. troops in Vietnam. The dining room is massive, air-conditioned and equipped with wide-screen televisions. If you don't want to eat there, there's a Burger King.

If you're in the States and want to chat with Jerrod Gaertner, you dial a local New York state number and he answers. "But we can't call out," he grumbles. As we chat, another call is coming in from home. It's his friend, the kennel master at Wright Patterson Air Base. "I'll talk to him later," he decides. Apparently staying in touch with home is not a problem. This is communication at the front line in modern warfare.

While Gaertner talks on the phone in the hallway, Oowen rests in his room just a few feet away. This is about as far apart as these partners ever get.

"He sleeps at the foot of my bed every night. He's with me all the time. And I love it."

That's one of the things that attracted him to dog handling. "I always loved dogs. Everyone in my family has a dog. But the thing I like most about this job is the fact that every day you go to work, you have the same partner. I used to see the K-9 handlers on the base, and their dog would be with them every time. It seemed a lot of fun to have that kind of bond. And that's exactly the case. The work becomes fun, because your dog is with you."

Being together all the time has put the two more in tune with each other, Gaertner says. "He has a very high drive to please his handler, which is me. So he is always ready to work. He'll do anything I ask him. If he understands it, he'll do it."

Oowen is a PED dog, which means he is trained in patrol and explosives detection. Some dogs specialize in only one or the other duty. Walking down a street in Iraq, Gaertner watches as Oowen sorts out the people he sees. "He knows a U.S. uniform," he says. "He'll sort of ignore them. But if he sees an Iraqi, particularly in Arab dress, he is very alert. He pays close attention to that person and always knows where he is.

"Same with coalition forces from other countries," Gaertner says, a little sheepishly. "He knows they're not Americans. He pays attention to them."

Why is he paying such close attention? "To protect me," Gaertner says simply. "That's what he cares about. He's a loving, friendly dog. But when it comes to my safety, it's like a light switch flips on and off. He will do anything he can to protect me. And the other soldiers around us as well. He'll do it just by natural instinct. I won't have to cue him up and give him a command to protect someone. He'll just do it."

Sgt. Gaertner claims that when not on protection duty, "He's a very friendly dog. Very social. I have a lot of trust in him. I can allow him to be around a lot of people without worrying that he's going to bite somebody."

Even though they've been in the country such a short time, Oowen has already alerted an American patrol to the presence of explosives. Since he can't say where it happened or what the explosive was, Sgt. Gaertner just talks about Oowen's training.

"The dog has a final cue—an alert built into their training to let the dog handler know that there is some sort of explosive odor the dog has detected.

"The old style would be for the dog to sniff out an area and if he finds any explosive, he sits down. He would look at the dog handler to basically receive a reward."

Oowen's reward is his Kong. Find the explosive; get to play with the Kong.

"The newer method being used is the deferred final response. Instead of sitting down and just looking at the handler, the dog will stay and stare at exactly where he believes the odor is coming from. They will continue to stare until the handler comes up with their toy." Gaertner laughs. "In training, you throw the toy somewhere near the source. Over here, you're not going to throw his toy at something that could possibly be an IED or a weapons cache. You're going to pull the dog away from it. You give him praise for doing a good job, and somebody else comes to confirm it, explosive ordnance disposal or engineers or whoever."

The dog handlers bunk together. They exchange tips and stories. They understand each other. There are about two hundred canine teams deployed in Iraq, among all the services. The bond they establish with their dogs is deep and trusting. "These dogs are like our children. I'm closer to my dog than I am to anyone other than my wife," said Staff Sgt. Charles W. Graves, the kennel master at Forward Operating Base Kalsu, about twenty miles southeast of Baghdad. Before he left the States, he wrote in his will that if he and his dog, a yellow Labrador Retriever named Udo, were to die together, they should be buried together.

It's an unusual request, but it's happened before. In July of 2007, Cpl. Kory D. Wiens and his Labrador retriever, Cooper, became the first soldier-dog team killed in action since Vietnam. The partners are buried side by side in Wiens's hometown in Oregon.

Since the start of the war in Iraq, about a thousand dogs have rotated through the country. Three have been killed in action.

Gaertner feels lucky. "We go outside of what's called the wire, which is the secure compound. Not everybody gets to do that. The majority of the people are here to support the ones who go outside the wire. They never get out into the country." Does Oowen like going outside the wire? "I think he loves it, personally. He's a very curious dog. Going to a bunch of places he's never been before and seeing a lot of things he's never seen before is fun for him."

He's also very aware that all Iraqis are terrified of him. "He's a great psychological asset. A lot of people are genuinely terrified of dogs. It keeps a lot of distance between people and the U.S. patrols when the dog is out. People aren't as prone to walk up to Americans when a dog is with them.

"Pretty much so far, I've never seen an Iraqi who was willing to come to close to my dog."

When they're not on a mission, they're training, or taking a rare chance to relax. "We'll go out and I give him an opportunity to just be a dog. So he's not constantly working."

An unfortunate aspect of life in Iraq is roving packs of wild dogs, running loose through the cities. "When it's time to work, Oowen doesn't care, to be completely honest with you. There could be a bunch of dogs sitting on the road barking at him, and he just still keeps listening to me. He doesn't seem to mind that they're there at all."

Here is one of the nice things about being a dog handler in Iraq: the infantry are always glad to see you. "They like having us around. They're not ever afraid of him. We'll pack into military vehicles and be tightly confined with a bunch of soldiers Oowen's never met before and there's no problem. He knows they're on our side. They know we're there to keep them safe."

Oowen's nose is constantly searching for TNT, C4, AK-47s,

wires, metal, and the other threats that insurgents have planted across Iraq to kill American soldiers. If he gets too close and sets one off, Oowen is in the lead and would take the brunt of the blast.

It's not just the fact that he protects them. "We go way out to an outpost in the middle of nowhere. These guys are in danger all the time. They're not in the big installation. They're on their own." The men watch as Gaertner scratches Oowen's back, and grin when he rears up onto Gaertner's chest, like a dance partner. They are standing around in full battle gear with loaded weapons, but they take a break to talk to Gaertner about their own dogs back home. Having Oowen there brings up pleasant memories, much the same way it does for patients in the hospital who are visited by therapy dogs.

How does he feel a month into this assignment? Tired and ready to come home? "Personally, as soon as I get back home, I'm going to be trying to figure how to come back. Because I actually love my job. I really really enjoy what I do. I don't think I'd like to have it any other way. You can spend your whole career training to do something and this is the time you get to actually put that into effect. You're better utilized here than anywhere else in the world. At this point, I'd rather be here."

But a tantalizing duty awaits back in Ohio. Gaertner and Oowen will support the Secret Service by protecting any presidential candidate who visits the Midwest. A lot of travel will be involved. Instead of marching down dusty streets, they will get to know the hill and plain cities of their homeland. Instead of searching pastures and markets, they will escort politicians into hotels and stadiums. Some of it will be the same; there are always vehicles to search and houses to clear.

Oowen has been on civilian duty before. They were training at Wright-Patt one day when a call came in from the police department in one of central Ohio's small towns. A suspect had escaped. They couldn't find him. Could the military dog team help them out?

Gaertner and Oowen were out of there like a shot. Oowen likes car rides. They met up with the civilian police in the parking lot near the Huffman Dam. The police had pulled over a car and arrested a man, who fought and got away. This suspect had a previous conviction for the armed robbery of a restaurant. He was dangerous. He was hiding in a massive area of woods near the dam. There was no way the police could locate him.

Oowen was happy to be out in a big park with the handler he loved. He began a search and instantly picked up the man's scent. Now it was a game, to catch up with the man and hold him. He worked his way through the woods.

The suspect knew he was well hidden. He was planning to stay where he was for a few hours. He knew the police couldn't find him in such a huge area. He'd simply wait them out, and then be on his way. But he heard Oowen's excited barks. He realized Oowen had scented him and was on his trail. He got up and ran. He changed course and tried to run in a different direction. But Oowen was still on the scent.

"We were able to scare him to run right into where the local police were waiting. Oowen was not the one who actually caught the guy that day. But without Oowen, they might never have found him."

Another call came in from a really small Ohio town, Mechanicsburg. It was the first day back to school for all the town's children. As soon as the kids got to school, a bomb threat had come in. School was dismissed, much to the dismay of parents. They wanted the school reopened so the kids could at least use the library and gym. But the small police department had neither bomb squad nor K-9 unit.

Wright-Pat was the closest place that had those things. Oowen leaped into the car again and traveled forty miles to the town's assistance.

Sgt. Gaertner says, "The world kind of stops in a small town like that. All the local businesses were shut down because they all had kids in that school." He was dismayed to see how large the building was: 169,000 square feet. There was no indication where a bomb might be placed, so they would have to search all of it. Oowen was relaxing and watching all the people. But when Sgt. Gaertner gave him the command, "He flipped on like a light switch and went full speed ahead." The partners cleared every desk, every locker, every cupboard, and every library shelf. They made their way through stacks of boxes in the kitchen and piles of paperwork in the file cabinets. "That took quite a few hours," Sgt. Gaertner said. "But there was no way they could use the school until we cleared it. So we did."

When he got Oowen, did he know they would make a good team?

"At the time, I liked the previous dog, Nisan, more. But over the months, Oowen's quirks have grown on me. Owen thinks he's a lot smaller than he is. He will constantly want to try to fit through areas when there's no way he can get through. He constantly runs into stuff and knocks things over. He's kind of a meathead. Some of those little quirks are frustrating at times, but I've really grown to love him. He's so friendly; he'll just jump on your lap, not knowing that he weighs about one hundred pounds. He's fun. Sometimes painful, but fun."

The handlers are constantly reminded that when it comes to understanding the human mentality, dogs advance only to about the age of a three-year-old child. So you get a lot of the kind of silly tricks a three-year-old might pull, as in the case of a Navy search dog, Pluto, who is now deployed in Iraq. Pluto made headlines when he decided to take a break from searching a cargo ship in New York Harbor and jumped overboard. Since there is no beach to scramble up, Pluto had put himself in danger of drowning. So his handler, Navy Petty Officer 2nd Class Blake T.

Soller, jumped sixty feet down into the Hudson River as well. A Navy boat picked them up. Neither was injured.

Gaertner sighs. "I can only hope that I will stay with Oowen as long as I'm a dog handler but there are never any real guarantees. It's hard to drop a leash and pick up new one. But at the same time, it makes you a better handler. The more dogs you experience, the more you learn."

He explains the Catch-22 of his next career move. "I'm in a huge dilemma and personal debate. I will test for a promotion again when I get back. If I were to be promoted, it might mean I will no longer able to be a dog handler. I could get promoted out of my own job."

Military dog handlers spend a lot of time hashing over their dilemma. Some of them intentionally fail the promotion exam just so they can continue to do the job they love. If they leave the military, it's almost impossible to find a police department that will hire them directly into the dog handler program.

"You would think that because of our on-the-job experience that we bring to the table they could possibly guarantee us a slot. But unfortunately, a lot of people are interested in it. It wouldn't necessarily be fair for them to bypass their own people who have been putting their time in and to hire me directly into the program."

He had to put in his time before he could take the Lackland dog handing course. That meant six years as "straight leg" Air Force police. He always knew he wanted to be a dog handler. But then he got assigned to Iceland. There was no K-9 unit in Iceland. "I really, really liked Iceland. It was a beautiful, beautiful country. It was the best duty I've ever seen. To become a dog handler, I would have had to leave, with no assurance of where I'd be going. And there are some posts in the military that are not that favorable. It might just be me, but I'm not exactly trying to go to places like North Dakota or Wyoming."

Iraq is where he wants to be. One of the unexpected benefits has been the closeness he and Oowen now feel. "Since we got to this country, I've noticed a huge change in our bond. In the States, I'm a police officer as well. So he doesn't get to work as much. Here, all the work we're doing is canine specific stuff. He gets to spend a lot more time out of the kennel here than he ever would at a stateside base."

Yes, it's currently the most dangerous assignment on earth, but other than that, life is good.

"I love what I do. It's hard not to be a good employee when you love your job. I think almost every dog handler I've met feels the exact same way."

Danger, he points out, is not strictly confined to the Middle East. His sister is a law student at Northern Illinois University, where just two weeks ago, a gunman shot thirty-two people, killing five. It's a strange irony that the brother on the front line feels relatively safe, but the sister on the university campus is fearful, even in her own classroom building.

"It turns out she is just as much in harm's way as I am."

Indeed, when I check out this statement, U.S. daily news sites are full of details about the shooting, which was the work of one of the university's own students. Reading down the paragraphs, some students say they are still fearful, jumping out of their skin every time they hear a loud noise. What have the local police done to make them feel safe? The same thing the military and the Secret Service do. They brought in a K-9 unit, and swept every room in every building for armed miscreants, weapons, and explosives.

Sgt. Gaertner warns me that he has to go. He and Oowen are leaving shortly for another weeklong mission in insurgent territory. I wish him luck.

"It's another fun day in Iraq," he says, with only slight irony. "Anyway, I already have good luck. His name is Oowen."

WITH REX BY MY SIDE

WHEN JAMIE HIMES was a little girl, she remembers her family members rushing off to the fire station when the alarm rang. It was an eerie high-pitched wail, a sound that made the cows shake their heads and stomp their feet in the fields. From those early days, Jamie wished she could be part of the community efforts to help other people. She admired her relatives for racing out in the night, coming back tired, dirty, with clothes that had burn spots where hot cinders floated onto them. Jamie and many of the farm kids were deeply affected by the patriotism and volunteerism of their parents. After her senior year at Hamlin High, 1998, she joined the Air Force.

She set out to become a military war dog handler. She attended the eleven-week training course at Lackland Air Force Base. She specialized as a handler of bomb detection dogs, and in 2002, Dana was paired with a purebred German Shepherd named Rex. Rex was great at bomb detection; not so great as a guard dog, where he was required to aggressively pursue, bite, and bring down a perpetrator. He would do it, but Jamie and the other handlers could tell he didn't really like it. Humans were his friends. He was uncomfortable biting one of them.

Jamie liked all the military war dogs, but from the beginning, there was something special about Rex. When he fell in line at her side, she felt that he had always been there. The two trained well together. They got their first assignment in 2004. Rex didn't care for the long flight hours in the C-130 transport. But he was fine as soon as they got back on land in Pakistan. Since Pakistan has long been friendly to the United States, there are several air bases there. But Al Qaeda extremists have tried to take control of the border area and have infiltrated many cities. The twenty-seven thousand U.S. troops in Pakistan and Afghanistan have to be on constant alert to the danger of an Al Qaeda attack.

Jamie and Rex worked at keeping their base safe. Security work in Pakistan meant long days inspecting vehicles, boxes, and buildings for explosives. Jamie felt confident that when he cleared a vehicle to enter the post, that vehicle was safe. But when they were on patrol together, she again noticed his reluctance to be aggressive. At training, many of the other handlers' dogs were terrifying and obviously enjoyed taking down the suspect. But Rex was not naturally inclined to "run after someone and grab ahold of him." Especially in hostile zones, "you want him to be ready to bite someone," she said. "I never knew if my dog would."

Jamie kept Rex's spirits up by playing with him several times a day. Three times a day, she got out his brush and groomed his coat, a bonding time for the two of them. They slept in a tent together on Pakistan's hard, scratchy soil.

Six months passed that way. Then it was back on the C130 and home to Peterson AFB. Jamie and her husband, Mike Dana, found an apartment in Black Forest, a small rural community fifteen miles north of Peterson. Black Forest encompasses two hundred thousand acres that are heavily wooded with dark Ponderosa Pine in some spots and open grassland in others. The area abounds in wildlife, and horses are a common sight. It was settled mostly by German immigrants. All of that made it a lot like Jamie's hometown, Smethport, Pennsylvania, which neighbors Alleghany National Forest.

And she found a cause close to her heart. She volunteered to help with the animals at the Black Forest Animal Sanctuary, a rescue and rehabilitation farm dedicated to helping abused, neglected, and unwanted horses, farm animals, dogs, cats, rabbits, birds, and goats. She'd spend about four days a week at the sanctuary. Tracy Hudock, who runs the sanctuary, said, "She would come out and ride the abused horses. She's the first person that has gotten on probably four of the horses that were unrideable when they got there." Jamie adopted two of the horses as her own. She was devoted to them and to her other pets, three dogs and two cats. Working at the sanctuary reinforced her determination to become a veterinarian. Through the Air Force, she started to take the biology and science courses she would need to get into vet school.

Jamie had a new, more immediate goal in life. She wanted to be deployed to Iraq. "I begged for it," she said. "I wanted to deploy. You want to feel like you're a part of it, not just watching it on TV."

Jamie and Rex were deployed in June of 2005. Their deployment was to last six months. They worked as a team scouring houses and villages for hidden explosives. Jamie was happy to have Rex by her side in Iraq. Together they walked patrols at night. It was hard work, but Jamie was upbeat. She sent e-mails to Tracy Hudock nearly every day. She missed the sanctuary and her animals and wanted as much news as possible about them. She wrote about the most dangerous part of her job—going on convoys.

"We feel safe inside the camp," she wrote one day. "But driving around among civilians, you never know what's going to happen. There are so many IEDs placed everywhere. Rex can warn me when we are walking on patrol, but when we're in a vehicle is when it's the most dangerous. Those things can go off right under you."

On Saturday, January 25, she wrote to Tracy, "I have to head out on a mission now—that's the only time I'm ever in any real danger over here. We go off base and have to interact with the public—most of them are nice; it's the troublemakers that make all the bombs and shoot rockets at us. The main thing I look forward to over here is pictures. I put them up in my room to cheer me up. I don't need anything else yet—but give it time— I've got five months to go. I'll talk to you later—tell everyone I miss them. :-) Jamie."

That e-mail was prescient. Jamie and Rex completed their mission in Kirkuk, clearing deserted houses where rebel activity was suspected. They were in a Humvee, riding back towards camp. They weren't scared, but they were eager to get back to a good meal and some rest. The Humvee sped along through the streets, and then—the world blew apart. An explosive device was blown up by one of the extremists as the Humvee passed over it.

The blast was so powerful the Humvee flipped over three times.

Jamie Dana was so critically injured that she was nearly dead. She was bleeding internally, her lungs collapsed, her spine fractured, and her pelvis was broken. In her last moment of consciousness, there was only one thing on her mind. She asked in desperation, "Where's Rex?"

When no one answered, she grabbed a medic's arm. "Where's my dog? Is he dead?"

"Yes," the medic said.

"I felt like my heart broke," she recalled. "It's the last thing I remember."

Jamie Dana was twenty-six years old, and it didn't look like she was going to get any older. The IED had blown up directly under Jamie's seat, shattering the Humvee and sending metal shards through her body. The three other passengers were only slightly injured.

Jamie was rushed to Kirkuk Air Base, where a team of twenty doctors and nurses went to work on her crushed body. This medical trauma team had done amazing work in keeping wounded soldiers alive. The total death toll during the war would have been much higher without their skilled work. This team had seen many wounded soldiers and they were experienced in repairing every part of the body. Even so, Jamie Dana was a real challenge. One of the doctors who treated her, Maj. (Dr.) Paul Morton, said simply, "We didn't think she was going to make it."

In the chaos of the emergency room, the team worked to stem the massive internal bleeding that would have already killed her if medical help had not been so close by. Again and again, they strung up units of volunteers' blood, working through more pints than they'd ever had before for one patient. In all, Jamie needed nineteen blood transfusions. "Our entire team thought she was going to die," Morton said. When they had her somewhat stabilized, Jamie was lifted into a Black Hawk helicopter and evacuated to Balad Air Base, accompanied by Dr. Morton and a team of medics who were concerned with only one thing— keeping her alive.

"That helicopter ride was the scariest forty-five minutes of my life and career," Morton said. "Jamie almost died multiple times, and I remember myself vividly praying for her."

During the helicopter flight, one of the team of medics said, "We've lost her."

Dr. Morton refused to give up. Using all the skill he'd acquired in his career, he got her heart going again and blood started once again to pump through her arteries. But Dr. Morton doesn't give himself the credit. "She had an inner strength and something deep inside of her to stay alive that was outside of this world," he said.

Back in Colorado, the phone rang inside the apartment where Jamie's husband, Mike, was sleeping. He was drowsy when he answered, but quickly alert when he realized it was the dreaded "notification of relatives."

"The initial prognosis, which really rattled everybody, was they didn't think she was going to make it," said his friend, Scott Hudock. Friends and neighbors gathered to wait with Mike for updates. They couldn't help but wonder if a chaplain would knock on the front door with the worst possible news.

"She's a strong-willed person, which is probably what kept her alive," Tracy Hudock said. "Mike is a big, hunky guy, but I've never seen a big guy like that so hurt and upset. I actually packed his suitcase for him. He was beside himself. He didn't know what to pack."

What the doctors wanted to do was stabilize Jamie further and evacuate her to a military hospital in Germany where she could receive even more skilled care. Dr. Morton was never far from her side in those first days. What he saw was a slow, determined improvement. They were keeping Jamie in a medically induced coma to reduce her pain and give her body every chance to heal. It was working.

Jamie doesn't remember anything about the flight to Germany. She woke up in Landstuhl Regional Medical Center. It was difficult to talk. She wanted news about what had happened to Rex's body. Had he been buried in Iraq? Was he given some sort of funeral? It was hard for Mike and the nurses to understand her questions. When they did, they were far too busy worrying about her to spend time investigating. Everyone had heard that Rex had died. They thought that pursuing the matter would only depress Jamie further.

In July, doctors in Germany decided she should make the trip home to the United States. She was flown to Walter Reed Army Medical Center in Washington. Her mom, Karen Riekossky, other family members, and Mike were there. It was a joyful reunion.

She had been at the hospital just a few days when a friend came in with some shocking news–Rex was alive! Jamie gasped. In the few hours of consciousness she'd had since her injuries, she'd wake and remember that Rex was dead. It sent a pain through her heart that was almost too much to bear. She felt that a part of herself had died. She was grieving for her dog. The world was a lesser place without him.

"Are you sure?"

Mike confirmed with members of her unit; yes, Rex was alive. He'd been injured in the explosion. His paws and nose were cut and burned. But he was recovering from those injuries. Where? At a military war dog unit right there in D.C. "When I was told Rex had been killed, it was like being told your child would never be coming home again," Jamie said. She started to look forward to the day when she could see Rex again.

A friend brought the dog to see her in the hospital as soon as she was out of intensive care. When she heard them coming in the hallway, she whistled — and Rex made a rush for her, leaping into her bed and tangling himself in her intravenous tubes. "I just wanted to touch him and pet him and feel him and know he was okay," she said. "It was hard to imagine life without Rex."

Rex was enjoying some down time, but he had recovered from his injuries and was due to go back to Iraq with another handler. When she heard that, a thought was born in Jamie's mind. Rex had served his country and he'd been injured, just as she was. Now, he belonged with her. His job should be to see her through her recovery, which the doctors told her would take months. She'd been told that even if she were able to walk again, she would be in pain for the rest of her life. If the Air Force really wanted to help her, it needed to let Rex be with her.

On July 18, several military dignitaries entered her hospital room. Jamie felt uncomfortable because she was still in bed, unable to stand up, and it didn't feel right to be sitting when the Former Acting Secretary of the Air Force, Michael Dominguez, Air Force Chief of Staff General, John Jumper, and Chief Master Sergeant of the Air Force, Gerald Murray, were holding a ceremony for her. In a pinning ceremony, Jamie was awarded the Purple Heart and promoted to Technical Sergeant. Another important visitor came to call the first weekend in August, the Secretary of Defense, Donald Rumsfeld, and his wife.

Rex made his second visit to see her at Walter Reed during that week. Once again, the visit with him worked wonders. When she put her arms around Rex, her constant pain seemed to recede. She had had several major operations in those two months, as doctors tried to rebuild her shattered spine and hip and repair internal damage. There was a major operation still ahead for her when she was stronger. Rex worked better than the pills at keeping her pain off her mind.

On Friday, August 12, Technical Sergeant Jessica Pierce visited, representing the Air Force Security Police Association. She told Jamie that her story had made newspapers and touched many people. Many sent her Get Well cards. She brought gifts: a peace lily potted plant, a current copy of *Tiger Flight*, and an AFSPA challenge coin. Jamie was delighted to hear about her popularity. But she was unable to sustain a long visit. She was in too much pain. She joked that she needed to save her strength because country singer Travis Tritt was due to visit her ward later in the day.

She was getting stronger with every passing day. Jamie often thought of Rex. She knew what happened to a war dog who lost his handler. He was evaluated to see if his injuries, physical or psychological, would affect his duty. Then he would have been given to another handler and put to work. Not long after she started to rally from her injuries, Jamie wrote a polite letter to Air Force leaders, asking if she could adopt Rex. The answer was no; it was against the rules, and Rex was still valuable to the military.

A month later, Jamie made a second formal request. The Air Force turned her down again. Lawyers pointed out that Rex was just five years old. The earliest retirement age was ten. Adopting Rex, officials said in an October 21st letter, would not be "a legal or advisable use of Air Force assets, in spite of the sentimental value and potential healing effects it might produce." The letter explained that as an MWD, Rex still had "five to nine years of good use" left. It noted: "MWDs are worth about $18K out of training. Consequently, Rex is very valuable to both the unit and the Air Force."

Jamie didn't give up. She contacted her congressman. That's how Jamie found out that federal law stood in the way. Under Title 10, U.S. Code 2583, the Air Force could not allow the wounded airman to take her combat dog home until the animal was too old to be useful. It would take an act of Congress for Rex to stay with Jamie.

The Air Force let Rex remain with Jamie on leave. The two returned to Peterson Air Force Base. Jamie could walk now, but because of the nerve damage in her legs and feet she was unsteady, and needed a cane to stay upright. The military medical board was evaluating her case to determine whether she should remain in the Air Force or retire.

When reporters called and asked why she thought Rex should stay with her, she answered, "He's my best friend. I thought he was dead, and I was almost dead, and that made the feeling to be with him a lot stronger."

In Congress, several lawmakers took up her cause. Representative John P. Murtha (D-Pa.) began work to attach a provision to a Defense appropriations bill. A committee approved the measure, but both houses of Congress had to vote to approve it. Representative John E. Peterson (R-Pa.), who represents Jamie's hometown district, lobbied on her behalf. "This young lady came as close to death as you can come and still be alive," he said. "She was extremely seriously wounded, and I think a person who came that close to death deserves to have the dog who went through it with them. I think that's the least we can do for her. It's not a matter of 'if' it passes," he said. "It's a matter of 'when.'"

Air Force officials said support for granting Jamie's request started to grow as people considered what she'd been through. "You add things up, and this is the right thing to do," said Brig. Gen. Robert Holmes, Air Force Director of Security Forces and Force Protection. Air Force officials said that as family, friends, and members of Congress weighed in on Jamie's behalf, Moseley, who was to become the Air Force's new chief of staff, took a strong interest. His view, Holmes said, was that "she's a wounded warrior. They went through this together; they need to heal together."

"I was shocked," she said, but she tried not to get her hopes up. "I'm waiting to see what happens." It was hard to count on the legislative efforts, "until I have it in writing that he's mine."

On December 1, Jamie and Rex sat for an interview with NBC News. She was nervous when she spoke of her request to adopt Rex, because the bill had not yet been considered. It could go either way. Sometime during December, she'd learn if Rex had to leave her side or if he could stay and join her in her civilian life.

December 2 was another big day in the life of Jamie and Rex. After more than five months, eight thousand miles, and countless prayers, Jamie received a visit from the physician who had saved her life, Dr. Paul Morton. He was stationed at the U.S. Air Force Academy in Colorado Springs. The two met on a cold winter day in the calm of the Black Forest Animal Sanctuary. They had been in touch via e-mail for the past month, but this was the first time since Iraq they were able to meet in person. Upon seeing each other, the two embraced, and Major Morton said, "You look a lot better than the last time we met."

Jamie had to admit that she didn't remember much from their first meeting. All she remembered was a split second of confusion and asking the urgent question about whether or not Rex had survived the blast. Dr. Morton remembered how amazed he'd been that in spite of massive internal bleeding, a fractured spine, and collapsed lungs, Jamie had never stopped asking about Rex, refusing to believe he had died.

"We were all worried about you that day," he told her. "We thought you were going to die."

Friends and coworkers set up a Web site dedicated to supporting Jamie, took donations, and offered many prayers on her behalf. Today, the Web site has received hundreds of heartfelt messages of encouragement and support from family, military, and civilian friends around the world. That support remained constant throughout her painful months of recuperation. "Jamie's recovery was nothing short of miraculous," said Maj. Paul Cairney, Twenty-first Security Forces Squadron commander. "She is very blessed to be alive."

On December 13, Republican Senator Wayne Allard of Colorado got up to speak in front a Senate session. His message was clear. An Air Force technical sergeant who was injured in Iraq ought to be allowed to adopt the canine companion and colleague who was at her side while both were fighting for their country. "An amendment to the Defense Authorization Bill will allow T. Sgt. Jamie Dana to be reunited with Rex. Both Jamie and

Rex gave their best in the fight to protect the ideals of liberty and courageously participated in the spread of democracy across the globe," Senator Allard said. "The least this country can do to honor their service is to allow this friendship to continue."

The Senate voted to pass the amendment. The vote was 100-0. All the Senators were in favor of Jamie and Rex's retirement. In Colorado, Jamie was delighted to hear the official outcome.

The day before Christmas, Congress passed Jamie's bill. Rex's retirement now had the approval of both houses. But there was another hurdle. The bill needed the president's signature to make it official. Thankfully, he didn't hesitate. On December 30, President George W. Bush signed the Defense Appropriations Bill including a clause allowing military working dogs to retire early and be adopted by their handlers following traumatic events.

On Friday, January 13, 2007, at a small ceremony at Peterson, Jamie received a certificate signed by Secretary of the Air Force Michael W. Wynne approving the adoption from squadron Comdr. Maj. Paul Cairney. Rex seemed unaware that he had just made dog history. He growled and rolled in the grass as only a happy German Shepherd can.

On January 30, the two received a great honor, one not bestowed on many veterans. They sat directly behind Mrs. Bush as President Bush delivered the State of the Union address. When Jamie arrived, she saw that every seat had a name card on it, so people would know where they were to sit. She grinned when she saw the card on the seat next to hers, *Rex*.

Rex has been at her side throughout her recovery, a faithful, loyal friend, always ready to go for a walk or accompany her to physical therapy. Jamie struggled to put into words all that Rex has meant to her. "Rex was my buddy," she said, trying to describe her affection for the dog. "We went to Iraq together. We got hurt together. We almost died together. It's such a wonderful feeling knowing he can't be taken away from me."

Rex is happy in retirement. No one asks him to be aggressive anymore. He is free to be his friendly self. But there is only one person who really matters, one he keeps his eye on at all times, one whose safety means more to him than his own life. As long as he is by her side, all is right with the world.

THE LAST FULL MEASURE OF DEVOTION

ON A COOL DAY in June 2006, Ron Aiello gathered with five other dog handlers, all of them veterans, just outside the Holmdel Vietnam Veterans Memorial Education Center. It was a moment Ron had been anticipating for seven years, ever since he and these same men had banded together in 1999 to create the U.S. War Dog Association. The six men tugged a green canvas curtain from a statue, revealing to the crowd of supporters a bronze soldier, balancing on one knee, his left arm tight around his military war dog, a German Shepherd.

Extensive fund-raising efforts had gone into this moment. Ron and his organization, The U.S War Dogs Association, had hired a renowned sculptor, Bruce Lindsay, of the Johnson Atelier to create the bronze. The vets had approved a small-scale model of the project in 2002. They'd chosen the Holmdel Veterans Memorial as the site. Ron and the men had been touched by the enthusiastic support they'd received from Boy Scouts, Girl Scouts, and the children who listened to the presentations they'd done at grammar schools and high schools.

"That was one of the reasons we wanted to put it in Holmdel, because it's one of the best Vietnam vet memorials in the country, and because they bring in a lot of school children to teach them about Vietnam. When they come out of the educational center, it's the first thing they spot. Children love dogs. The day we were installing it, a busload of schoolchildren saw us and ran over and got all excited about it. We want children to learn about how these K-9s worked for us."

By the end of the war, six thousand dog handlers had served in Vietnam. Every one of them has a story. Every story has some unbelievable elements in it, until you consider the combined weight of all the stories. When you hear from the twentieth person you interview that his dog saved his life multiple times, you have to go back and start believing all of them.

Ron has one of those almost unbelievable stories. "The first mission we led, Stormy and I were in front of this patrol. Suddenly she stopped and stared up at the trees. I dropped down to her and said, 'What is it?' Exactly at that moment, a bullet whizzed by my head. If I had been standing, it would have killed me."

His description of that moment sounds familiar. It sounds exactly the way this statue looks, with the soldier dropped down on one knee, his arm around his dog. Ron's lifesaving moment has been captured in bronze for eternity. Ron Aiello might have been happy at this ceremony, but there is no smile on his face. His head is bowed. Before he walks away from the bronze, he pauses to rub the muzzle of the metal shepherd in a movement so natural, so familiar, that I realize he is repeating a gesture he must have made hundreds of times with Stormy.

The story of Stormy breaks my heart. Ron Aiello was a young Marine in 1966 who served a dangerous year in Vietnam as a dog handler with his partner, Stormy. The two led many patrols safely through the Vietnam jungle. They guarded the perimeter of the base. Then Ron was transferred back to the states. Stormy was not transferred. She stayed on, and another handler was assigned to work with her. Ron's research discovered a total of four other men who handled her.

"It felt terrible to leave her behind, when she had saved my life so many times. You form a bond that is so close… that dog is like your closest friend. It was one of the hardest things I've ever had to do. I thought about that dog every day, and I've thought of her every day since."

As soon as he got back in 1967, Ron wrote to the Department of Defense, offering to take Stormy off their hands when she was no longer useful. He explained that he would be willing to pay any costs associated with flying her back to the States.

He wrote again in 1973, when the U.S. started shuffling out of Vietnam. Stormy would be ten years old, probably too old to be useful. He never got a reply. "At that point, I figured something wasn't quite right, but I had no idea what it was," he says.

In the 1990s, with the Vietnam War twenty years behind him, Ron had not forgotten Stormy. He discovered that none of the other dog handlers had forgotten their dogs, either. A.P Smith said of his partner, "Duke was and still is my best friend. After almost thirty-eight years I have never forgotten how much he meant to me. He was my life savior." Larry Laudner of the 377th Security Squadron said, "In Vietnam dogs were the best psychiatrists. I talked to Buck about everything. He was a person to me. I enjoyed talking to Buck because he actually listened."

Since most documents relating to the war were now declassified, Ron thought he might be able to research and learn what had happened to Stormy. What he discovered sickened him. "I found out they had given two thousand of our dogs to the Vietnamese," he says, with bitter irony. "The Vietnamese didn't want those dogs. They didn't like dogs. One of our German Shepherds weighed about ninety pounds. Their soldiers weighed about eighty-nine. There was no way they could control those dogs."

The only thing they liked about dogs was eating them. Ron figures all two thousand ended up in somebody's frying pan. As for the thousands who were still in the country, they were euthanized. Only 204 dogs out of 5,000 were brought home from Vietnam.

"They gave us years of service and loyalty, and that's what we gave them," he says sadly.

It turned out that many other veteran dog handlers were discovering this bitter truth. It rankled with all of them. Most had fallen out of touch with each other, as veterans of an unpopular war. As older, more mature men, they wanted some connection to that part of their lives. That was made a lot easier by the invention of the Internet. Day after day, the handlers talked back and forth through various lists. Each had tracked down some part of the story. They shared all their information.

"The military didn't want to talk about it. What I found out was there was a document signed in 1966, the early part of the war, stating the dogs would not leave Vietnam. It was what they had planned to do all along. They never told us that. They made us think that when the war was over, the dogs would come back to the States. They probably knew it was a terrible thing to do. And since it was an unpopular war, they wanted to sweep all the unpleasant incidents under the rug. If people in the States had heard that we were going to abandon all these canines, people would have been up in arms. Many of them were people's pets.

"When we asked if we could adopt our old military dogs, they gave us all these excuses. They said, 'the dogs are too aggressive.' Well, they were aggressive, but they could have been used at other bases, around the world or back in the States. The ones who weren't so aggressive could have been retrained into civilian lives.

"Then they said, 'these dogs have a blood disorder; we can't take them back because they will pass it on.' Well, that was true. They did pick up a blood disorder. But it was something that was well-known in the southern United States. A lot of dogs had it. We found out later; it was easily treated with antibiotics."

That's when Ron Aiello and the others conceived the idea of a memorial to the war dogs. They needed some way to mark the brave service of these dogs who had been such a big part of their lives. Larry Laudner said, "It was like having a brother. Did he get a decent burial? Did anybody say anything nice over him? Did he suffer?" He pauses to wipe away tears.

"Back then, when I asked to adopt Duke, I was told there was a new law passed that said animals could not leave Vietnam. It wasn't accurate. But that's what we were told.

"The American people should know that this is wrong. These dogs should not have been abandoned. Because they saved many lives. They don't have a voice. They don't have a vote. They don't have any money to contribute to some politician. So nobody gives a darn."

A handler from North Dakota said, "I have mixed emotions when I see the memorial. I am happy to see that the canines who have worked beside the soldiers, in times of war, have been honored. I also feel a great deal of sadness for the dogs that served in the Vietnam War. The fact is, that many, if not all, of the dogs that were used as guards or lookouts were left behind. After serving so bravely they were discarded as if they were nothing more than a tool.

"I hope in the future, we show our four-legged brothers and sisters the kind of respect, compassion, and loyalty they deserve. They know nothing about war or conflict, they only want to live and bond with man, as they have done for thousands of years." Then he gave the signature cry of the Marines, the phrase that is meant to demonstrate their spirit and perseverance, "Ooh-rah."

Once they were back in touch, the Vietnam veteran dog handlers represented a powerful force. Many of them got involved with sending K-9 care packages to dog handler teams in Afghanistan and Iraq. They formed a sort of "adoption" system, so that a veteran dog handler kept in touch with a young handler currently serving in the war.

Next, the vets focused on having a law passed so that what happened to their dogs could never happen again. They wanted the law changed so that MWDs could not be discarded like spent bullets. There were many of them willing to work extremely hard for this cause. They were helped by an incident regarding a congressman and an elderly MWD, Robby.

—

CONGRESSMAN ROSCOE BARTLETT of Maryland was taking advantage of some few rare moments of relaxation in his Capitol Hill office to glance through the daily digital issue of *Stars and Stripes* news. As ranking member of the Seapower and Expeditionary Forces Subcommittee and also as a member of the Subcommittee on Oversight and Investigations of the Armed Forces, he had plenty of reason to keep up with what was happening in the military. It was late September, so the afternoon sun slanting through the windows was bright and strong, and made him wish he were not inside working in the government, but outside mowing hay on his 145 acre farm.

An article about a military working dog named Robby caught his attention. Robby was a Marine Corps dog, sick and nearing the end of a distinguished career at Quantico. Robby was eight years old and suffering from bad hips, arthritis in his elbows, and a painful growth on his spine. But his handler, twenty-six year-old Lance Cpl. Shawn Manthey, kept him working as a training and exhibition dog anyway. It sounded cruel, until Manthey explained that under the current military rules, if Robby was no longer useful to the military, he had to be put to sleep. That was the law.

Congressman Bartlett was shocked. He had been raised on his grandfather's farm in Kentucky and animals had always been part of his life. He'd raised ten children and taught them to love and care for their dogs. He was fond of saying, "We have an obligation to be not just owners of our animals, but responsible stewards of their lives." To hear that the government actually had a law requiring dogs to be put to sleep upset him. He made an appointment to visit Quantico.

Early one autumn morning, Bartlett arrived with a group scheduled to watch a Military Working Dog demonstration. First, another dog, two year old Tanja, was given a command to stop a suspect. She leapt forward, full of speed and power, and grabbed the arm of the "suspect" as he ran away.

Her handler, Marine Sgt. Terrell Lambert, ordered, "Out!" She instantly released the suspect and went to Lambert's side.

Lambert ordered, "Do not move or my dog will bite you." The suspect froze, but when Lambert began searching him, he tried to overpower him. Tanja charged and subdued the suspect again.

Manthey was supposed to put Robby through a similar drill. But running was so painful that Robby couldn't reach the suspect. When he finally bit him, his gums bled. He was in so much pain that the demonstration had to be halted.

Now Bartlett was really upset. Manthey told him he would

happily adopt Robby and take him home. He would pay for his medical expenses. Robby had served his country well for eight years. He deserved some rest. But a law passed in 1949 made that impossible.

Bartlett returned to Washington and researched the issue. He learned that officials were afraid that the dogs were too aggressive to ever become pets. "I don't think you can really deprogram these dogs," said the Quantico handler, Lambert. "The training might get toned down, but she'll always have it in the back of her mind." Sgt. Brice Cavanaugh, Quantico handler of a Belgian Malinois named Irac, said, "I'd rather see a dog put down than have the handler take him home and have him bite a small child out of fear and pain."

Bartlett got in touch with William Putney, who was once the Marine's head veterinarian, who had been responsible for deprogramming and re-homing 525 MWDs after World War II. "Not one of those dogs presented a problem," Putney told him. Both men agreed the law was ill considered and inhumane. As with so many things, at the root of the issue were lawyers who claimed the military would be liable if the dogs bit anyone. Bartlett had a name for such government bureaucrat lawyers, "the no-men."

"They would rather say no than look for a solution," he said.

But if the military could transfer liability to the new owners, that would solve the problem. Bartlett wrote this into the law. "The fear that these dogs might pose a danger or a legal liability after adoption is understandable, but unwarranted," he said. "These dogs are not a hazard."

He wrote in another requirement that the military must provide a report on each euthanized dog. "We can have hearings," he says, "and they'll have to get up there and explain why they killed that dog."

Publicity about Robby generated a massive letter-writing campaign across the country. Bartlett's press secretary, Lisa Wright, says, "We got more letters about the dogs than any other issue we'd been involved with." Many were supportive, but some, she pointed out, told Bartlett to get back to important business and forget about helping dogs. But Bartlett mostly got a lot of support, and soon got the law passed. On November 30, 2000, President Clinton signed H.R. 5314, which contained the provision for "the adoption of retired military working dogs by law enforcement agencies, former handlers of these dogs, and other persons capable of caring for these dogs."

Ron Aiello says, "Now, as long as the dog is healthy, he has to be put up for adoption. They have no choice."

Sadly, the new law came too late to save Robby. His daily medication bills came to more than Manthey, with a new baby at home, could afford. Robby was euthanized at a military facility.

Betty O'Neill of Tennessee drove eleven hours to San Antonio to pick up Reza, who was retiring as a K-9 training aide. "Now, she doesn't leave my side, except when she sees a police officer or someone in a military uniform. Then she ignores me and gets all excited and goes up to them and sits by their side as if she's found a long lost friend. I guess I'll have to buy some fatigues."

Betty says Reza adjusted well to civilian life. "She is my constant companion, physical trainer, and comedian. I couldn't have found a better dog or friend anywhere. I'm very proud to own a four-legged soldier."

When other dogs were adopted, their new owners said the same thing. The adoption program has been very successful. Officials at the Military Working Dog School said they have not had to euthanize any dogs for lack of someone to adopt them. In fact, in some places they've had to establish a waiting list because there are not enough dogs to meet the requests.[1]

In the spring of 2003, Army Special Forces Sergeant Russell Joyce asked the Vietnam dog handlers for their help with a different problem. With the help of Maslawi Kurds, he'd conscripted a German Shepherd that had been trained as a military working dog by Saddam Hussein's soldiers. Sgt. Joyce had retrained him to guard and protect Americans. He was good at the job. His bark warned insurgents to leave the sleeping Army men alone. He accompanied Sgt. Joyce on patrol. He'd switched allegiance to the point where he now wouldn't allow an Iraqi anywhere near them. So when Sgt. Joyce got orders to leave Iraq, he knew he couldn't leave the dog, ironically known as Fluffy, behind. But he wasn't able to traverse enough of the red tape to bring Fluffy back with him on the plane.

His plight made the veteran dog handlers furious. Each one, working on his own, called his senator and congressman and demanded that the dog be brought back to the States. The request quickly landed on Secretary of Defense Donald Rumsfeld's desk.

Ron Aiello says of that effort, "The dogs in Vietnam didn't come home. Our dogs. They served with us, just as hard, just as loyal. And we betrayed them. We left them behind. The Vietnamese probably ate most of them. We were going to get this one home. Like I wrote to Donald Rumsfeld, 'If we bring this dog home, it's kind of like a living memorial to the dogs who served in Vietnam.'"

The Secretary of Defense himself ordered that the dog be brought back. Fluffy now lives in comfortable retirement with Sgt. Joyce's family in South Carolina.

Ron Aiello had a lot on his mind, that day at the Vietnam

---

[1] The Department of Defense maintains a list of available dogs on their Web site. There are also a number of Web sites devoted to helping people adopt MWDs. www.militaryworkingdogfoundation. com, www.militaryworkingdogadoptions.com, and www.uswardogs.org.

Memorial dedication in June 2006. The pain and suffering so many Vietnam handlers felt over the loss of their dogs now had a focus. They have formed several organizations across the country, and, by gathering together and sharing their stories, there is an outlet for the pain. It's hard to see grown men cry. But you see it every time they allow themselves to think back and remember a time when their dog was their best buddy, their friend, and the one who would protect them and take a bullet for them. They knew that their dogs had given what Abraham Lincoln called, "The last full measure of devotion."

Those dogs deserve to be proudly remembered. But so do the men who reclaimed them from obscurity They are all heroes. "I had no idea they had just abandoned those dogs," Ron Aiello remembers. He chokes up. He has fixed things so that the government cannot abandon any more. But that is never going to allay the pain he feels in his heart when he recalls leaving Stormy behind. The song that plays on his Web site explains his feelings best, "I Can't Cry Hard Enough."

"When handlers discussed the need for a memorial, it's not just because of their dogs' heroism," Ron says. "It's because the dogs shared their lives as well as saved their lives. I don't know how you can honor the military without honoring the dogs."

"I want everybody to know that these animals existed and served this country." There is a long pause. I don't want to ask any more questions. "When you give your life, that's most you can give," Ron says.

> It was extremely painful to come home to such a
> cold and thankless attitude. Finally we can feel a little
> better about doing what we did.
>   Don, handler of Rebel, 1968–1969

Duke was and still is my best friend. After almost
38 years I have never forgotten how much he meant
to me. I took him to various places in country and
through many situations. He was my life savior.
Duke was euthanized on my next to last day in
country. He suffered from hip dysplasia and was
only two-and-one-half years old. It makes me proud
to have had the honor of his friendship.

AP Smith, handler of Duke, 1970–1971

Great idea and one a long time coming. A part of me
was left behind when I left my dog in Vietnam.

Greg Dunlap, handler of Blackie, 1968–1969

My wife and I were at the opening service for the
War Dog Memorial at March Air force Air Museum
on Feb. 21, 2000. That is where I found out about
the VDHA and joined that same day. The memorial
touched me so much that I ordered a plaque for my
dog. Now everyone who passes by can see that REX
766E was my buddy and I will never forget him.

Ronald T. Carlton, handler of Rex, 1966–1967

My partner and I are in Afghanistan right now.
We will be here for about eleven more months.
Through it all he has been the constant companion,
friend, and motivator for me. He would give his
life for all of us, and I would give mine for him. He
helps everyone here at this FOB to forget the daily

drudgery and death. When you pet or play with him he helps you forget about this place for a while. He puts joy on everyone's face. Without him, I don't think I could handle the rest of this deployment. He is my best friend.

Jim Hall, 2006–2007[2]

[2] In April, 2008, Jim Hall notified me that his partner, Denis, had been killed in Afghanistan. Details of his death are not available for security reasons.

HEROES OF THE MTA

ON A CLEAR DAY in the spring of 1999, Lt. John Kerwick hurried towards the headquarters of the New York Police Department's Transit Bureau in Brooklyn Heights. As the head of the K-9 Unit, he had been busy searching for qualified dogs to join the force. Now, he was in a hurry to get back to the office to finish some paperwork. The Transit Police are responsible for the protection of New York's subways and bus lines, and Lt. Kerwick was convinced that they should have additional K-9 partners to help them do that.

The radio on his hip suddenly came alive. The emergency operator's voice notified all transit police that a man had been reported down on the subway tracks. Lt. Kerwick stopped and considered. Although he was on his way to his administrative duties, he was very close to the specified location. He looked down at the partner by his side, and two bright, dark eyes looked up hopefully at him.

"Spike, we better see what we can do," he said. Spike wagged his tail happily in agreement. As much as Lt. Kerwick loved his job, he sometimes thought that Spike loved his job even more.

He quickly made his way to the man's location. He saw him

at once. The man was naked and clearly upset. He was standing on the train tracks, holding a can in one hand and a stick in the other. Lt. Kerwick called to him and tried to move up to his location. Spike bounded alongside. The dog understood that he had to leap over the dangerous, electrified third rail, the system used to supply power to the train through the tunnels. While generally safe, it can supply as much as seven hundred volts of electricity when needed, more than enough to kill a man if he touched a live rail. There was even a rumor from Chicago that a drunken man had been electrocuted when he peed on the third rail because his stream of urine completed the electrical circuit. If trains were nearby, all rails could possibly carry current.

Lt. Kerwick wasn't sure the distraught man knew about the dangers. Maybe he was too disturbed to realize that walking on the tracks was perilous. It was best to get him out of there safely as soon as they could. Lt. Kerwick saw the man spray something on a parked train. While he did, the officer managed to move closer to him. Lt. Kerwick got close enough to determine that the man was probably high on drugs. At the time, the city was experiencing an epidemic of crack, a solid, smokeable form of cocaine, which produced an intense psychoactive high.

"Calm down, sir, and let's get you some clothes," Lt. Kerwick told him. When he got within two feet, the man startled him by whirling around and spraying him with the contents of the can. Lt. Kerwick recognized that it was butane; the colorless, odorless, highly flammable liquid used as lighter fluid or a starter for barbecues. For a minute, he tried to grab the can, but the attacker seemed to have inordinate strength and it was impossible to wrest it from his grasp. In the meantime, Lt. Kerwick was being soaked with the entire contents. Lt. Kerwick took out his mace and sprayed the man with that, in an attempt to subdue him.

"He was so high, he didn't even feel it," Lt. Kerwick said.

The man started to run into a tunnel. If he kept on running, he'd come out on the other side, and Lt. Kerwick knew how to get there before he did. After years on the job, he knew all the entrances and exits to the tracks, even some that were hidden from public view. He jumped in his vehicle and drove four blocks to the other end. He reported the location over the radio, and hoped another officer would catch up with them soon.

Sure enough, when they reached the other side, the attacker was running towards them. He was wild-eyed, and now he had something else in his hands.

"Let's get you some clothes," Lt. Kerwick told him encouragingly.

Instead of responding, the man fumbled with something. Lt. Kerwick saw that he was struggling to strike a match. His hands were shaking so much that at first he couldn't do it. He threw the unlit, broken match at Lt. Kerwick and started to light another. His hand steadied and it seemed that this time he might succeed.

Since he was soaked in lighter fluid, Lt. Kerwick knew that if that match came anywhere near him, he would light up like a bonfire. There was almost no chance he would survive an attack like that. He was in extreme personal danger. He took a step back and stumbled, and at the same moment Spike sprang from his side.

"I hadn't said a word to him. It happened too fast. He saw the danger. He got between the perpetrator and me and made him back off. When he didn't, he went right at him and bit his arm and held on, exactly as he had been trained to do."

Even with an eighty-pound German Shepherd attached to his arm, the man was still mobile and violent. But he couldn't get both hands together to light the match. Spike saw to that. Lt. Kerwick went forward and managed to get one of the man's wrists into a handcuff. When he did, Spike released that arm and grabbed the other. "We still struggled for three or four minutes to get him subdued."

During the struggle, the man kicked Spike so hard he needed veterinary treatment when the fight was over. Even though he was badly injured, Spike refused to back off. He didn't run away in pain. He hung in there like a good police partner.

Once the handcuffs were on, Lt. Kerwick took a look at the things the man had with him: a police scanner and his own set of handcuffs. He seemed to have been on some delusional military mission.

Spike guarded the man as others officers ran up to them. Then he let go. The natural instinct of a guarding dog would be to savage and even kill an attacker who tried so hard to harm a member of his pack. But Spike responded only to his training. He never for a minute overreacted. He never tried to harm the man. He simply held on to him.

With the incident over and the man on his way to prison, Lt. Kerwick had time to change his clothes and reflect back on what had happened. "Spike saved my life," he said. "The guy had probably been doing drugs for a week. He was trying to kill me. If Spike wasn't there, I probably would have had to use deadly force to stop him—if he didn't get me set on fire first.

"The dog didn't hesitate. He went right out and did his job. It was a moment when all his training came together and he made the right decisions." He paused for a moment. "If Spike hadn't been there, I probably wouldn't be talking to you today."

Spike's assistance didn't end there. The man entered a plea of "not guilty" to a charge of attempting to murder a police officer. When the case went to trial, it was assigned to Judge Jerry Sheindlin,[1] who Lt. Kerwick knew was both an animal lover and a supporter of the NYPD K-9 unit. Judge Sheindlin issued an official subpoena for Spike to appear in court with his medical records to

[1] Judge Jerry Sheindlin was the host judge on The People's Court syndicated television program from 1999 to 2001. He is the husband of Judge Judy, who had her own show of that name.

document the injuries he received during the struggle.

It was a non-jury trial, but reporters were on hand when Lt. Kerwick led Spike into the courtroom.

"Well, I guess we don't have to swear him in," Judge Sheindlin joked.

Spike's hip and ribs still bothered him from the hard kicks he had received. Lt. Kerwick asked, "Judge, may I let him sit down?"

With the judge's permission, he told Spike to get into the witness chair and sit. "The funny thing was," Lt. Kerwick remembered, "the minute he sat down, he lifted his right paw, and put it right down on the Bible. It was like he was going to swear that he'd tell the truth, the whole truth, and nothing but the truth."

The defendant was convicted of attempted murder and escorted to prison.

Shortly after this incident, and possibly because of it, Spike's injuries turned to painful arthritis, forcing him to retire after eight years of work. He went to the Kerwick home to finish out his years. Lt. Kerwick was assigned a new K-9, this one named Tonto. Spike had been born in Germany and received his initial training there. Tonto was born and trained in Czechoslovakia. Most dogs in police work come from Europe, where they cost from three to six thousand dollars.

Lt. Kerwick says, "Tonto was a typical German Shepherd. He was a calm, methodical dog who could be perceived as a pet 80 percent of the time."

The only sad thing was having to say good-bye to Spike every morning. Even though he could barely walk, he dragged himself to the door and begged Lt. Kerwick to take him back on the job. "It broke my heart," Lt. Kerwick said. Spike's sad eyes followed the car until it disappeared down the street.

Tonto was smart and willing and quickly learned his role. He became a devoted partner, never too tired to put in long hours. Most K-9 work, like most police work, is routine. The MTA is one of the most extensive public transportation systems in the world, with 468 passenger stations and 842 miles of track. It is among the few rapid transit systems in the world that operate 24 hours a day.

The partners checked the tracks and patrolled the stations. Lt. Kerwick told me that sometimes, just having a dog present calmed a volatile situation. When a person got angry and began to behave violently, "He may figure he can take on the police. It's just another human. But he knows he can't escape the dog. If he gets out of line, the dog will nail him." Violent people start to inhibit their own behavior in order to avoid a K-9 confrontation, he said. As their behavior becomes less violent, there is less chance a policeman will have to use his gun which makes it safer for everyone.

One day, Lt. Kerwick and Tonto were sent down on the platform to find two men who were suspected of carrying guns. Another officer arrived to help. The two officers had the suspects lean up against the wall while they searched them for weapons. Tonto sat nearby, observing.

"I could hear a train coming in on the tracks, going fast, sixty or seventy miles an hour. These two guys looked at each other. I could sense something was wrong, but before I figured it out, they suddenly began to push off the wall—they were going to shove me in front of the train. And just in that millisecond Tonto came roaring in. He bit one guy on the buttocks and then bit the other on the buttocks." He shakes his head in wonder. "He acted totally on his own. If there'd been time, I would have given him the order, but it didn't click. He figured it out. These dogs can think. He didn't hurt them, he just squeezed them on the buttocks, to let them know he was there."

The good thing about having a K-9 with you, Lt. Kerwick

says, is not because they can use force to help you. "Sometimes that's necessary. But countless times, we escape having to use force. Hundreds of times. If we drew our weapons, deadly force might be used. There's that chance. But the dog is force that is not deadly."

One day, Lt. Kerwick and Tonto were on duty in the Bronx. They answered a call to a station where someone reported a man down on the tracks. Lt. Kerwick found the man and asked, "Are you okay?"

"The guy shot up and he towered over me. He must have been six-foot-six, because I'm six-three and he was way bigger. He came at me. He had just decided, 'It's time to fight the cop.'"

Lt. Kerwick was caught off guard. He was facing a bigger adversary. The man turned out to be well-trained in martial arts. He punched Lt. Kerwick hard in the chest, a blow that took his breath away. As he fell, a train entered the station. It was too close to stop. Lt. Kerwick had no time to get out of its way. He was off-balance and on the way to being crushed—when Tonto leaped forward, grabbed his clothing and pulled him off the tracks. Lt. Kerwick still marvels at the incident. "I could have rolled right under the train and been killed. He definitely saved my life." Tonto had been totally aware of his partner's predicament and had acted immediately to save him.

In the meantime, the man seemed determined to get in front of the train and kill himself. Lt. Kerwick went after him to prevent that. Tonto stuck by his side, helping to subdue the man. Tonto was struck repeatedly with martial arts blows to his body. But he didn't run. He stayed right there with his partner through the fight.

"That turned out to be the last job that dog had," Lt. Kerwick said sadly. "He had nerve damage several places in his body from that. I ended up having to retire him. I always felt bad about that. He wasn't ready to retire. He wanted to stay on the job. When I think back, I would have been under that train if it hadn't been for the dog."

Two of his partners had saved his life. Lt. Kerwick felt blessed to have them. But he couldn't convince the new chief of the Transit Police of that. The boss didn't think dogs were useful enough to keep. He closed the K-9 unit. Handlers took their dogs home to live as pets.

Then came an event that changed the way transit law was enforced in the United States—the terrorist attack on the World Trade Center on September 11, 2001. Armed with box cutters and pilot training, nineteen Al-Qaeda extremists hijacked four commercial passenger jets and flew them into the World Trade Center towers and the Pentagon, killing three thousand people. This led to the creation of the Department of Homeland Security, with one of their highest priorities being to prevent any kind of explosive from entering the United States. Security screeners could peek into everyone's luggage. But to smell inside the luggage, you need a dog.

DHS wanted a rapid deployment Mass Transit K-9 program started immediately. They felt dogs would predominantly be used in special threat environments. With the DHS providing the funding, police departments in all the big cities set out to find working dogs as quickly as they could and train them. Lt. Kerwick acquired his next dog from Czechoslovakia, a handsome, muscular German Shepherd with a very strong work ethic who needed only a name in the English language to start on the job.

Lt. Kerwick had a name picked out, a name that would remind him always of his good friend, fellow officer Stephen Driscoll, who worked on truck four of the Emergency Services unit in the North Bronx. When the two hijacked airliners slammed into the World Trade Center towers on Sept. 11, 2001, Driscoll did not hesitate. He got to the site so fast that he was there, administering emergency medical aid, when the North Tower collapsed, killing him and hundreds of others.[2] For Lt. Kerwick, his friend was the very definition of the word *hero*. That's what he named his new partner.

The partners cover primarily Grand Central Station and Staten Island Rapid Transit. But they responded to a home invasion in progress when they were nearby in White Plains. Two men armed with handguns had burst into a couple's home, tied them up, and took their cash and jewelry. When they heard police sirens, they ran out the back door. Both men hid their weapons. One man seemed to disappear. The other kept running, and was apprehended right away. Police found his gun. But they couldn't find the other perpetrator or his weapon—until Hero came onto the scene.

He quickly picked up the scent and led Lt. Kerwick to the backyard, to an area where trashcans were stashed, and started barking. Lt. Kerwick had his weapon drawn. He didn't see anyone, but he called out that the criminal should stand up with his hands on his head. Slowly, a head appeared among the trash. Kerwick quickly handcuffed him. The thief did not appear worried that the cop would shoot him. But he never took his eyes off that eighty-pound barking dog.

Lt. Kerwick gave Hero a command to find this man's weapon. Hero raised his nose into the air and began to search the backyard. He went over to a large rock and hit it with his nose. Officers dug up the handgun. "They probably would have found that gun eventually," Lt. Kerwick said. "But Hero found it for them instantly."

The unit is normally on duty for ten-hour shifts, four days a week. For political conventions and gatherings of the U.N. General Assembly, they work twelve-hour days, all week. "Our

[2] *New York Newsday* Victim Database 9/26/2001

dogs get tired, but we have all kinds of medical assistance," says Lt. Kerwick. During big events, veterinarians from the Federal Emergency Management Agency are on hand to check the dogs' respiration, pulse, and hydration. Some of the dogs are so eager to work that handlers have to keep them from becoming overheated on a hot day. In Penn Station, there's a special patch of turf that serves as a doggy restroom.

Hero is trained to react quietly if he detects a potentially deadly explosive. He signals the find by coming to a halt and sitting down, which looks to passerby like a nice, obedient dog. That way, there's no panic or stampede by a terrified crowd. To keep Hero and the other K-9s sharp, the handlers occasionally hide a small amount of explosive for them to find. It's a game of hide and seek. When he finds it, Hero's reward is a brief game of tug-of-war.

Much of a K-9 team's work these days involves recovering evidence. Lt. Kerwick says, "Everything you touch carries your scent. They can find stolen property and any weapon that was used because it was touched."

Dogs who work with the police seem to develop abilities for the work that are beyond their sense of sight, hearing, and smell. Lt. Kerwick gave the example of a K-9 team who boarded a train car on a Saturday night, not knowing it had just been robbed. Three people sat still, tense, and quiet, because the fourth man, sitting in a corner, had threatened them with a gun and taken their cash and valuables. They feared that if they moved or pointed him out to police, they'd be shot.

Although there was no visual sign that something was wrong, the K-9, Coffee, became agitated and led his handler immediately over to the robber, who tried to get away. Coffee stopped that. Why did Coffee react? There was no visual sign that anything was wrong. And as it turned out, there was no weapon—the man was using his finger in his jacket pocket, pointing it and pretending it was a gun. So there was no gun for Coffee to smell.

Lt. Kerwick says, "My belief is that if someone does something wrong, they are emotionally upset, whatever the reason. Being agitated ramps up the cells that come off the human body. Cells are falling off all the time anyhow. But in a situation of emotional distress, that accelerates the process. The dog can smell it."

Auburn University is doing advanced studies into dogs' ability to smell. Lt. Kerwick pats Hero as he sighs. "If only we could get them to talk, we'd know."

He's had three K-9 partners now. I ask which one was his favorite. "They were all my favorite at the time. I really can't say. They were all very different. Their abilities were different. Some recovered evidence better. Another was better at tracking down suspects, or subduing assailants, or sniffing out hidden explosives. They were all great at their job. But all did it in their own particular way."

He's noticed over the course of fifteen years that each dog has more drive to work than the one before. "If I take Hero out of the car in a large parking lot, he starts searching the cars as we walk by. I don't tell him to do it. He's checking each one out because that's his job. When we walk through Grand Central, he's doing covert searches. People don't know it, but he's checking out their luggage.

"Hero couldn't care less if you pet him. If someone starts to pet him, he'll walk away. He just wants to know it's okay to go to work. His reward is to be able to do what he does as much as he can.

"At home, as soon as the uniform goes on, he can't wait. He wants to go to work. I wish all cops were like that.

"Working K-9, it's great. It's a comforting feeling, having someone by your side who unconditionally loves you. I tell my family, I'm luckier than most cops because I have a set of eyes watching out for me. Not just me, I have a set of eyes watching out for everyone. They are trying to keep us safe. Even the other cops take comfort in knowing that.

"Having a dog at your side is a very big advantage. He will gladly step between you and the bad guy any time. That's why we try to never use them unnecessarily."

On a recent morning, Hero started a shift in Grand Central Terminal as commuters streamed into the historic hub. Guided by Kerwick, he briskly padded through the dank and dimly lit bowels of the station. Only MTA workers know how to tread through this maze. As he walked, Hero scrutinized everything that could be used to conceal a deadly device, including dumpsters, trashcans, discarded paper bags, pallets, and stacks of metal pipes. Hero didn't hesitate to enter rooms where pipes hissed loudly and plumes of steam filled the room. He is agile and unafraid of narrow, winding stairs. He can even climb ladders. Today, his journey took him into a cavernous equipment room 160 feet below street level. The room houses critical equipment to power trains and reduce the voltage of electricity once a train has passed.

The police radio summoned them back to street level to check out an unattended package just outside the station. Hero sniffed it and moved on, looking for something else to investigate, so Lt. Kerwick knew it contained no explosives. A pedestrian suddenly ran up, begging the policeman's pardon for forgetting his bag when he boarded his bus. MTA Police Chief Kevin McConville said, "The K-9 teams permit us to investigate reports of unattended and suspicious articles without unnecessarily interrupting the movement of trains, which would delay a lot of passengers."

When his shift is over, Hero travels in Kerwick's SUV, which is rigged to turn on the air-conditioning and fans if it gets too hot inside. If that should happen, its sirens wail and bubblegum lights flash and Kerwick is paged to get out there and help his partner.

Is a police dog worthy of such luxury? "Hero is ready to give his life, anytime, any day, without a thought of his own safety, to protect me and the public," said Lt. Kerwick. He gently touched his partner's soft head. "So I treat him like a hero every day."

BENTLEY'S BORDER

ON A CLEAR San Diego afternoon, Brent Barber hustled out to a landing pad where a military UH-1, better known as a Huey, was noisily waiting. His K-9 partner, Bentley, leaped in, and he followed; securing himself and the dog as the chopper rose vertically into the warm, dry air.

It was a routine mission. Four Air Mobile Unit agents of the Border Patrol were being airlifted into the Otay Mountains, a remote and nearly inaccessible patch of Southern California, right along the California-Mexico border. The mountains were a wonder of rugged natural beauty, with their jagged boulders, hundred foot cliffs, waterfalls, and saguaro cactus.

It was an incredibly treacherous place to cross illegally into the United States. Many people got lost and never made it. Dozens of others broke ankles and wrists trying to navigate the steep rock. But increased enforcement at San Diego and El Paso crossing points had made those areas a veritable no-man's-land. In the wake of 9/11, money had come pouring in from the Department of Homeland Security. The number of border patrol agents doubled. They added floodlights, armed soldiers, infrared night-vision scopes, low-light TV cameras, ground sensors, and other high-tech tracking devices. Helicopters and all-terrain vehicles moved up and down the border all night.

So the coyotes—slang for illegal crossing guides—had moved west, and now led tens of thousands of immigrants into the inhospitable Otay Wilderness. Brent Barber and the Air Mobile Unit's mission was to find them, arrest them, and send them back.

Brent patted Bentley's side and ran his hand along her shining, silky black coat. Like the agents, she was in top physical condition. He was proud of her, not only because she was a successful tracking dog, but because she was also the unit's first dog. It had been his idea to arm Air Mobile with K-9s, after discovering how useful the Search and Rescue dog, Malcolm, a black Labrador, was to his friend, Agent Roy Lopez.

"I was just amazed from the first day at the force multiplier that his dog was for us. He could run into the canyons and very quickly clear layouts and areas that we were patrolling for concealed humans. The wheels started turning in my head. I thought, 'Man, we could really adapt this kind of thing for our work.'"

Historically, the Border Patrol's K-9 program had always been at checkpoints, to sniff vehicles for concealed narcotics and hidden humans. The dogs were incredibly effective at that job. It could take human searchers several hours to do a complete check of a vehicle, if they have to look into every cranny of the transmission and body and even the tires. Even a cursory search by an officer requires at least twenty minutes. A dog can screen a vehicle in seconds and do a thorough exam in minutes. But though their effectiveness had been well documented, there had never been a push to get dogs out into the field with patrols.

After applying up the chain of command, Air Mobile was granted three dogs. From the first, the bosses had been impressed. "We were showing them results in the form of one hundred-plus apprehensions a month, of absconding subjects who otherwise would not have been apprehended without the dog. If we didn't show them tangible numbers, they weren't going to sign the checks. They keep track of every pound of drugs confiscated and every person arrested. The dogs were incredibly successful."

Almost every day meant a ride through the mountains to scour the boulders for subjects. Then, suddenly, the whole world came crashing down.

"Ten minutes into our flight, flying over the north side mountain peak, the pilot struck some new heavy transmission power lines. They ran perpendicular to the canyon we were flying through and they were completely invisible to the pilot. They were gray on a gray sky just before sundown. He had no idea they were there. They weren't mapped. The power company had not notified us. We were at five hundred feet when we struck the wire. The first wire took out the tail rotor. The second wire wrapped around the main rotor. The pilot was able to auto rotate across the canyon and crashed into the opposite side canyon wall."

The wreckage of the chopper was so crushed, rescuers who rushed to the scene feared all eight people on board had been killed. But none had. Barber and the female pilot were the most seriously injured. "I broke my back, my L2 vertebrae, cracked my forehead open, and broke my sternum and two ribs. She broke the same vertebrae but her fracture was worse. She had to have an operation to fix her back. I was able to recover by being put into a cast for four months."

But one of his injuries was different from anyone else's. Bentley's head, pressed against his chest, had broken his sternum. "I don't remember anything about the accident, but what I was told was that as soon as we started to go down, I grabbed Bentley and wrapped her up against my waist. So when we crashed, her head was against my chest.

"I was unconscious for about forty-five minutes. All guys told me I kept waking up and asking, 'Where's my dog? Where's my dog?' Then I'd go back out again.

"They said they kept reassuring me that she was okay. Then I'd come to five minutes later and start asking them all over again. I had no idea I'd woken up and asked before. They said I did that multiple times."

Everyone on the chopper had various types of injuries. Bentley had a partially collapsed lung and internal bleeding. She was in the veterinary hospital for four days, but came out charging and ready to go back to work.

Why would he grab the dog? Why not grab a cushion and try to save himself? Barber seems slightly shocked by my question. "She's my partner. My partner. Everyone else in the helicopter knew what was happening. But the dog… she'll follow me off a cliff if I ask her to. When I became a K-9 handler, I quickly formed that bond that exists between the dog and the handler. I'd do anything to protect her. I don't remember making the decision. I don't remember anything. It was just instinct. The dog doesn't understand what's going on. She can't defend herself. She doesn't realize the helicopter is crashing. Everybody else knew what to do. But not her."

Barber pauses to reassure me that he'd work just as hard to save a human partner. "In our line of work, we all look out for each other. We go out and get dropped off in the middle of nowhere. Places where it may take a day and half to hike out. There's no backup. There's no way to call for assistance because the radio doesn't work out there. All you've got is you and the guy next to you. In a unit like mine, it's a real tight group of guys. It just becomes second nature to watch out for the guy on your right and the guy on your left."

There are eleven thousand agents in the Border Patrol. They have a big job; their duty is to prevent terrorists from entering the United States, and deter, detect, and apprehend illegal immigrants and malfeasants involved in the drug trade. The international border between Mexico and the United States is almost two thousand miles. It runs from Brownsville, Texas, in the east to San Diego, California, in the west. It traverses a variety of terrains, ranging from major urban areas to dry and desolate deserts. It follows the course of the Rio Grande from Brownsville to El Paso. Winding west, it crosses the Colorado River Delta, vast tracts of the Sonora and Chihuahua Desert, before reaching the Pacific Ocean.

It is the most frequently crossed international border in the world, with about 250 million legal crossings every year. Barber's unit is not interested in them. Their job is tracking the million people who cross the border illegally. Those people leave behind homes and families in fading towns where they can't find work, and reach out towards the north, heading to the effervescent American dream. They are unfazed by the fact that they are unwanted by government policy and many American citizens. They know they will be hunted by Border Patrol agents and pursued by sheriff's deputies. They know they may have trouble getting jobs and will be forever haunted by the possible sighting of an immigration official. But some deep longing in their souls says, "Go! Try!" so they pack knapsacks with tuna, bread, bottles of water, rosaries, prayer books, and all the money they can scrape together, and try their luck with a border crossing. Every year, thousands of them are successful, which is why thousands more keep making the attempt.

Some come from Guatemala, Honduras, Costa Rica, El Salvador, Belize, Panama, and Nicaragua, the Central American countries connected to the United States by land passage. But overwhelmingly, in numbers that dwarf those from other countries, the illegal crossers are Mexicans.

People like Maria Lupino Cantanta, of San Vicente, a small town in the Mexican state of Baja, California. She is twenty-seven and has a five-year-old son. Her husband left for California two years ago. He still sends money and letters once a month, but he's been unable to find a legal way to bring her to the States. In desperation, they have decided that Maria must cross the border illegally, as he did. Her son will live with her parents, a seamstress and a knife sharpener. They make little money, but Maria plans to send them enough for his clothing and school. Remittances sent from the United States are Mexico's third-largest source of income, after oil and tourism, especially in poor rural towns.[1]

Many people from Maria's town have left for the United States over the years, former classmates from elementary school, drug dealers who travel to Panama to pick up high profit cocaine, and many of the laborers who work the potato fields that surround the town. What she has noticed is that those who come back have more funds than when they left: enough money to rent a home with a bedroom for every member of the family and white dresses and white shoes to wear to Father Guillermo's Mass on special Sundays—things Maria would like to have, but doesn't, things she sees no way to obtain, ever, in this town with this economy. The lure of the north started tickling her dreams years ago, and now it has taken hold. She will go.

She takes a bus to Tecate, a small border city about an hour east of Tijuana. Casual visitors to Tecate like to tour the local brewery, but potential migrants have no time for that. Unlike most U.S./Mexico border crossings, there is no town on the U.S. side, which means no local police force being put on alert. But there's a reason there's no twin town for Tecate. The city faces the terrible terrain of the Otay Wilderness. Even the shortest of the smugglers' paths through this area takes two days to navigate. Many paths take longer, up to five days.

Maria hears, "Looking for passage, senorita?" the moment she

---

[1] In 2003, former President of Mexico, Vicente Fox stated that remittances of Mexican nationals in the United States, both legal and illegal, totaled $12 billion, and were the largest source of foreign income for Mexico. Signonsandiego.com, 2006.

steps off the bus. She follows a slouching young man to a small group gathered around an older man, whose skin is tough and rugged like the earth, but whose body is fit and lean.

"Loaf of bread, tuna, candy bars, flashlight, and plenty of Gatorade," the man is saying. The group nods their understanding. They will meet here at nine o'clock tonight, drive out the Tecate Highway to a lonely staging area, and start their walk. The older man counts fifteen people in the group. "If anyone fails to show up, we will have to call the expedition off," he warns. He and his two partners are asking eight hundred dollars from each group member. They will have to pay before they start the journey. No credit. No IOUs. "It's not a two hour hike," the man, whose name is Luis, warns. "You need enough food and water for two or three days. And very strong shoes."

The Tecate Highway was built in very close proximity to the border line. Looking at it on a map, the highway winds like a snake in and around parts of the mountains. Next to it is the border, neat and straight and tight, demonstrating clarity on paper that it lacks in real life. The smuggler's old truck lurches to a stop next to a river valley canyon that runs east-west. Maria tightens the straps on her backpack and reties the laces of her new Nike shoes. The ring of a cash register has been sounding in her ears all day. She imagines shelves full of colorful blouses and a single family home, all her own. She would face the problem of how to bring her son, Jorge, and her parents over to enjoy it all with her. But that's a problem for another day. She joins the line of hikers, full of anticipation and energy.

Agent Brent Barber stands outside of headquarters in the May sun, awaiting the arrival of another Huey. This will be his first mission since the crash. Bentley sits by his side. He can sense her happiness and anticipation about being back on the job, and it eclipses his own. He's glad the long months of rehab and physical therapy are ended. He's proven to physicians and

Border Patrol bosses that he's as fit as ever and certainly ready to leap back into the business of risking his life. He's so glad to be released from a desk and piles of paperwork that he forgets about the possible Post Traumatic Stress Disorder the hospital's psychiatrist warned about. The partners surge forward the minute the chopper lands.

"A soft dog would never have gone near that helicopter ever again," he says about Bentley. "But she didn't even hesitate. She knows that getting in that helicopter is the ticket to finding her toy. She jumped on with no fear."

He admits that the helicopter crash was the worst accident of his eleven-year career with CBP. "I've been in three different shootings and numerous assaults. And been hurt many, many times. That's my line of work." He shrugs, a movement that dismisses further worry about such things. This is a man who loves his work.

They load into the chopper and lift off to a mountainous part of San Diego County to check out a report of migrants seen stumbling over one of Otay's peaks. If they determine the people are injured, BORSTAR will be called in, the Border Patrol Office Search and Rescue team. Border crossings in this area are so dangerous, thirty-four people are known to have died trying so far this year. They fall off cliffs into Otay's deep streams, or break their legs or backs in precarious leaps among the boulders. BORSTAR's dogs, like Roy Lopez's Malcolm, are trained to run off leash and find injured people, then come back and lead their handlers to them. Their work is different from Detection and Patrol dogs like Bentley, who is trained to catch and hold suspects.

"Our dogs have a good reputation for what they call, 'bark notices.' You go into a canyon and make your dog bark and tell the guys, 'Hey, come out with your hands up!' Nine times out of ten the guy shows himself right away. They're afraid you're going to release the dog."

That's the power a dog holds over a human; you can't outrun him, his bite really hurts, if he goes for the throat he could kill you, and he can do all this before you get your pistol steadied enough to shoot him. Agents armed with guns and confinement in a detention center are less terrifying than the thought of that sixty-pound dog with his inch-long fangs locked into your thigh.

The team is dropped into a remote canyon, which the pilot knows is near the border. Starting near the border doesn't always make sense but it's necessary for the legal system.

"With the tracking certification that our dogs have, the dog alerting on the border area and following to source of odor is probable cause for arrest. I may track them eight miles north of the border, but I've still tied them into crossing the line with my dog."

Barber carries a heavy load. "I secure everything in my pack for both of us, extra water, food, and medical gear." He harnesses Bentley and deploys her, asking her to find a fresh track of human footsteps. Her head goes up; he knows she's caught a scent in the air. Then her head goes down, and she scoots back and forth. She pulls him over a boulder and grows excited at a narrow, winding trail among the rocks. He knows for sure that she's found a fresh trail, and given the location, it's from a group that's crossed from Mexico into the United States. He has to run to keep up with Bentley's eagerness to find them. The two agents sprint nimbly behind them. It takes an hour before they come up behind the group.

Maria Lupino Cantata sits side by side on a boulder with two other women, exhausted and discouraged. So far their experience has been hot, dry, painful, and horrible. Their legs and feet started to ache hours ago, but they had to keep on going to stay with the group.

Night will fall soon, their third night on this god-awful mountain. She and the others suspect that Luis lost his way yesterday but won't admit it. They think he has led them twice around the same set of rocks. Several people have run out of water. They are waiting for Luis now. He and his partner scurried up the cliff a few moments ago, explaining they needed to reconnoiter to find the best way down to the road, where they will radio to summon a U.S. partner and truck to carry the group to Los Angeles. Luis says they are close to the Otay Truck Trail that leads down into Dulzura.

She was staring into the twilight for Luis when she saw instead a black dog running towards her, followed by three men in uniforms. She felt the instant sweep of fear of being caught in the act. It was over. She knew it. There wouldn't be any small house and white shoes. At least, not this time. She turned her head to look up the cliff, but there was still no sign of Luis. He must have seen the agents and taken off.

Bentley the Belgian Malinois runs happily up to Maria's group, her tail wagging. Barber calls out in Spanish, "Stay where you are, and the dog won't hurt you. If you run, the dog can run faster. Just stay on the ground."

Barber tosses Bentley an eight-inch jute toy, a tough tug toy made of the kind of rough fiber used in making twine, rope, and sacking. She catches it and brings it to him to tug. She loves this game. She loves setting out on an empty trail and letting her nose guide her to people. It's her job and she does it well.

Barber and the other two agents continue to speak to the group in Spanish. Maria and the others are reluctant to say anything. But finally the woman sitting next to Maria tearfully nods in the direction where they last saw Luis. The agents ask her about the group's departure point and their trip. They inform everyone they've broken the law and will be escorted out of the mountain and into federal custody. Barber and the agents consult briefly, and then move through the group, binding their wrists with plastic twists.

One agent stays with the group. Barber moves in the direction the woman pointed, and asks Bentley to find another track. She is delighted at that idea. She casts back and forth in a small clearing, then charges in one direction, pulling Barber behind her. Barber and his partner run for about an hour. At the bottom of another canyon, Bentley stops and casts around. Barber knows what this means. The two men have split up and gone in different directions. Bentley is not sure which track to follow.

The agent calls out, "Sabemos donde usted está. Nuestro perro le encontró. Salido con sus manos para arriba. Si usted no, enviaremos el perro después de usted. Ella no es tan agradable como somos." ("We know where you are. Our dog found you. Come out with your hands up. If you do not, we will send the dog after you. She is not as nice as we are.")

There is a brief pause. Then one head rises over the scaly leaves of Tecate cypress. Not long after, an older man emerges from behind chaparral shrubs. Both are taken into custody. These two are the real targets. Illegal border guides can be fined and imprisoned for up to six months. Repeat offenses can bring up to two years in prison.

Barber says, "They're the criminal element of the group." What's great about having Bentley with them, Barber says, is that in the past, too often, the smugglers got away. But now, "They can go anywhere they want to, they're not going to hide from the dog. It's just a matter of time before I catch them. What that means is the dog is a huge force multiplier. You've now created a safer environment for the officers, you created a safer environment for the migrants you have in custody. We don't have to rush. I can let them run away. The dog knows where they're going. The dog can track them down wherever they went."

The Pew Research Center released a report indicating that illegal border immigration may have peaked. It showed a marked decline in border apprehensions: 288,000 in January to March

2007 compared with 404,000 in the same period of 2006. I ask Agent Barber if he's seen any sign of a decrease. He considers the question. "I've been a border agent for eleven years. It's been a steady flow since day one. I don't ever remember seeing more or less; they'll shift around to different areas and it becomes a different sector's responsibility. They'll be changing traffic patterns. It'll be busy in one area, for whatever reason. We'll beef up enforcement in that area and kind of shut it down. Then it'll shift over to another area. And we'll shift over to there. We basically play this game on a constantly rotating basis."

Because of the success of Bentley and others, a specific breeding program was begun at the National Canine Service Facility in El Paso to supply agents with just the right kind of dog for this work. "We need a good, hard, confident dog. We look for really high drive."

Bentley is from the "B" litter, the second generation. "The dogs go through five or six weeks with a professional trainer, then another five or six weeks with their new handler, to see if the two can meld as a team." Dogs who make the grade will lead a good life. "Our dogs are with us 24/7. We take them home; we don't kennel dogs in any situation, unless I'm going on vacation. For the K-9, you need two vehicles, one to secure her special traveling kennel, which is a converted four-door truck. For field work, we also have a Jeep Rubicon converted for her."

The center is breeding Belgian Malinois. Why that breed for border patrol? "Mals seem to work best for us, mostly because of their body style. The Malinois are usually low body fat; very lean, very agile, able to negotiate the really arduous terrain where we work. There are areas where we have fifty to one hundred foot waterfalls that we have to negotiate in a canyon. If you have a big eighty-five-pound German Shepherd, that's a great tracking dog and a great patrol dog, but when that dog gets to the bottom of a big boulder that you have to climb over, he's looking at you to lift him up because he can't make it. It's a little tough to lift an eighty-five-pound Shepherd over a rock."

The lighter, more agile Malinois are likely to scramble right up. But even if you have to lift her, Bentley's weight is not prohibitive; fifty-eight pounds. There are two German Shepherds employed in Border Patrol here with the Air Mobile Unit, but they are both small females, weighing around sixty pounds.

But Bentley's most important asset is one thing you hear about over and over from law enforcement handlers: her drive. Malinois want to work. Nothing else interests them as much. They never want to stop. Barber says that if the dog is at home with him and having a bad day, he'll let her sit in the truck for a couple hours. It makes her feel she's been to work, and, "she's happy as a clam."

One particular incident stands out in the list of Bentley's accomplishments. "Our first real criminal apprehension involving a track and trail was about eight months ago. There was a car chase from a sheriff's department that started out of Ocotillo Wells. It went almost seventy miles up into the city of Poway until their car became disabled and couldn't run anymore. There were five occupants in the car and they all jumped out and ran down into the canyon. It was a real rugged area. Big boulders shored the side of the rural highway where the car chase stopped. For fifty feet there was no dirt, no vegetation, just boulders. They called for K-9 assistance. I was about an hour away.

"Meanwhile, a sheriff's dog arrived and tried to pick up a track, but he said, 'Because of the boulders, I can't locate a track. I can't help you. I'm sorry.' And he left. I got there almost an hour after the whole thing had happened. The officers on scene had caught three of the people. But there was still the driver and another person unaccounted for. When I showed up, they told me that the other dog couldn't find a track. They said, 'Thanks anyway. Looks like these guys got away.' I said, 'Well, I'm here;

Let me give it a shot.' So I took Bentley out and geared her up and deployed her. She broke to an apparent track going down through the boulders. I said, 'Hey, I think I got a track. I'm going to go.' So I went after them. About forty-five minutes later hiking down into the canyon, she located both subjects.

"They had dug themselves into really thick brush. The terrain where I was tracking them was a steep canyon full of manzanita. Manzanita is a brush that's typical for this area. We like to use term 'impenetrable' because it's so thick and strong that it can literally suspend you off the ground while you're trying to climb through it. If you get stuck in manzanita, you can't move. They had broken through a lot of this manzanita to get off the trail. Without the dog, I would have gone right by them. I never would have seen them.

"When she found them, the male subject tried to get up and run away. She immediately let me know by running back and forth and barking and growling. I had to hold her back on line and convince him to give up. He didn't want me to let her off the leash.

"I arrested them. It wasn't a unique situation. I've had a few of those since then. But it was the first time that I really learned, 'Trust your dog.' She was tracking them on rock on a contaminated trail. It had been walked over by numerous officers. But she had good, solid odor recognition because I started her from the car, from where the subjects ran. She trusted her own nose. I trusted her. Between the two of us we made the arrest. It was such a prize to walk out of that canyon with these two people they had basically written off as escaped. That was a good shift."

There are an estimated 9.3 million undocumented immigrants in the United States;[2] 5.3 million are from Mexico. The Mexican government has worked to make illegal immigration to the United

---

[2] The United States Current Population Survey, 2002.

States easier, by producing a comic book that explained how to cross the border. The state of Yucatan produces a handbook and a DVD that instructs citizens on how to avoid notice as an illegal immigrant once the border has been crossed. This guide also tells immigrants where to find health care, how to get their kids into U.S. schools, and how to send money home.

So Agent Barber and Bentley probably won't be unemployed anytime soon.

TRAINING TO DETECT
AND PATROL

THERE IS AN EMPTY office building near Mercer County Airport, past the Courtyard Marriott and behind the low one-story highly manicured complex used by the Department of Environmental Protection. The building comes into view, but I can't find the entrance. So I pull over in my green Honda next to a white truck with *DEP Stack Emissions Monitoring Unit* stenciled on the side and dial Sgt. Craig Bunting on his cell phone.

"I can't find you," I groan.

"I can see you," he replies. He must be peering at me from one of the many identical windows of the building. I squint, but it's reflective glass. I can't see anything inside.

"Keep following the driveway around. See the white van? Make a left just past it. You'll see our vehicles. Wait for me there."

The vehicles of K-9 units are unmistakable, mostly because K-9 is painted in vibrant red on the side of each one. They also seem, to my way of thinking, the nicest of the vehicles on the force. They are SUVs with black glass and air conditioners that are left on to keep the temperature inside comfortable. K-9 handlers prize their dogs and don't let them become overheated.

Lt. Craig Bunting, the K-9 trainer for the Mercer County Sheriff's Office, invited me here to observe police dog training. Today, he's testing one officer's potential new dog, and reinforcing the training of several others. If you ran into Craig Bunting when he was off duty and out of uniform and had to guess what he does for a living, police officer might not come to mind. He is open and affable. There is no suspicious nature. His eyes are not constantly measuring his surroundings. He is nearly always smiling. You could see him as a friendly father who plays baseball with the kids, or the knowledgeable auto mechanic who helps out his neighbors with their cars, or even the manager of the Marriott who finds a room for you even when the hotel is fully booked. But a guy who carries a gun? No. The tough part of Craig Bunting is deep beneath layers of genuine gentleness and kindness.

He introduces me to Vinnie, another smiling officer who surely must be asked to play Santa Claus when Christmas rolls around. On his leash is a big chocolate Labrador Retriever, tail wagging heavily from side to side as he greets us, that big silly Labrador grin on his face.

"You think they're searching for bombs," Craig tells me. "They're not searching for bombs; they're searching for their toy. Since he's new, what we're trying to do here is build up his drive."

Vinnie acquired this Lab recently from Labrador Retriever Club rescue. He needs a second dog because his older dog, a nine-year-old chocolate Lab named Grady, is slowing down. Already, he's being relegated to less strenuous searches. "We take him along for cases of domestic violence," Craig says. "When there are restraining orders on the wife or husband and we want to get them apart. They'll listen to you if you have the dog." Craig chuckles. "The last case of domestic violence I did was in

Bordentown Township. The guy said he didn't have any weapons in the house. I asked the dog, and he went right to a drawer where the guy had a box of ammunition. I told the guy, 'Bring me the gun that goes with these bullets.' He did."

This prevented at least one husband or wife being shot to death that evening.

On Craig's command, Vinnie throws a rolled-up towel across a long, empty room that used to be a cafeteria. When the Lab bounds after it, he yells, "Good boy! Good boy! Good boy!"

The dog turns around to bask in the praise. He forgets about the towel.

"Vinnie, you hollered praise before he touched the towel," Craig corrects. "Wait till he goes for it. Wait till he gets it. Then you praise him."

"The first time I worked with this dog, I was not impressed," Craig whispers to me. "You've got to see a lot of improvement in that drive."

Vinnie repeats the toss; the Lab bounds after it, and this time goes all the way up to it. Vinnie goes wild praising him, "Good boy! Good boy!"

Craig corrects him again. "You've got to wait till he touches that towel! When he touches, then you praise him."

The pair sets up to try again. "Now let's get it right this time. Throw the towel. Say fetch fetch fetch fetch fetch. Nothing else. No other words."

Craig explains, "This is only his third time in training so he really doesn't know the game yet. I want to give the dog every opportunity to make it."

The towel is thrown; Vinnie screams, "Fetch fetch fetch fetch fetch!" The chocolate Lab bounds down the room and picks up the towel. He carries it in his mouth in a little circle. He seems unsure of what to do. Finally he drops the towel and comes over to Craig, who pats him and praises him and leads him back and urges him to pick it up again. The dog picks it up. "Good boy!" Craig says encouragingly.

To me he says, "You want the dog to hold that towel. At first, nice and easy like that. That's how you build up the drive. You build up the tug. You let him win. That's progress. That's what I want to see. If we can keep building up his drive...well, we'll see. This dog has had three homes in the last six months. That's not good.

"As long as he has the towel, he's being imprinted. You can see how proud he is. We're building his confidence up. That's what you want to do. With scent work, everything is positive. No negative. Praise is everything."

Vinnie comes up to us. "How was his drive that time?"

"Getting better. If he keeps improving, you're getting somewhere. Along the line you might level off, and you got to wait and bring him along. Praise is everything for scent work."

Craig is also the trainer of the K-9 Task Force in New Jersey. "It's a lot harder teaching the handlers than the dogs," he tells me. "A lot of guys take to it, but in the police you have a lot of guys who aren't going to praise and baby talk the dog. Maybe they came out of the military. They're tough. Maybe they don't have the patience. They want to yell at the dog, or slap him. If they do, that's it. They're out. Maybe 10 percent of the handlers don't make it."

But an even larger percentage of potential dogs they try are not suitable for police work. Craig doesn't want to name a specific percentage, and I think it's because Vinnie, the guy who's so anxious for this chocolate Lab to make the grade, is listening. "Not too many make it. It takes a special dog," is all Craig will say.

Vinnie returns with his nine-year-old dog, Grady, also a

chocolate Lab. There is a piece of colored vet wrap on his tail, the kind used to bind an injured dog or horse's leg. Craig laughs, "I think the tape is so he can tell the two apart." He's right; except for a slightly graying muzzle, the two chocolate Labs look exactly alike. It seems to me that Vinnie is trying to replace his old partner with one who could be a clone of him. Vinnie throws the towel and screams, "Fetch it! Fetch it! Fetch it! Fetch it! Fetch it!"

Grady knows the drill. He grabs the towel and returns it to his handler. Even an experienced police dog gets regular training to keep his skills sharp.

Craig has hidden a bag of C-4 explosive somewhere in this mostly empty cafeteria. He orders Vinnie to begin a search. Vinnie takes the dog to the corner farthest from us and snaps his leash on the dead ring of his choke collar. "Find it!"

We watch the Lab methodically sniff through the room. "We get a lot of bomb threats at the courthouse. The main thing is to check the common areas, places where lots of people are walking in and out, like waiting rooms, bathrooms, kitchens, around garbage cans. The secure areas are pretty secure. So they are your secondary search. The handler's got to observe the dog. You have to know everything about that dog. You have to be able to tell, just from his body language, that he found something, but it's a baloney sandwich, not a bomb."

A dog can work intensely for about fifteen minutes, Craig says, and then he'll start to get tired. The handlers take them out for water and play break. Then back to work.

While we talk, Grady completes his tour of the main room of the cafeteria and moves into the adjacent buffet area. He starts to show a lot of interest at the end of a row of cabinets. He sniffs, and then sits down. Craig opens the closet and "finds" the bag of explosive he planted there.

"Good boy! Good boy!"Vinnie says enthusiastically. He throws the towel and Grady happily plays with it, bringing it up for a tug of war.

"Lot of times, people take out bricks or wood planks to hide the things. We don't have time to do that, so we just hide it out of sight."

Craig warns me that a large German Shepherd is coming in next. He wants me to stand up against the wall, and not move. I'm not to make any approach, not even to pet him. I mustn't move my arms at all. I understand that I'm about to see an aggressive protection dog, one who doesn't put up with any nonsense. "He's nailed me a number of times," Craig sighs.

An extremely large and handsome German Shepherd named Brock enters. He flicks his eyes over me, measuring in an instant that I'm a wimp and no threat. He never breaks stride. He seems very serious. His accompanying officer, Joe, is handsome, fit, and serious, like the dog.

Craig hides the C-4 again. He tells the officer to begin.They start at the same corner where Grady started and begin a methodical search.The German Shepherd is using his nose a lot more actively than the Lab did, bumping it up against heaters, windowsills, and the edges of rugs. When he enters the buffet area and gets to the cabinet, he sits and turns his head to the handler. "Good boy!" His prize is a tennis ball. He and the handler bound away for a game of catch.

"He does a sequence," Craig explains. "When you start training, it's like starting your engine up on your car.You always do the sequence. When I bring in my dog, I'll take him over here, and put the lead on the dead ring, so he has no restriction on the choker. Then I say, 'Go to work!' That's the only time I use that, to get him going. You want to get him ready. Some guys say, 'Find the bomb!' but you really don't want to use words like that when the public may be listening."

Craig radios down for the next dog. "Now you'll see something,"

A cop and a Belgian Malinois come bounding into the room. The Mal is a classic example of his breed: well balanced, square, with a proud carriage of the head and neck. He looks like a smaller, thinner, more elegant shepherd—strong, agile, well-muscled, alert, and full of life.

Craig tells the cop to begin. Again, they go to the farthest corner. The dog rushes past a set of windows with heaters underneath. "Take him back," Craig instructs. "Make him search." To me, he says, "Now you'll see his sequence. It's really important how you start the dog off. He has to work the pattern so he doesn't miss anything."

The cop pulls his dog back and points to the heaters and says, "Search!" The dog understands. He starts the search over. I don't think he skipped those heaters out of laziness or because he's not well-trained. I think it's the opposite. I think he tested that wall for the scent so quickly we didn't see it. He knew there was nothing there, so he went on. But he doesn't mind being called back and asked to do it properly. "We don't want to oversearch something," Craig says. "But we don't want him to miss anything, either."

In short order, the Mal enters the buffet area and checks out the lingering smells. There must have been a lot of food here at one time; hamburgers, French fries, ketchup, hot dogs, baked beans, fried chicken, fish on Fridays, potato chips, Pepsi, and donuts. Then there would have been all the cleaning up, with soap and disinfectant and bleach and Windex and air fresheners. I can't smell any of those things, but the scents must be there, because I see this dog smelling them. He sniffs along more slowly here than in the big room. When he reaches the corner cabinet, he bounces happily in the air and looks at his handler, then looks at the cabinet. His handler says, "*Guter Junge!*" then takes out a big plastic Kong and throws it across the room. The Mal joyfully grabs it and plays. He came from Germany, so his handler gives him all his cues in German.

Craig and the handler have a brief discussion. They agree the dog is sharp on his skills. Craig cautions him about the dog's tendency to skip a spot. The cop assures him he watches very carefully when they're called to search.

"Now wait till you see this," Craig tells me. "This is why we like the Belgian Malinois." He radios down, and a few moments later another handler and Malinois appear in the hallway. This Malinois is slightly lighter in build than the previous one, but he is so charged up he looks like he might explode. His handler laughs as he tries to hold him back, but the dog has been detonated and about to go off. He knows he is here to make a find, and he wants to do it.

"That's what we call, 'high drive,'" Craig says. "You can't keep that dog from his work. He's got to work. It's all he cares about."

"But how do you live with a dog like that?"

There is a whisper of a smile across Craig's lips. "It can be a problem," he admits. "You've got to keep them working. Guys who have these dogs at home spend a lot of time throwing balls for them to chase. It's hard to burn off all that energy."

The handler moves closer to us to get his directions. He's holding the dog by its collar, but even so, when they are about ten feet from us, I see the dog's head snap around and a light go off behind his eyes. The corner cabinet is right behind me, and this dog already knows the C-4 is there. He hasn't even begun his search, according to the approved method, but he knows.

The handler gets him back to the corner and tells him to search. Then he has to flat-out run to keep up. The dog doesn't miss a spot. He is thorough. But the way he does it reminds me of the saying, "faster than a speeding bullet, more powerful than a locomotive, and able to leap tall buildings in a single bound," the Superman motto.

When they get to the buffet area, I see the dog's eyes flicker over to the corner cabinet. He *knows* the target is there. But he moves down all the cabinets, anyway, giving each a sniff, then stops at the corner cabinet and sits. The handler says, "Good boy!" and opens his arms for the dog to jump up and grab his toy.

"In a real situation, you pull the dog away before you reward him like that," Craig tells me. "If it's a real bomb, you don't want to take any chance of setting it off."

The bag of C-4 weighs at least a pound. "Once we get them scent trained, we use only minute quantities. You want to get the dog used to finding a small amount."

Craig goes out to get his own Belgian Malinois, and asks another cop to place the C-4. When he and Balco start the search, neither of them knows where it is, so it's impossible for Craig to give some unconscious signal.

Balco is a handsome dog, serious and all business. He is ready to go to work, but it's a relief to see he does not possess the uncontained enthusiasm of the last Mal. We walk around the building and check a dozen rooms before Balco suddenly alerts on a desk. He tries to push his head behind it, but Craig stops him and looks at the cop walking behind us, the one who hid the explosive. He nods. Out comes the toy, which sends the dog into paroxysms of joy.

Watching these men train their dogs illuminates the closeness of the bond each one feels. I've learned to read Balco's cues a little bit. I saw him tense when we entered that last room, which meant there was something interesting there. I saw him alert to the desk. But the clues are small. Tensing of the body, turning the head, facing in the direction of the bomb, looking back at the handler—they are little motions that would be easy to miss if the handler didn't know his dog very well. The dogs don't talk. The cops don't want them to bark, which can be upsetting to the public in a real situation. Craig told me that training now is switching from the passive "sit" to a slightly more active "stare." The dog stares at where he knows the explosive is until the handler rewards him.

Craig tells me there is only one instance in which he would punish a dog, and that's for trying to bite. That is absolutely not allowed. Then he pauses, remembering something. "I got bit by my own dog," he admits. "Everyone in K-9 will tell you they've been bitten sometime." He explains how he was working Balco in a training exercise, like this one, while at the same time explaining to a visiting fire chief and a new cop what was going on. He was distracted when, "he got his towel tangled with his lead. I reached down to grab it but I wasn't paying attention, I was talking. He went for the towel at the same moment and got me. He laid my lip wide open from here to here." He indicates a scar across the side of his face. "I didn't holler at him. He didn't mean to do it. It was not his fault. It was my fault. It was human error. I was bleeding like you wouldn't believe. Blood was gushing out. Never got mad at the dog. Hooked the dog up and took him out.

"The dog knew something was wrong. He was upset. I patted him on the head, then went back in and put something on my lip. I didn't take it out on the dog. You have to maintain that good relationship. You build all that drive up and then if you smack him for no reason, you bring it back down. You can lose everything you worked to build. I built that drive up to go for that towel. So when he went for it I should have moved. I wasn't paying enough close attention."

Another cop is told to place the C-4. Another German Shepherd comes up. He searches the room but passes right by the windowsill where the explosive is hidden. Craig says, "He's off source. Can you take him back around and try again? Start at the beginning again and work your way back. He didn't pick it up."

Craig listens carefully to the sounds the dog makes as he works. To me, it sounds like just a lot of panting and heavy breathing. But I can see that Craig is reading significance in minute changes in the sounds. He nods. "He's on it now."

The dog makes the find. Both men praise, "Good boy! Good boy!"

A question had been bothering me; those Labrador Retrievers— do they really make successful police partners? When you ask them to bring down an escaping felon, do they do it?

Craig laughs. "No," he said, "you'd never convince them to bite anybody. They are detection dogs. They are detecting bombs, or drugs, or people, or whatever you train them to. They can't work patrol because they're too sweet. They want everybody to like them.

"That's the main reason a dog fails in a police department; he doesn't want to bite. Not even when you ask him to. I guess he figures humans have always been pretty nice to him and he doesn't want to hurt one."

The patrol dogs are practicing their exercises downstairs, but they don't want me there. Those dogs are grabbing fleeing "suspects" and wrestling them to the ground. They are going for "criminals" who move in the direction of their handler. They are serious cops and serious dogs. They don't want tourists dropping in on their lives.

—

WITH DOGS able to do so much for the police, why doesn't every police department have one?

"Money, mostly. Small departments, like Hunterdon County, don't have the manpower. With the K-9 unit, you've got to be training a couple days a month. A small department can't function with three or four guys out training.

"But it's a necessity nowadays. There's a lot of grants out there now for these smaller departments. They pay for the dog, pay for the vehicle, pay for upkeep for about a year. That's why you see a lot of little townships now that have K-9s. It's one of the priorities of the Department of Homeland Security. They know what the dogs can do. They want them in all the transportation hubs, checking for bombs. When we had Code Orange,[1] we had checkpoints at the airport and we stopped and searched all trucks and all vehicles coming in. You need dogs for that. We used the Bloodhounds a lot on that job."

This is the first time I've heard about Bloodhounds who are currently working at a police department. Many chiefs have told me, usually fondly, that they used to have Bloodhounds, but replaced them with German Shepherds or Belgian Malinois. I ask how the Bloodhounds are used.

"We use them to track people, mostly. They've brought back a lot of elderly patients who wandered off. And kids. They can

---

[1] In October 2001, a cluster of cases of bioterrorism-related anthrax poisoning was discovered in Trenton. Three were post office workers, one was a bookkeeper, and two intentionally contaminated letters were mailed to U.S. Senators Thomas Daschle and Patrick Leahy from a West Trenton mailbox, near the Mercer County Airport. Investigators worked on the case for seven years and announced on August 7, 2008 that a Fort Detrick, Maryland scientist was responsible.

always find kids."

Another cop passing by stops to say, "Remember when we used them to track that rapist one time?" Craig smiles and nods.

"Did you find him?"

The cop gives me a look which I would say is the police equivalent of a word my friends use when someone is asking something that is perfectly obvious to everyone else, "Duh!"

But he doesn't say that, he says, "Oh yeah. It was a couple years ago. The guy was long gone, and the scene was contaminated, but we started the Bloodhound at the house and he hit on the trail right away. We tracked the suspect a good mile. The dog took us right down Broad Street, right through the center of Trenton, up to Pat's Diner! The guy was having a meal!

"They didn't want us to take the guy out, not to upset the public. We couldn't let the Bloodhound finish. He was very keyed up about it, trying to get in the diner to say hello to the guy. They knew they had the guy, so they called the dog off."

Craig adds, "A Bloodhound will do anything to find the person. A Bloodhound will track, and they won't stop. Those dogs will just fall over dead if you don't watch them because they don't know when to stop."

The court accepted the Bloodhound's decision that the man in the diner was the one who had committed the crime.

"A German Shepherd will tire out and let you know it. Malinois and Bloodhounds, they'll work until they collapse. If they're tracking, that's it."

Craig reveals that when training Bloodhounds, they always send the "suspect" out with a big piece of liverwurst, which the dog gets the minute he makes the find. "That's their reward. They don't want to play with the towel, they want that food."

Craig's proud of Balco, who was imported from France. "Not

long ago in Trenton, there was a robbery, two guys robbed another guy with a gun. While they were getting away, one of them tossed the gun. The cops caught the suspects. But they couldn't find the gun. That's when we were called in."

"Why did you want the gun?"

"Evidence. That's something the dogs are used for a lot, evidence searches. You need the gun for the case to hold up in court. Otherwise the suspects claim there was no gun. 'What gun? We didn't have a gun. We were just kidding.'"

Balco searched the backyard and went right to a particular spot. His training was to sit when he found the gun, but this time he didn't sit, he kept moving back and forth. He'd pretend to sit, then straighten up and move. Craig knew he was trying to communicate something. He said to one of the cops, "Check the other side of the fence."

The suspect had thrown the gun over a ten-foot-high fence, into bushes on the other side. "He made me look good that time." The dogs are not trained to find guns, they are trained to find nitrate. What Balco smelled was the tiny bit of powder inside a bullet.

"In the old days, we used to search as much as the dogs did. Now, we know what the dogs can do. We just try to stay out of their way."

Do the dogs ever make mistakes? Do they give false indications?

Craig considers. "When you run into problems with false sitting, usually there's a reason for it. We try not to train on diesel fuel now, because when you're searching trucks, there's a lot of diesel and you don't want the dog to hit on diesel all the time. Then, you train them on fertilizer. But if we're out here and there are a lot of potted plants around, he's going to indicate on a potted plant. Is he totally wrong? There are nitrates in it. Lot of bombs are made with fertilizer."[2]

If you own a dog, there is an inevitable moment when you wonder what separates your dog from one of these. Could your dog learn to find explosives? Could your dog signal you with just the slightest movements that something is wrong? They are all canines, brothers under the skin. The difference, I would say, first and foremost is *attention*. Few pets give this amount of intense attention to a task. That has partly been bred into these dogs but mostly taught through encouragement.

The other thing these dogs have that your dog doesn't is *consistency* in their training. Since they spend nearly every waking minute with their handlers, their behavior is constantly monitored and adjusted.

And how many owners have the *patience* for this kind of training? You have to teach and praise and teach again, never getting upset or annoyed, never giving up.

Bichons, Poodles, Dachshunds, Cockers, Yorkshire Terriers, Boxers, and Shih Tzu; what I've learned about dogs in my research has convinced me that nearly all of our dogs can be trained to search. They need willingness to please, which is part of what the K-9 officers describe as "drive." But drive can be built.

When I was researching my previous book, about the healing power of dogs, I learned about a study in which dogs detected bladder and prostate cancer in urine samples. Other scientists in other cancer studies had gone straight to police K-9 units to find dogs and trainers. But the doctor in England, for whatever reason, didn't think about that. He just asked among

---

[2] On April 19, 1995, a truck loaded with five thousand pounds of agricultural fertilizer blew up the Murrah Federal Building in Oklahoma City, killing 168 people. Military veteran Timothy McVeigh was subsequently executed for the crime.

his secretaries and nurses if anyone had a dog they would volunteer. Dr. Church had already heard about a Dachshund, Border Collie, Dalmatian, and Labrador Retriever who had each, acting on their own, notified their owners that they had some type of cancer by continually calling attention to one spot. Since all dogs have pretty much the same nose, he thought all dogs must be able to smell it.

His team consisted of three Cocker Spaniels, a Labrador Retriever, a Papillion, and a mutt. All of the dogs except the mutt performed with a far greater rate of success in detecting cancer than any other known test, such as a visual exam, blood work, or an MRI. They did not perform as well as the police dogs, who were professionals at working with their noses. But they had no trouble learning scent detection.

Your dog could learn to do it. Most likely, the biggest deterrent to his learning is you.

—

A MONTH LATER, I called Craig's cell phone to ask for an update. "Did the chocolate Lab make it?"

"No," he sighed. "I could have got him trained with a little more time, but we didn't have it."

"Any interesting cases since I spoke with you last?"

It turns out Balco had been busy; he's cleared vehicles and hotel rooms and auditoriums and stadiums for Governor Corzine, Secretary of State Condoleezza Rice, former President Bill Clinton, and the King of Jordan. And once, the Secret Service called and asked the K-9 unit to meet them just across the Scudders Falls Bridge over the Delaware River. It forms the border between New Jersey and Pennsylvania. They got out of their cars and asked Craig and Balco to check them.

"Their *own cars?*"

"That's right."

"Why?"

"I didn't ask questions," Craig says. Both of us are silent for a moment as we consider the audacity of terrorists bold enough to try to plant bombs in the *Secret Service agents'* cars. Thank God for detection dogs.

"I love my job," Craig says. But I already knew that.

ARSON DOG:
WHAT WINCHESTER
SAYS

ON A FRIDAY EVENING in April, Assistant Chief Steve Gallagher was busy with paperwork at his desk in the Chillicothe Fire Department when he heard a call coming in on the loudspeaker. He glanced down at his chocolate Labrador Retriever, Winchester, who was snoozing in his crate. Winchester raised his head, ears alert, listening to the loudspeaker, as was Gallagher. If the call was for a building fire, it meant a quick run to an official vehicle to get to the scene. In Chillicothe, a city of about twenty-six thousand in southern Ohio, calls to real structure fires came in about two or three times a month. This time, the 9-1-1 operator gave a street address which meant that the call was intended for another station. Gallagher watched as Winchester lowered his head and dropped back off to sleep.

"I swear he listens to the calls and knows what they're saying," Gallagher said admiringly. "I'll guarantee that he knew exactly what that was. That was an EMS call. So he really didn't show too much interest in it. He'll turn around and look and if he sees me moving, he knows we are going to do something. If it's a structure fire, he's out of that bed like a shot and waiting for me at the car."

Winchester is an Arson Dog, also sometimes called an "Accelerant Detection Canine" or "Combustible Detection Canine," terms which more specifically spell out what he does.

Even structure fire calls often turn out to be minor incidents. "It might be food on the stove. Or somebody burned something in the oven. Sometimes people set off fire alarms with burned toast. We've got several apartment buildings here in town with elderly people that automatically dial in the report for things like that."

The next call that came in was for a fire in a four-story building, right in the center of downtown Chillicothe. Winchester rushed out of the office to the car, with Chief Gallagher right behind him. They bounded into the special vehicle provided by the city for their arson K-9 team. Winchester was one of only three dogs in southern Ohio trained for arson work. Since then, and because of Winchester's success, the State Police have added three arson dogs to their arson investigation unit. One indication of how highly valued Winchester is to the Chillicothe FD was that a special vehicle had been outfitted for him to travel. If the temperature inside got too warm, it was programmed to sound a siren, flash its lights, lower the windows, and start a fan.

"They got all the bells and whistles on it," Gallagher told me. Chillicothe city officials did not want to risk losing their highly trained K-9 in a hot car while Gallagher was working a fire. "I always have the temperature sensing system on. And the vehicle is always in my sight. I watch him pretty close."

Firefighters found the Carlisle Building fully engulfed in flames. They began pumping water immediately. The building was four stories of former offices. But in changing economic times, the owner had given up trying to rent it out and when the last tenant left, simply closed it. Its windows were boarded up and a fence was placed around it. It was an eyesore for the downtown area, right across from the courthouse. Bricks sometimes dropped from it, damaging parked cars.

Chief Gallagher quickly put on his equipment and moved in to direct operations. Gallagher's job at a fire is "Incident Commander." With an empty building, there is always a concern that either homeless people or kids are inside, occupying empty rooms. Vacant and abandoned buildings are ready targets for vandalism and fire.

This was a big fire that took many hours to control. Whenever he glanced back at his car, Gallagher could see Winchester's nose, pressed up against the window, watching. "He keeps an eye on things to see what's going on." From long experience, Winchester knew that it would be hours before he got to go inside. "There's a process they call 'overhaul' where they make sure all the fire is out. Then we use fans to clean out a lot of the smoke and heat. If it's dangerous he doesn't go in. That's my call and solely my call. Believe me, I'm extremely cautious about where I put him. The last thing I want is to see this dog get hurt because of something that I did."

Firefighters extinguished the last of the hot spots smoldering beneath the rubble. The building was so badly damaged that early estimates put the damage at several million dollars.

Inside, investigators discovered another problem. The three million gallons of water that had been used to fight the fire had swollen many of the old floors and walls. "Water weighs eight and a third pounds per gallon. We had no idea at that point how much had been soaked up and created additional weight that the building wasn't designed to bear. We didn't know if the weight of the water could cause the building to collapse."

Instead of going into the scene, a disappointed Winchester was driven back to Gallagher's home. There, the chief arranged some exercises for him, putting drops of evaporated gasoline on a piece of wood and hiding it in the backyard. When Winchester found it, as he very quickly did, his reward was his food. "The only way he eats is to find an accelerant. He doesn't eat out of a bowl. He's fed by hand."

All the arson dogs are trained to work for food. Instead of regular meals, their two cups of kibble a day is doled out for every find. It's one reason why Labrador Retrievers are the breed of choice for arson. They are always hungry and they're eager to please. Working for their supper suits them to a T.

Gallagher trained with Winchester in the summer of 2000 at a rigorous five-week course at Maine Specialty Dogs run by Paul Gallagher, who has trained more than half the arson dog teams working in the United States. Winchester took to the training immediately, maybe not surprising since he comes from an accomplished family. His parents were both drug detection K-9s with the State Police in Arkansas. His brother, Hunter, went through the same training and is an arson investigation dog in Houston, Texas.

The next day, the city engineer was able to ascertain that the building was so old that water had drained quickly off its hardened surface. It was structurally sound.

Investigators are always eager to get into a building as soon as possible. Fire investigation is extremely difficult because the first thing that has to be established is whether or not a crime was committed. In most police investigations, the crime is obvious. In fire investigations, it is not. Plus, the evidence needed to prove that a crime took place is usually consumed in the fire.

From the beginning, this fire was suspicious. Now agents needed to begin searching inside for clues that could tell them what caused it. Fire investigators need knowledge of both human and fire behavior, and as much forensic evidence as possible. That's where Winchester comes in.

Chief Gallagher went through by himself first, getting a map in his head of where he thought the fire started and where accelerants might be found, and more importantly, looking for any weak spots that might not support their weight. "We had an idea where the fire had started simply by looking at the burn patterns." Then he put the eager Winchester on a leash and climbed to the building's third floor. He wanted to get all the way up to the fourth floor, but the stairs were so badly burned that there was no access. The search always starts at the top of the building and works down.

"We started working down in the common areas. We even worked rooms where there was no fire. Even if there's nothing in there, sometimes we'll find something that didn't ignite. So we always check those, too.

"In the main common area, he showed some interest, but the floor was weak, so we didn't actually go in there. We pulled some stuff out for him to smell. He showed some interest, but not enough that he alerted.

"Where the stairs discharged, near the front of the building, that's where he alerted to the accelerant. When he got into the scent cone, which is where the vapor comes off and widens, he put his nose in that and worked towards the source."

Then he looked back at Chief Gallagher for food. The handler carries a pouch filled with either Iams or Pro Plan kibble. Most handlers use fanny packs, but Gallagher had abandoned his because he was losing pounds of kibble that spilled out every time he leaned over. That had been a distraction to Winchester, who of course felt that every available kibble should be his. "I didn't want him eating anything off a burned floor," Gallagher said. He had settled on a "Prison Control Bag" that attaches to the belt. Jailers use them to collect shivs they find in the cells of inmates. "Through the months preceding getting this thing,

I tried camping pouches, I tried first aid packs, I tried military surplus, I tried anything I could put on a belt. I saw this bag in a Black Hawk Industries catalog for holsters and gun belts. I've been using it ever since."

While Winchester munched happily, Gallagher placed a forensic evidence marker on the spot. He asked the dog to continue. Winchester hit on the next step, stopped, turned around, and got his reward. The team descended the entire staircase that way. Every step was another hit.

"When you flow three million tons of water through a building, there's a really good chance that whatever evidence was there is going to be washed away. So that worked against us. Where he alerted was between the planks of wood."

Chief Gallagher and other forensic investigators stopped to scrape each place Winchester pointed, collecting evidence to be sent to the lab. Gallagher was now absolutely sure that someone had used an accelerant to purposely start this fire. But the lab samples came back from the lab several days later as "negative."

The lab was saying that Winchester was wrong. They had not been able to find traces of accelerant on the sample. "The possibility was that we didn't collect a sufficient amount of material that the lab could sense. But the dog could. The dog is more sensitive. Most of the instruments the labs are using are calibrated to parts per million. But the dog will detect down into parts per billion. That's way beyond the calibration points for the crime labs."

In fact, Dr. James Walker, head of the Sensory Research Institute at Florida State University, documented the fact that a dog can detect chemicals in concentrations as small as a few parts per trillion. He was using n-amyl acetate (nAA) a chemical which he diluted one part to ten, then one to one hundred, then to one thousand, and so on. He found that at a minimum, dogs could smell ten thousand times better than a human. [1]

"When he's working, I'm leaning over him to point out where I want him to sniff. I'm actually walking beside him or walking backwards in front of him, pointing out things I want him to check. If something looks weird to me, or there's a strange burn pattern with some degree of intensity, I have him check that."

The question now was who had started the fire? Police had evidence that two teenagers had been seen in the area. They picked them up for questioning in the late afternoon. At the same time, Gallagher and his dog had been working the scene for hours. "We were taking a break because I was getting tired."

They had walked over to the law complex and sat in the lobby, discussing the fire with an investigator from the state fire marshall's office and a policeman. Gallagher paid no attention when another policeman walked by, guiding a fifteen-year-old boy and his mother down the hall.

Suddenly, Winchester's head went up. He snapped around and went to the end of his leash, straining in the boy's direction. "When they walked by, he wanted to follow. He smelled something. He turned and looked back at me, then back at him, three times, like he was saying, 'Let's go check him.'"

Gallagher didn't know why. He had no idea who the boy was. But he knew his dog. His dog alerted to accelerant. "He'd been working for so long that he was still on alert. He was still seeking because he associates that to food. I said, 'Wait a minute. Do you mind if we walk this dog by you to check?'

"We asked first, because we didn't want to blow potential evidence because of a constitutional issue. If we walked the dog

---

[1] "Naturalistic Quantification of Canine Olfactory Sensitivity." *Applied Animal Behavior Science*, 2003.

by him without asking, found something, and then had it thrown out because of a constitutional issue—we didn't want it thrown out on a technicality."

The boy and his parent agreed, so Winchester came close and sniffed him. When he got to his shoes, he pointed to one particular spot, then looked to Gallagher for food.

Gallagher said, "Show me."

Winchester put his head down and touched the shoes with his nose.

"I told one of the detectives who was working with us, 'That's a positive alert.' The kid had changed clothes since the fire. But he still wore the same shoes. That's when the detective told him, 'We need the shoes. We're taking them as evidence.'

"Winchester had just been sniffing so hard for so long that he was still on alert in his head. He hadn't separated himself from that. Once they're off alert and not working, they don't react. Normally, I can be working a fire, put him in the car, and go to a filling station and get gas, and he'll show no interest. This time, he made a definite connection to the fire scene."

The lab was able to identify the material on the shoe as lighter fluid, the same fluid they eventually identified from the burned building. But even better, the tread pattern of the boy's rubber deck shoes matched the tread pattern of footsteps found entering the building through a broken window from the tar roof of a shed. "It wasn't even so much that we got accelerant off the shoes; we had probable cause to collect the shoes for evidence. That was actually more important to us. We were trying to prove who was in the building."

The Ohio Bureau of Criminal Investigation technicians were able to match the zigzag pattern from that shoe with 99-percent accuracy to footprints on the roof. At the same place, they found the juvenile vandals' fingerprints.

Once they realized that the dog's clues had proved that they were in the building, the teenagers, ages fifteen and seventeen, confessed. They said they broke in looking for a sort of clubhouse. They claimed the fire was an accident. They said they were carrying a torch looking for some kind of extension cord.

They couldn't explain why they decided to use a torch instead of a flashlight. But to Chief Gallagher, one of the most interesting parts of their statement had to do with where they built the torch. The kids said they had put it together at the top of the stairs near the front of the building, exactly where Winchester had alerted. They said they had soaked it with mineral spirits and some had dripped on the floor. Even though the lab results were negative for that spot, the kids confirmed what Winchester had found.

"They said they dropped the torch. Which was nonsense, but neither here nor there. They pled guilty to an arson charge."

Even with the lab saying Winchester was wrong, it was still his evidence that broke the case, as it had many times before. "He's been proven right plenty of times, enough that I'd be willing to bet on him."

Right enough that, during their first years, Chief Gallagher and Winchester were busy covering the whole lower half of Ohio. Eventually, the state fire marshall's office obtained three arson dogs, and took over K-9 assistance when local fire departments called. Winchester works Chillicothe, but he's on call for whoever needs his help.

State Farm insurance helped to create the arson dog program, and continue to support it by awarding ten scholarships to local fire departments every year. They currently have one hundred teams active in forty-one states and three Canadian provinces. The head of the program, Dawn Fones, says a department must show a heavy enough fire load, which warrants having dogs and make a five-year commitment. "We want to help the community protect their property and lives. This is one way we can do it. It's very difficult to determine that a fire is arson, let alone try to find the person who set it. This is one tool for the investigators to use."

The Bureau of Alcohol, Tobacco and Firearms conducts a similar program of training Accelerant Detection Dogs. They have about one hundred teams operating throughout the United States. Most arson dogs are certified by one of these two programs.

Arson is probably one of the oldest crimes known to man, practiced against competing clans ever since they learned how to light a fire. Arson and suspicious causes remain the number one cause of property damage due to fire in the United States according to a Department of Justice study, "Next to war, arson is humanity's costliest act of violence."

Fires cause three hundred thousand deaths per year worldwide and destroy families, workplaces, cities, and woodlands. In 2003, the Cedar Fire whipped through San Diego, Los Angeles, San Bernardino, and Ventura counties, consuming 280,278 acres, burning down 2,820 buildings and killing 15 people. A hunter who said he was signaling other hunters eventually was found guilty of starting it. Of the twenty largest California wildfires, sixteen were acts of arson or under investigation. In the United States in 2006, fires caused 3,245 civilian deaths. That's one death every three hours of every day of the year. There were 524,000 structure fires which did $9.6 billion in property damage. Between 1992 and 1996, ATF investigated 2,970 arson-related fires in the United States that caused 349 deaths, 1,031 injuries, and approximately $2.9 billion in property damage. Arson is the highest dollar crime and the most violent means of death.

It's interesting to note that since the arson dog program

was inaugurated, the number of incendiary and suspicious structure fires has been falling, even though the actual number of fires went up. Back in 1978, there were 160,000 incendiary or suspicious structure fires reported. Twenty five years later, in 2003, that number was down to 37,500, which means there were 68 percent fewer suspicious fires. And it keeps falling. The year 2003 saw 15 percent fewer than 2002 (National Fire Protection Association estimates). This may mean that while there are more fires, investigation has been better able to separate accidental fires from intentionally set ones. Chief Gallagher points out that it may also be the result of more accurate methods of reporting.

In 2003, among those fires designated as arson, only 17 percent were cleared or solved, according to FBI statistics. Only an estimated 2 percent of the people arrested led to convictions, a figure that shows how much more progress is needed in investigation and forensics. Juvenile fire-setters accounted for roughly half or more of those arrested, 51 percent in 2003.

The most common motive for arson is profit. Owners who can't sell a building think the insurance companies will cough up cash when they burn it down. Some arson is committed in an effort to conceal other crimes, such as murder. Protection rackets may set a building on fire when their targets fail to pay extortion. Revenge drives some arsonists. There has even been arson committed in the service of political beliefs.

"I have a strong belief that the dog has actually prevented a lot of people from using gasoline and kerosene. When we first came back from Maine, we were finding all kinds of things. We were getting lots of hits. We don't get near the hits that we used to. We haven't had near the fires. These dogs are a huge deterrent."

Gallagher thinks that television programs like C.S.I. have helped spread the word by showing dogs on the scene, sniffing out evidence. Then he laughs. "C.S.I. has also been terrible for us, because the jury expects us to have the DNA done in half an hour! In real life, that testing takes weeks sometimes."

"The dog basically is a tool. He's not the one that calls the fire.[2] He's a tool that increases the odds that we're going to have positive samples."

Chief Gallagher recalled the details of Winchester's assistance in a case in which three people died. The partners rushed to Hillsboro, a small town of about six thousand, thirty-eight miles west of Chillicothe, in the early morning hours of March 4, 2002. A small building on Main Street had been thoroughly burned. It was a chiropractor's office, and on the second floor, an apartment. Three people had been at home, sleeping. They were overcome by smoke and flames and had no chance to escape. While extinguishing the blaze, emergency personnel found their three burned bodies. It was important to know if these people were victims of an accident or if their deaths were the result of a criminal act.

Because of the intense burn pattern on the stairs, firefighters suspected that someone had intentionally set it. They asked Winchester to check.

"When we got there the fire was out, and it was freezing, in single digits. The place had cooled down. The fire marshal investigator was the only one there then. The police had just left, and one of the private investigators got there shortly after me." At the scene, "They don't give me a whole lot to go on, other than, 'There's a weak spot on the floor.' Because they want a blind read. They don't want any kind of predisposition. So they don't say 'This is what we think,' or 'This is what we were told happened.' I just know there was a fire."

In the building, Winchester immediately alerted along the

---

[2] Investigators "call" the fire when they determine the cause and whether or not it was arson.

steps. "He hit on every step as we came down, in a perfect line. We don't collect the samples immediately. We put down a marker, like a golf tee. So it was obvious he (the arsonist) had poured a trailer down the steps. The samples that went to the private lab came back positive for lighter fluid."

"Each time he alerted, he'd get a few pieces of food. On each stair. He had a good time with that one." Winchester's evidence showed that it was not an accident. The three people had been murdered by the fire. Hillsboro and state officials were now investigating to find out who did it.

A few days later, Gallagher got a call from James Lyle, the Hillsboro fire chief. He wanted to know if Winchester was available to sniff some clothing. He showed up at the firehouse with a shirt, jacket, pair of pants, and shoes. They put them on the floor and brought Winchester in.

"He alerted to a shoe and the pants leg. It was the clothing he (the suspect) had been wearing at the time. They did a rush on the lab test from the marshal's office. And it came back positive for lighter fluid." Gallagher says proudly, "Winchester is the one who tied the suspect to the fire."

When Winchester does well, Gallagher says, "It's like watching your kid hit a home run in Little League. My kids are grown. He's kind of like a new kid to me."

The first trial for the suspect, David Jones, ended in a hung jury. Eleven jurors voted guilty, but one who wasn't convinced refused to change his vote. The District Attorney examined their case and decided to bring in Chief Gallagher and Winchester to give evidence at the second trial.

First, Winchester needed to be granted status as an expert witness. Chief Gallagher designed a test in which he put a drop of lighter fluid in one can and a burned wire and piece of burned wood in others. Winchester was brought in, and, while the judge and jury watched, sniffed the cans.

"He went by and showed some interest to the wire. Not alerting on it. But it was something he's smelled a lot. But when he got to that lighter fluid, it was like somebody turned a faucet on. He was drooling. He made a wet spot in the carpet on the floor. It was a 100 percent positive alert." Gallagher noticed the jury members paying close attention.

The defendant was convicted of both arson and murder. "Some people think Winchester was the factor, but that's not totally true. It was not Winchester who got him convicted. It was the manner in the way that the case was presented, and some of the information was different from what was offered at the first trial."

More and more courts are testing the arson dogs and granting them expert witness status. Dawn Fones related a recent case in Iowa. "One of our K-9s was involved in two court cases, within three months of one another. The canine was asked to do demos in each of the cases. They happened to be in the same courtroom. Back in February, he (the handler) put down the drops to show the court what she does. Then brought the dog in, and she found them right away.

"Three months later, they had to be in that same courtroom and were asked to do another demo. They had to move into another area of the courtroom because the K-9 was still alerting on the drops he had put down three months earlier! It was three months ago and she was still able to alert on the drops." Her point is even more impressive when you consider how many times the courtroom floor would have been washed and polished, and that dozens, maybe hundreds, of police officers, witnesses, lawyers, judges, jurors, and defendants would have passed through the room, all leaving some trailing scent.

Chief Gallagher points out, "When we identify stuff on the

fire scene, we're not just looking for the guilty. We're not out to just put people in jail. We're looking for the truth. When we go in and use the dog and show that there's really no accelerant there, it helps clear suspicion. That helps protect the innocent."

If Winchester doesn't find an accelerant on the scene, "We pretty much take it as gospel that it's not there. He's been proven right much more often than he's been proven wrong." Gallagher won't say that his dog is *never* wrong. He just can't remember any incident in which that happened.

Gallagher says about his partnership with Winchester, "It's a lot of work, but it's some of the most rewarding work I've done."

Fire officials have been trying for years to come up with an electronic arson investigator. The current model is supposed to beep when it's in a room where accelerant has been used. It only works *sometimes*. It doesn't have millions of scent receptors, perfected through years of the "survival of the fittest" evolution theory of Darwin. It doesn't have mucus to help the foreign scent infiltrate its nasal glands. It's a good invention. But it's not a dog.

"We've been more accurate than the electronic instrument," Gallagher said modestly. What's been particularly satisfying is to see Winchester alert to a certain spot, have the lab declare the samples, "negative," and have the suspects later confess to pouring accelerant in exactly the spot where Winchester found it.

Sometimes, just knowing the dog was on the scene and alerted to accelerant has caused suspects to give up. "We've had multiple cases where he's alerted and people confessed right away. They didn't wait till we got the samples back from the lab. They just figured, 'The dog got me.' "

Winchester alerts to any hydrocarbon, a compound of hydrogen and carbon, the chief components of petroleum and natural gas. Gasoline, kerosene, diesel fuel, paint thinners jet fuel, Coleman lantern fuel: "Anything that is a flammable liquid, he will alert to. We train him to weathered gasoline. Then we test him against other stuff. Just to make sure he'll alert to diesel fuel, I'll put some in a can. He'll alert to it. So that way we know he's alerting to other substances."

With a dog like Winchester, training is a daily matter. He's tested briefly at home before work. At the firehouse, he'll make his rounds to say hello to all his friends, the firefighters and the secretary. Then it's into his crate for a nap until he hears that all-important call. "We go home and he gets a walk and he's basically like any other animal. He's a pet outside of the way he is fed."

At home in the evening, the partners will do a few more scent discrimination exercises. Gallagher puts drops of raw gasoline on ceramic tiles and hides them around the house. "I do anything and everything I can think of to give him some training. That's life with this dog. He's trained every day. I don't put raw gasoline on the carpet anymore, though. My wife gets a little upset when I do that."

Winchester is nine now, but Gallagher says, "He's still jumping around like a little puppy. He's not really changed in that affect at all. He's one of the friendliest animals I've ever had."

Gallagher keeps complete records on his partner, his work, his health, and everything he eats. They're kept in a full, four-inch binder. Every summer, the pair returns to Maine for a check-up and renewal of their certification. The master trainer goes over all the records.

"They told me when they screened the applicants; this is going to be a life-changing experience. It's not something you can just stop doing; you're going to have to train the dog all the time. Most people don't understand that. But it's become a way of life.

I enjoy it. I'm close with this dog, and to see him succeed just tickles me to death."

Ross County recognized Winchester's achievements by awarding him the Ross County Heroes Pet Award at a breakfast ceremony in 2007. The Mayor Joe Sulzer pointed out that Winchester has saved the county a lot of time and energy. The man hours that go into any investigation cost money, so by the accuracy of his nose, he had earned his keep. A city councilman pointed out that Winchester was also an asset to the community because he helped teach kids about fire protection. Chief Gallagher added that he also very happily assisted on tours of the firehouse.

The first attempt to train an Accelerant Detection Canine in the United States was a yellow Labrador Retriever named Nellie, acquired by the Bureau of Alcohol, Tobacco and Firearms in a 1984 pilot program. The results of this study were sent to the American Academy of Forensic Sciences, which determined that the dog's work was in fact useful to forensic investigation. In May 1986, a black Labrador, Mattie, became the first certified Accelerant Detection Canine and began work with the Connecticut State Police. She learned to detect seventeen different odors. Connecticut State Police Trooper Douglas Lancelot, Mattie's handler, said that on several occasions, Mattie alerted him to an onlooker who was watching the fire. She had detected accelerant on his clothing, which led to an arrest and later conviction on an arson charge.

Many arson dog handlers told me the same story; their dog would pick out a bystander in the crowd, who later turned out to be the arsonist. This is not something they are asked to do, but the power of their scent detection is so strong that they led firefighters to a specific person. Some suspects started to run when they found the dog had identified them. But they were not able to outrun the dog, investigators, and an arson charge.

ATF trains their canines at the 250-acre Canine Enforcement Training Center (CETC), in Front Royal, Virginia, which they share with the U.S. Customs Service. They now have a breeding program underway, to create even better arson dogs.

Arson Dogs have their critics. First, there are the laboratory technicians, who prefer the simple and unemotional methods of detection with test tubes to a dog's nose. Their electronic detection machines often mistakenly alert to the oils and resins present in both soft and hard woods. They claim the dogs must also be alerting to burned wood. Since burned wood is everywhere in a fire gutted building, this would mean the dogs' evidence is not useful.

Gallagher scoffs at that idea. "Absolutely not. I'm not buying that for a minute. We do scent discrimination work at least once a week. We use a daisy wheel and concrete blocks. He'll walk right past burned wood. He's trained to not alert to those things. We don't care whether its yellow pine, whether its hickory, hemlock, whatever it might be, he'll walk right past it. You can have the same wood and put a drop of gasoline on it, and he'll find it.

"We start with scent discrimination work very early on, probably the second day of training. We get them imprinted with typical Pavlovian responses. Once we get that accomplished, we'll start into burn materials, carpet padding, that kind of thing. That's just part of their daily training. They're highly accurate. In all honesty, we've been doing this for eight years and I don't ever remember him hitting on burned wood. Or even showing an indication that he wanted to."

Private investigation firms are paid by insurance companies to do what's called "origin and cause investigation." Gallagher feels the private investigators are generally glad to see the dogs on the scene, as an additional investigative tool. But one firm, Unified

Investigations & Sciences, Inc., has a definitely negative opinion. The firm's CEO, Carter D. Roberts, wrote on his Web site, "Dogs should not be allowed on fire scenes! The only circumstance under which a dog has a proper place at a fire scene is the need to search for a fire victim or a body."

There are three reasons he believes dogs should not be used. "First, there is potential for health problems. When we as humans change an animal's habitat, or use an animal for purposes other than that for which it is naturally prepared, we have a moral responsibility to protect it from any increased hazards.

"Secondly, there is a common problem of assigning dogs capabilities they do not possess. They serve us so loyally, and have such distinct personalities, that we tend to believe they have greater mental capabilities than they really do. In spite of their exquisitely sensitive olfactory systems and intelligence, dogs are not capable of determining intent.

"Finally, the use, even presence, of a dog at a fire scene can be an influence, direct or subconscious, that destroys objectivity. Without objectivity, a fire investigation is like a ship without a rudder—any random current can throw it off course, with no way to get back."

An ATF official pointed out that the first arson dog, Mattie, worked for eleven years and lived to be seventeen, which would not be possible for a dog whose health was compromised. Other arson dog handlers are angry at the suggestion that they would do anything to endanger their dog's health.

The University of Pennsylvania School of Veterinary Medicine has an ongoing study of one hundred Search and Rescue dogs who responded to the collapse of the World Trade Center Towers on September 11, 2001. These dogs spent weeks sniffing through debris, much of it burned, but after seven years have not suffered from environmentally induced breathing problems.

Chief Gallagher says he wouldn't argue with Carter's second premise: Dogs cannot determine intent. That's the investigators job. The dogs are there to find accelerant.

And as far as destroying objectivity simply by being there, couldn't the ATF vehicles be accused of the same thing? Wouldn't their presence at a fire scene make the public think an arson investigation was underway?

David Latimer, head of Forensic Sciences & Investigations in Alabama, says he's keenly aware of how frustrating and disappointing it can be to try to work with a poorly trained and motivated dog. But he says, "Poor performance is not the dogs' fault; dogs know only what they are taught."

Latimer thinks that properly trained dogs are a huge help in scent detection. "Rather than trying to force dogs to conform to human methods and what we think the dog should be doing to search for an odor, we encourage dogs to use their natural predatory instincts to stalk and capture prey, following odors to the source much like they would a deer or rabbit." [3]

Chief Gallagher believes that Winchester has made a difference in his life, in the work of fire investigators, and in the mind of potential fire setters, who now realize how quickly an Arson Dog can find an arsonist. "They're just an incredible tool. They are absolutely an amazing, amazing tool. I don't know if the other handlers get as attached as I am to this dog. He's like my kid. I know how hard he works. Whether he finds something or not, I'm just as proud to call him my partner. We're partners. I never imagined I could be this close to an animal. Since he comes to work with me, I spend more time with him than I do with the rest of my family. We're pretty much attached, would be the best way to put it. To see him succeed has been a lot of fun."

---

[3] Basic Instinct Training© is the dog training method Latimer has created for use at his detection training school, Forensic & Scientific Investigations K-9 Academy.

As he speaks, the head of a chocolate Lab rises. Winchester has been listening. He stares directly at me, as if carrying out a 100 percent positive alert, and I realize suddenly that I can hear his thoughts. "I feel the same way about him," Winchester says. He looks adoringly up at his chief. Then he starts thinking about dog food.

A JOB FOR SNOOPY:
THE BEAGLE BRIGADE

AIR FRANCE FLIGHT 12 lifted gracefully from Charles de Gaulle International Airport on a cool October morning, banking over the webbed steel of the Eiffel Tower and the white travertine arches of Sacre Coeur before heading west, to America. I'd been traveling with friends through the Languedoc-Roussillon region of France, exploring the fortified medieval city of Carcassonne, hiking along parts of the Santiago de Compostela pilgrimage route, and enjoying the region's specialty wine and cheese. We took off at 9 a.m. and found ourselves at JFK in New York eight hours later, at which time it was 11:00 a.m. Passengers pooled eagerly around the baggage islands, eager to grab luggage and get home or begin their long-awaited holidays.

My magenta bag tumbled over several black ones and became wedged, upside down but upright, between a rumpled American Tourister and a bashed Samsonite. Un-wedging it sent me stumbling backwards. Now it was on to Customs inspection, which meant finding my declaration form in whatever safe, unforgettable pocket I'd placed it.

That's when I saw the dog.

The form in my hand declared that I was not bringing any

fruits, plants, food, or insects into the United States. My signature ran across the bottom. The form was a lie, and also a federal crime. As just one more disheveled American woman bumbling through with bulging bags, I had expected to slip through Customs unnoticed. But I knew I couldn't get past the dog.

He was a sweet little Beagle, white, black, and tan, with that happy-go-lucky Beagle charm. Beagles love the company of humans. That's what makes them one of the most popular family pets. He was wearing a cute blue jacket, which had *Protecting American Agriculture* on the left side and *Beagle Brigade* on the right.

Since I'm an American Kennel Club dog show judge of the breed, I knew the National Beagle Club's standard was one of the few with instructions on how to judge Beagle manners: "The hounds must all work gaily and cheerfully, with flags up—obeying all commands cheerfully." That same standard declared that the Beagle was "the hound that can last in the chase and follow his quarry to the death."

All good news in the show ring, but depressing to contemplate now, because this darling little Beagle was going from passenger to passenger, and while he seemed to be welcoming each one with a little wag of his tail, he was on serious business. He was highly trained in agricultural detection. If you had any sort of food or plant in your luggage, he would know. He would alert the uniformed officer who held his leash. You would be arrested. You would be fined right on the spot.

Kiss three hundred dollars good-bye.

Travelers formed a line which halted at a tall white desk, where a vigilant official scanned their forms and cast a skeptical eye over their appearance, quickly profiling and "thin-slicing," Malcolm Gladwell's word for making a snap decision based on hundreds of tiny clues that entered your unconscious from long experience. Dozens of times in the past, I'd passed right by officials like this, a confident yet tired expression on my face. They never cared.

But that damn little Beagle and his handler had positioned themselves in front of the desk. Most entrants smiled warmly at the Beagle, probably not realizing that he was using his 200 million scent receptors to examine them more thoroughly than any human or machine ever could. A dog's olfactory epithelium contains a hundred times more scent receptors per square inch than a human's.

There is no theory that completely explains the complexity of canine olfactory perception. Most scientists believe that odors are distinguished by different shapes and sizes of odor molecules, a theory that was verified when Linda B. Buck and Richard Axel were able to clone olfactory receptor proteins in the laboratory. They won the Nobel Prize in 2004 for their work. But there were still many unexplained pieces to the canine olfactory puzzle.

In humans, the brain decreases or eliminates the stimulus of an odor after approximately ten minutes. But the more sophisticated canine olfactory system instead locks on to the odor. The stimulus remains fresh as long as the canine searches; no matter how long that takes. Can you imagine picking up the scent of rotting freshwater mussels from the Netherlands, and having that scent in your nose just as powerfully an hour later if your partner was still searching the carrier? Fortunately, scientists believe that dogs have a fold of skin they can use to close off odors. It must be true, otherwise how could Fido stand to lie on a pile of your dirty gym socks and underwear all day?

Futhermore, humans are only capable of detecting whether or not an odor is present. The canine brain is able to detect exactly where the scent is by which nostril has the greatest concentration of odor molecules, and therefore knows whether to turn to the left or to the right. When the concentration of the scent is equal in both nostrils, the dog knows that whatever they are searching for is straight ahead.

Also, canines can pick up *layers* of odors, meaning that while you are smelling hamburgers and French fries, your dog smells meat, pickles, onions, ketchup, and even the vinegar used to make the ketchup and the oil used to fry the fries. This ability has caused drug smugglers despair, because their drugs are detected by dogs even when surrounded by coffee grounds or strong fragrances or fabric softener sheets. They keep coming up with new substances they feel *guaranteed* the dogs won't be able to sniff through. But they do.

Humans cannot fully comprehend this tremendous sense of smell because we have no experience to compare with it. And no machine has been able to duplicate it. It is an incredibly valuable tool for law enforcement agencies. But it's a disaster if you're coming in with a suitcase full of *saucisson sec, Pate Forestier, poitrine séchée,* and several varieties of France's wonderful *fromages.*

Excuses started to form in my head. "I can't help it, I'm an addict," would probably not elicit any sympathy. Would he care if I begged that the *boudin blanc* is a brilliant example of French charcuterie, a combination of chicken and pork meats given a unique flavor and texture with the addition of fresh milk and cognac? Would he be impressed that *cervelas de Strasbourg* is a fine-textured sausage, rosy in color and lightly cured, impossible for an American amateur chef to recreate? What to say about the *Rillettes du Perigord,* a delicious combination of shredded duck meat and fat seasoned with herbs that would never be served at a diet-conscious American dining table?

Here's what was going to happen. The Beagle would recognize the wonderful meat and cheese scents emanating from my bag and give a passive alert, which meant sitting and pointing his nose at me. Death from embarrassment seemed an imminent possibility. My steps went from slow to sluggard. And then, the impossible happened.

The Beagle alerted to the man in a wheelchair right in front of me! He wagged his happy tail, sat down, and stared at a tan, canvas carry bag. The elderly man beamed down at him, and the officer asked sternly, "Sir, are you carrying any meat or plants?"

While the man and his companion tried not to look like desperate criminals, I slipped breezily around them. The officer at the tall desk collected my card and waved me through. He was busy watching the drama of the wheelchair man and the Beagle.

The Beagle Brigade program averages around 75,000 seizures of prohibited agricultural products a year. Animal and Plant Health Inspection Service officers nab more than 295,000 people, most of them travelers like me. The Beagle's job is to intercept illegal agricultural and food products in luggage and in cargo. If the United States Department of Agriculture has not inspected and approved the food at its source for import, they take the position that it has the potential to carry diseases, which could infect U.S. citizens and livestock. Animal and Plant inspectors also find nearly 104,000 plant pests and diseases annually that could be dangerous to the agricultural industry.

Lisa Beckett, Training Specialist at the National Detector Dog Training Center in Orlando, says about the Beagle Brigade program, "It's been exceptionally successful. They've been around for over twenty years now. They've grown from one handler to one hundred in the field. It definitely is a good way to get the job done."

APHIS chose Beagles for use at airports after auditioning many different breeds. Doberman Pinschers and German Shepherds were originally considered but abandoned because many people were fearful of having those guard dogs approach them. Labrador Retrievers are excellent sniffers but rather bulky for maneuvering around milling crowds of people. Beagles are small, they have an acute sense of smell, and they are renowned for their gentle nature. Beagles have no difficulty remaining calm in crowded, noisy airports. Beagles are constantly using their sense of smell. It gets them into trouble in family homes; they explore closets, empty garbage cans, chew jacket pockets, and get stuck under sofas in their quest for food. Beagles have such an overwhelming food drive that they are happy to work for treats. They are naturals at searching out food in luggage. It's what they'd do anyway if they were left loose in a room with a wedge of salami hidden somewhere.

"Basically, we train the dogs that a lot of good things happen when they smell certain odors. We use really good treats. They become very driven to find the odor, because they know once they find it, they're going to get something good."

That's why the Beagle in the airport missed me; he was excited, anticipating a treat from his handler as a reward for catching the wheelchair man. I wonder what forbidden substance the man had hidden? Sausage, like me? Or a clipping from a treasured grapevine? Or seeds from the hairy, scarlet perennial Peacock Anemone of the Riviera? If he'd admitted he had a banned food or plant on his Customs form, it would simply be taken from him. If he hadn't, he was subject to a fine. When a Beagle alerts, that passenger is taken aside and thoroughly searched by an agricultural specialist. Officer James Reynolds says, "We don't expect people to know the law. We just expect them to be honest. 'Do you have any food or plants? Yes or no?'"

"We start by hiding citrus fruit and raw meat from them in boxes," Lisa Beckett told me. "When they go to a box that doesn't have anything in it, we ignore them. When they go to a box that has a fruit or meat in it, we tell them how great they are and give them treats. The Beagles don't think they're working. They think they're playing a really cool game of hide-and-seek."

Before 2003, the Beagles wore green jackets and worked for the Department of Agriculture. Since 2003, the various departments of the Animal Plant Health Inspection Service, Customs Service, Fish and Wildlife Service, Public Health Service, and Immigration and Naturalization Service have been combined under one designation, Department of Homeland Security, and the Beagles now wear blue jackets.

In 1984, USDA started its detector dog program at Los Angeles International Airport with one team consisting of a Beagle and a handler. On the other coast, one of the Beagle Brigade's first and best-known detector dogs was Jackpot, who worked the international arrivals hall at JFK and happily incriminated hundreds of carefree vacationers. Jackpot's photo hangs in a place of honor in the customs agents' staging room, where new Beagles have to pass it on their way to work every day.

The Beagles were an immediate success, so much that APHIS eventually launched a detector dog program in Hidalgo, Texas, on the United States-Mexican border in 1997. The job of the Border Beagle Brigade is the same as their airport cousins; they sniff out prohibited agricultural products that may be entering from Mexico in vehicles and baggage. The canine teams worked quickly and saved a lot of officers from hour-long inspections. Next, USDA placed additional Beagles on both the northern and southern borders of the United States.

If you see larger breeds working in airports, you can safely pass them with your hidden ham sandwich. The big dogs are looking for drugs and explosives. They don't alert to food.

Beagle Brigade dogs live in kennels, not at home with their human partners as most police dogs do, because they are so sensitive to the smell of food that they can't relax. Beagle Brigade dogs are fed a high protein diet. I asked why they are not trained to work for food, as the arson dogs are. Beckett sighed. "A meal is such an important event in a dog's life; we like to give them that. The way they eat the treats, though, you would think they were starving." She shrugged. "That's a Beagle. That's one of the reasons we use them. That's the only handle we have on them, otherwise they'd be off running through the fields."

On a warm Florida afternoon in 2004, one hard-working Beagle, Trouble, roamed through the Customs area of Miami International Airport, sniffing luggage. He wanted to convince his handler, Agricultural Specialist Sherrie Keblish, to dole out some of the dog treats she kept in her pocket. The only way to do that was to find a plant, meat, or fruit somewhere.

Trouble had been recruited by an Agricultural Department trainer from an animal shelter in Texas, where a mother who found his eagerness and high energy level too much trouble had dumped him. It wasn't unusual for a trainer to stop into an animal shelter and have a look around. The trainers liked to rescue dogs from the shelters, knowing they would otherwise be euthanized. "We look for really high food drive," said Lisa Beckett. "We want high energy and eagerness to please."

Trouble had those qualities. He trained for four months at the Orlando center, a state of the art training facility on two acres of land, with large buildings, kennels for thirty dogs, five quarantine runs, postal and passenger training areas, and classrooms. From the beginning, his enthusiasm and intelligence suited him for scent detection. He was introduced to field inspector Sherrie Keblish and trained to become her partner at Miami Airport. Now, in 2004, he was a seasoned professional with three years of experience under his blue jacket.

Because they keep careful statistics, the Plant Protection & Quarantine officers know that after six months to one year of experience, Beagles sniff out prohibited material correctly 80 percent of the time. After two years, their success rate rises to about 90 percent. The Beagles are trained continuously to new odors throughout their career. Some have learned to recognize nearly fifty different odors, providing the nation with even more protection against plant diseases and invasive species of insects.

Trouble already had scored 115 "notable interceptions," according to Customs records. He alerted handlers to 1,834 prohibited items, including 1,541 plant seizures, 697 animal products, of which 853 pounds were meat. Keblish said Trouble is a great companion and one of the agency's finest detector dogs.

"Trouble's enthusiasm starts very early in the morning and is contagious. He is always ready to work."

Trouble and Keblish generally worked six to eight flights per day. Today they were assigned to meet planes coming in from Europe and South America; Alitalia 630 from Rome; LAN 570 from Bogotá; American Airlines 904 from Rio de Janeiro.

In a laughing group of foreigners, Trouble picked up a strange, strong fragrance, one he'd never been trained to recognize and had never sniffed before. It was heavy and overpowering, like a combination of fruits he *did* know, citrus, apple, and pear. Trouble approached a woman carrying a brown leather sack and sat down. Surprised, the woman tried to maneuver around him, but was stopped by Keblish. "Do you have any fruit or meat in that bag?" she asked her.

In a back room, inspectors unpacked the remnants of a lunch, bread crusts, packets of butter, an empty container of mineral water. But one more item caught their attention; a raw quince.

American consumers who've purchased quince in the market would be surprised to hear that someone was eating one raw. In the United States, the fruit has a heavy, apple-like shape, a rich golden color, and the rind is coarse and woolly. Biting into a quince is difficult because the flesh is hard, and the taste is unpalatable, both astringent and acidulous. In hotter countries, such as South America and the Mediterranean, the woolly rind disappears and the fruit is softer and juicier. It can easily be eaten raw.

This quince may have been delicious, but it had an overwhelmingly serious problem. Within the pinkish flesh, twenty Mediterranean fruit flies had taken up residence. This fly is one of the most destructive pests known to man. It is a major pest of citrus, and an even more serious pest of deciduous fruits such as peaches, pears, and apples. It attacks more than 260 different fruits, flowers, vegetables, and nuts. It lays its eggs beneath the skin of the ripening fruit. The larvae tunnel through the pulp, eventually destroying it into a juicy inedible mass.

The Mediterranean fruit fly is not to be confused with the common fruit fly you find in your own kitchen, buzzing around the ripened or rotting tomatoes, melons, squash, grapes, bananas, potatoes, onions, and other un-refrigerated produce. Those little fruit flies are *Drosophila melanogaster*, from the Greek words for *black-bellied dew-lover*.

The Mediterranean fruit fly, *Ceratitis capitata*, originated in sub-Saharan Africa and spread to the Mediterranean and South America. It is not established in the United States. When it has been detected in Florida and California, each infestation has necessitated intensive and massive eradication to save the state's crops. The first infestation on the U.S. mainland occurred in Florida in 1929. Since then, several infestations have occurred. A 1997 attack in Florida's Tampa Bay region lasted nine months and cost $25 million to fight. Med fly battles have cost taxpayers $500 million during the past twenty-five years. It infiltrated Hawaii in 1910 and is still a major problem there. Department of Agriculture scientists are working to find its natural enemy, something other than chemicals that will kill it. So far, they haven't found it.

Entomologist Bruce McPherson says, "The Mediterranean fruit fly may be the most beautiful pest in the world." It has colorful blue eyes and banded wings. They are small, almost impossible to detect with just the human eye. But once an infested fruit is cut, the naked eye can determine that larvae are present. It is the larvae that cause the real damage.

APHIS estimated that if the Med fly ever took hold in the United States, annual losses would come to about $1.5 billion a year. These losses would come in the form of treatments, reduced crop yields, deformities, premature fruit drop, and subsequent loss of market. California and Florida are at highest risk. They have the climatic conditions favorable to reproducing and two hundred varieties of fruit hosts readily available. The public opposes chemical control measures. California farmers grow $8.1 billion dollars of fruit a year; Florida farmers, around $2 billion. They are a significant factor in the economy of the states and the diet of the nation.

One little Beagle finding one little lunch fruit saved the state of Florida billions of dollars.

Trouble got his crunchy dog treat and was perfectly content.

That year, the Customs Service entered Trouble in a kind of "American Idol" search for America's number one dog hero.[1] People were invited to vote for one of the six dogs posted on the Pedigree Dog Food "Paws to Recognize" Web site. The vote was tensely watched by thousands of dog lovers, and, unlike American Idol, ended in a dead heat between two heroes: Trouble, and a Newfoundland named Gentle Ben who did therapy dog work. At the international salute, the winners had their paw prints enshrined in cement as a "Canine World Heroes Walk of Fame." Customs and Border Protection Commissioner Robert Bonner said in his speech, "Trouble will continue to spell trouble for anyone who tries to do our nation harm."

Sherrie Keblish spoke proudly of Trouble, "He is an amazing dog and it is always nice when that hard work is recognized."

Twice the Port Authority of New York and New Jersey have recognized the Beagle Brigade for outstanding customer service. The Pedigree All Star Hall of Fame inducted USDA's Beagle Brigade into the National Dog Museum in St. Louis, Missouri, as the outstanding service program. Several rescue organizations have recognized the Beagle Brigade for rescuing dogs and giving them a second chance.

In a back room of the maze that is JFK, APHIS inspectors showed me an array of items that had been confiscated from travelers: a full-grown rose bush; a dozen plastic baggies full of

---

[1] A program sponsored annually by the Pedigree Dog Food company.

high-fat cream; dragonfruit; jackfruit; bundles of figs, peanuts, mangoes; eighteen large, pale brown eggs from an unknown bird species; prickly pears; carrots; containers of chicken soup; avocadoes; limes; German sausages; Italian sliced salami; cabbage; tomatoes; pears; one coconut; a bouquet of flowers; green onions; squash; yams; potatoes; pistachios; and a bunch of little seedlings with soil attached to their roots. "That woman really fought with me," said Officer James Reynolds, indicating the seedlings. "She said they were precious grapes from her grandfather's vineyard." Two dozen dried birds' nests; ugly, prickled breadfruit; rhubarb plants; and a homemade rice, anchovy, coconut, and chicken dish known in Malaysia as *Nasi Lemak*. "Isn't that nice?" asked Officer Rudy Raghoo. "Grandma probably made it."

"Is this what you collected in one day?" I asked, amazed at the huge pile.

The officers laughed. "This is just a few *hours*," Jim Reynolds answered. "Some hours, there's even more."

The two agriculture specialists and their supervisor, Lee Lawrence, sorted through the pile, finding interesting items to show me. Their conversation was freckled with Latin. Reynolds picked up a fruit I pointed to and said, "*Artocarpus heterophyllus.*" Supervisor Lawrence disagreed. "*Artocarpus altilis,*" he said. They hunted for an English translation for me, and finally came up with *breadfruit*. I don't know what breadfruit is in any language.

All three had different opinions on another plant. "*Rha barbarum,*" said Reynolds. "*Rheum rhabarbarum,*" Raghoo corrected. "*Rheum x hybridum,*" Supervisor Lawrence mused, almost under his breath. I looked it up; all three terms may be used to describe rhubarb.

"Do you know the Latin names of *everything?*" I asked.

All three men nodded. They have degrees in horticulture or agriculture; it is one of the requirements of their job. The second requirement is a full-hearted love of dogs.

With blue plastic gloves over my hands, I punctured the skin of a dragonfruit and poked around inside a gallon container of rice stew. When people are determined to smuggle something, they can be quite inventive at hiding it. Officer Raghoo recalled asking a woman if she had any plants or fruits, and she immediately said yes. She opened her suitcase and handed out several mangoes. The officer glanced down at his dog, who alertly sat for a second time. He put on gloves and patted down the case. "The whole back of a pig was sewn into the lining!" he recalled. "She was taking it to a barbecue. She thought if we found the mangoes, we'd stop looking."

Flights from Colombia contain some of the most interesting contraband, so I thought sure the dogs would cover that one. But the officers said no. "We check everybody on those flights, whether the dogs are there or not," said Officer Reynolds. "It's not a good assignment of the resource."

Instead, we headed to a flight just in from Prague. I watched Officer Reynolds' Beagle, Rollo, go from bag to bag, sniffing each one. He worked deliberately. Sometimes Officer Reynolds gave a tug to tell him to move on. At a line up of unclaimed bags, Rollo gave a tug back, and when he did, Reynolds reached down to "breathe" the bag, pushing it with his hand to more fully release the scents within. Rollo promptly sat. Reynolds gave him a treat, then opened the bag and pulled out a bunch of bananas and showed them to the dog, who was still very interested in their smell. "Good boy, good boy!" Reynolds said. Rollo's tail wagged in happiness.

"They're taught five smells," Reynolds told me. "Apple, mango, orange, beef, and pork. Those are the smells that best represent what we're trying to stop. He was never taught bananas, but he's starting to generalize. He's thinking, 'Hey, this kind of smells like something I'm supposed to find. I'll try alerting on it.'"

The most commonly intercepted item is sandwiches. People who either forgot to eat them on the plane or didn't realize you couldn't bring stuff like that in to the States usually carry them innocently. The officers noticed a huge uptick in confiscated sandwiches when the airlines stopped serving food on board.

Why are they so concerned about even our sandwiches? Officer Reynolds says, "Because of the possibility that these products are carriers of bacteria which would be harmful to American crops. That's what we're doing here, protecting American agriculture."

"Think about the farmers," said Supervisor Lawrence, his agriculture degree showing. "These things may carry pests or diseases that are not known in the States. One disease can wipe out an entire crop. That's one farmer's livelihood, gone. It might take years for him to recover."

Some of the diseases APHIS inspectors are trying to keep out sound truly terrifying. Avian Influenza, Bluetongue, Bovine Spongiform, Encephalopathy Brucellosis, Chronic Wasting Disease, Classical Swine Fever, Contagious Equine Merits, Equine Herpes Virus, Equine Infectious Anemia, Equine Viral Arteritis, Foot-and-Mouth Disease, Johnes Piroplasmosis, Pseudorablies, Scrapie, Spring Viremia, Carp Tuberculosis, Venezuelan Equine Encephalomyelitis, and Vesicular Stomatits.

A Beagle Brigade dog's career usually spans six to ten years, unless he loses interest in working or has health issues. Beagles are generally among the healthiest dog breeds. To keep them fresh, handlers make sure they rest for at least twenty minutes of each work hour.

In 2007, as Trouble the Beagle entered old age, he retired from the service to spend his days at Sherrie Keblish's home. His muzzle is gray, but he still sparkles with eagerness at the mention of a car ride or a chance to earn a treat. For elderly Beagles whose handlers can't keep them, APHIS finds other suitable homes from a waiting list of people who would love to adopt one of these hard-working Beagles.

With millions of people participating in international travel, there are always going to be threats to American agriculture. Since

September 11, 2001, there's been a 17 percent decline in foreign visitors to the country. But the Department of Commerce projects by 2010, international arrivals will reach back up to 63 million.

In addition, millions and millions of pieces of international mail and countless commercial import and export shipments continue to enter U.S. ports. All of these people, all of these pieces of mail, all the packages and luggage and cargo need to be sniffed by detection dogs to make sure pests and plant diseases stay out. We need more dogs. We need more handlers. We need to take advantage of the greatest natural deterrent to pests and disease on earth, and give them a pat on the head. That's all they want. Praise and a Milkbone make their day.

Trouble, come back. We need you.

As for me, I consume my paté while I'm in France now, and then leave it forlornly behind. I don't want to cross paths with those Beagles with a smelly sausage in my purse. I know they'll get me next time.

In the course of researching this story, an APHIS inspector told me his Beagle had alerted him to a man in baggy clothing who turned out to have a small monkey buried under his shirt. The man had sedated the little animal, but it was starting to wake up, and the Beagle alerted to the man's strangely mobile jacket and possibly the smell of human blood (the monkey apparently bit him).

They find food and plants, but do Beagles alert to the presence of live animals? Lisa Beckett told me, "They're not trained for that. It would be up to the individual dog." She paused. "Of course, there's the Jack Russell Terriers on Guam. They're trained to alert to snakes."

Jack Russell Terriers on Guam? Snakes?

As it turned out, she wasn't kidding.

THE SNAKE
THAT ATE GUAM

THE MARIANA FRUIT DOVE is a glorious bird. Gazing at it from below, the birdwatcher notices the many colors of its breast; orange, green, violet, blue, yellow, silver gray: pastel colors, nestled right next to each other. The forehead is covered by a splash of magenta. The neck and back are silvery and green. The dove grows to about ten inches. A pair of Marianna Fruit Doves enters into a marriage-like arrangement; the female lays a single egg, and the male helps her tend it. It is a songbird, but sings very little these days.

The Mariana Fruit Dove is extinct in its homeland, the island of Guam. The last time one was spotted there was in 1984. There are a few small colonies on the nearby Northern Marianas Islands, but they are threatened and considered near extinction. There are a few in zoos.

Before 1960, there were twelve native species of birds on Guam. Walking in the forest, the air was filled with bird vocalizations, warbles, chirps, cheeps, trills, tweets, peeps, whistles, twitters, and chatter. Today, the forest is silent.

"Guam is beat up," says Richard Engeman of the National Wildlife Research Center.

Guam is beat up in part by general destruction from World War II, unrestricted growth of its cities, and loss of its woodlands. But one of nature's own creatures has taken part in the beating up of Guam, a small, slithery reptile called the Brown Tree Snake. "Anyplace else in the world, this is a *boring* snake," Engeman says. "It's small, it lives in trees, and it's very aggressive when confronted. It's mildly venomous, but it's not dangerous to humans. Except for small children. This is not a snake that's fun to have in your herpetarium." The Brown Tree Snake, *Boiga irregularis*, is not native to Guam. Guam, like Hawaii, has no native snakes. So the birds that evolved on Guam never adapted to having snakes around. There weren't any.

After World War II, Guam became an important mid-point in the Pacific Ocean. Cargo was transshipped from the Philippines, Japan, Hawaii, and New Guinea. The American government took over 75 percent of the island for military bases. Guam became a territory of the United States. Natives to the island, called *chamorros*, became U.S. citizens. Guam has its own area code, 671, and calls to Guam are billed as domestic calls, not international, even though when I call Guam from New Jersey, I have to calculate that it's ten hours behind (6 p.m. in New Jersey is 8 a.m. in Guam), yet it's tomorrow. Guam is on the other side of the International Date Line.

Tourism is Guam's primary means of support, particularly from Japan. Visitors to Guam enjoy pristine sandy beaches, twenty large hotels, a duty-free Shoppers Galleria, aquarium, and Las Vegas-style shows. There are ten golf courses and three American-type shopping malls.

But there are no birds.

There are no birds because the Brown Tree Snake slipped aboard some of the cargo ships and planes in New Guinea and Australia and hitchhiked a ride to Guam, possibly as early as during World War II. In its native homelands, the snake population was in balance with the rest of the native wildlife. The birds and lizards that make up the Brown Tree Snake's diet evolved alongside the snakes for thousands of years. They know how to keep from being eaten. The birds of Guam had no idea what a snake was. They were stunned to find a hungry predator sitting right next to them on a tree limb. They didn't try to fly away. Brown Tree Snakes are prolific climbers. Songbirds became their primary diet.

"When they come to a tree or a fence, they go up," Engeman says.

Once aloft, they began to pick off Guam's native birds. With so many innocent, delicious birds around, the Brown Tree Snake population exploded. The bird population began to decline.

The Brown Tree Snake has extirpated nine of the twelve species of native Guam forest birds. They are extinct. We will never hear their distinctive calls or see their delicate plumage. A tenth species, the Marianna Crow, is nearing extinction. The population declined to only five individuals before biologists transplanted some from the nearby island of Rota. Hope still exists for re-establishing two species, the Micronesian Kingfisher and the Guam Rail, which have been preserved through captive breeding programs. The bioinvasion of Guam by Brown Tree Snakes has been a disaster. At first, no one realized that it was the snakes that were killing off all the birds. Biologists claimed the cause was pesticides being used on the crops. Pesticides were halted. Then they thought it was somehow due to all the construction on the island. Thousands of acres were set aside as protected forestlands.

Biologists and the government did everything they could think of to save the birds. Yet the birds continued to disappear. There were fewer and fewer every year.

In 1984, Julie Savidge of the Wildlife Biology Department of Colorado State University took a field trip to Guam. She wanted to watch the remaining birds and see for herself what was happening to them. What she saw was frightening. These small snakes, which are never seen anywhere in the daylight, were gliding up trees and picking off birds who landed on the branches. At first, people on Guam were incredulous, because no one ever sees a Brown Tree Snake. They spend all day curled into a tight little hidden ball, away from the sun. Yet, there are an estimated three million brown tree snakes on Guam, probably too many to ever completely eradicate.

When Julie Savidge's research identified the Brown Tree Snake as the culprit, several federal and territorial agencies began researching solutions to the problem, among them scientists at the National Wildlife Research Center. The scientists made some depressing discoveries. The Brown Tree Snake has no natural predator on Guam. Introduction of any natural predators from New Guinea or Australia would mean bringing in another invasive species that might hurt Guam. (Richard Engeman says, "If it eats the Brown Tree Snake, it's going to eat other things, too.") They turned to pesticides. Methyl bromide, a gas used to kill insect pests in cargo, was found to be highly effective against the snakes. However, it was not a practical solution in Guam's tremendous cargo flow. That experiment was halted.

A special trap was devised which works very well. A live mouse lives in a chamber of the trap. Snakes slither in through a tunnel, and then find they can't reach the mouse and a one-way door traps them inside. Snake trappers tour around the airports and ports at night with large spotlights, which they shine on the tops of six-foot, chain link fences. Brown Tree Snakes are night rovers who like to look down on everyone else from up high. The trappers use a special pole to catch the snakes and put them in a bag.

One researcher discovered that acetaminophen, the ingredient in Tylenol, was deathly toxic to Brown Tree Snakes. One Tylenol stuffed in a dead mouse was perfect bait for a Brown Tree Snake.

Using various methods of control, the Brown Tree Snake

population stopped increasing on Guam. In the 1990s, the Wildlife Service began to think they had a handle on the Brown Tree Snake population. Their numbers were no longer expanding. But another terrible thing was unfolding..

The snakes were discovered in cargo areas in Hawaii.

"The danger of invasion on other islands and subsequent impacts similar to those observed on Guam is high,[1]" wrote Ms. Savidge.

The islands of Hawaii had previously been snake-free. Brown Tree Snakes on Hawaii would find the same advantages they had on Guam; a bird and reptile population that could easily be eaten because they didn't know anything about snakes, including the fact that they were deadly predators. The blue and green Omao, the bright red I'iwi with its hooked beak, the big-breasted yellow Amakihi, the endangered little Akiapolaau, the pale blue, equally endangered Hawaii Elepaio; all the birds of Hawaii who nested in trees would be easy prey for the Brown Tree Snake. They could go the way of Guam's Flycatchers, Rufous Fantails, Cardinal Honeyeaters, White-throated Ground Doves, and Nightingale Reed-Warblers. They could disappear. Hawaii could become an island without birds.

Something had to be done.

Clearly, the snakes had once again hitchhiked a ride on planes and ships. Working with the Departments of Agriculture and Customs and Border Patrol, fences were erected to encompass all cargo areas and long stretches of flat, unforested land were created as a buffer against the tree loving snakes.

"Nothing stops them," a Customs Inspector moaned. "When they get out to the planes' wheels, they wrap themselves around and go straight up. We've found snakes in every part of the plane.

[1] Biology and Control of Brown Tree Snakes. Principal Investigator: Julie Savidge, Colorado State University Fishery and Wildlife Biology Department. www.colostate.edu/Dept/ccpunit/research-browntreesnks.html

They curl into a small ball and hide. We've found lots of them around the wheel wells."

These are places where the hardest-working, best-intentioned inspector in the world can't find them. The inspector can't see them. They don't leave a visual trail to follow. They are invisible to humans.

Then an inspector on Hawaii started to think about those silly Beagles in their green jackets who greet planes coming in to Honolulu International Airport. The Beagles check over tourists arriving from Japan, Hong Kong, the Philippines, Taiwan, Korea, Thailand, Australia, Indonesia, and everywhere else, and often find forbidden fruits, vegetables, plant clippings, and insects which would be harmful to Hawaii's ecosystem. The Beagles alert their handlers and the harmful animals and plants are seized. Could Beagles perform the same service with Brown Tree Snakes?

Dog trainers employed by the Animal and Plant Health Inspection Service conducted tests. First, they used the scent of Brown Tree Snakes to teach Beagles to find it in the same way they were taught to find fruits. No problem.

Next, they tried the Beagles with the real thing; live Brown Tree Snakes that were hidden in boxes. A problem developed. Brown Tree Snakes are extremely aggressive when threatened. When the Beagles poked them with their soft, wet noses, the snakes struck.

The quick bite of a Brown Tree Snake doesn't really hurt, because they are opisthoglyphous, or "rear-fanged." Their venom is injected by means of a pair of enlarged teeth at the back of the jawbone. These fangs point back rather than straight down. In order to envenomate its prey, the snake must bite it, hold it, and move it to the back of the mouth where it can penetrate it. The fangs have grooved channels, which deliver venom into the victim. The body of a Brown Tree Snake is small, approximately the circumference of a man's index finger. They grow to about three feet in their native New Guinea, but with the rich birds of Guam to devour, they were getting much longer. Six- and eight-foot long snakes became common. Its head is large, but still nowhere near the size it would need to be to hurt a human, or a Beagle.

But the Beagle is a peaceable little dog. While they are excellent rabbit hunters, they were disturbed by the bellicose attitude of the snakes. They didn't like getting nipped on the nose. After only two or three hostile encounters, the Beagles stopped sniffing out the snakes. Who could blame them?

Instead of giving up, the trainers looked for a game-hunting breed that would be tenacious, courageous, and single minded. The breed would have to be highly energetic and agile to leap away from the snakes. They had to be small enough that handlers could easily lift them up on top of containers, and narrow enough to get between closely stacked cargo boxes. They had to give a vigorous alert; in other words, give the handler strong cues when they found a snake, through their excitement or barking.

They decided to try the Jack Russell Terrier.

The Jack Russell has traditionally been a working terrier. They were required to bark at prey so that if the dog had gone underground into a wild animal's tunnel, the owner could locate it and dig it out. Since in dog breeding, the specimens who are bred are the ones best at hunting down its prey, Jack Russell Terriers became very vocal dogs, and excellent diggers.

"They were bred to hunt vicious prey. A few little snakebites wouldn't bother them. It would make them mad," said Jack Russell breeder Michael Reed.[2] "They would keep right after those critters." Marcia Knoster, another breeder, added, "When they're hunting, we put electronic 'locators' on their collars so we

---

[2] The American Kennel Club and other dog registries divide Jack Russell Terriers into separate groups based on leg length. The longer legged variety, standing about fourteen inches at the shoulder, is registered as a Parson Russell Terrier.

can find out where they are. They'll follow a fox or a raccoon or a woodchuck into a hole that goes ten feet deep. You might hear the dog barking, but still don't know where it is. Hunters carry shovels, and they have to dig down to get the dogs out, because the dogs will never give up. Never."

They are intelligent, protective, fearless, high-energy dogs. Many families who adopt them as puppies find to their chagrin that although they are small, they are not lapdogs. They never seem to get tired. Even after a long walk in the park and twenty tennis ball retrieves, the Jack Russell is still fresh and ready to be busy again. If not kept busy, they get bored. Jack Russells that are not trained and exercised regularly often exhibit unmanageable behavior, including excessive barking, escaping from the yard, or digging in unwanted places inside and outside the house.

Jack Russell breed rescuers have to work constantly to find new homes for Jack Russell Terriers whose owners were not aware of the high energy level when they picked out the puppy. The little, bouncy Jack Russell, with his inquisitive black eyes and active manner, are very cute. Families don't find out until they get them home that they are dogs that require frequent and enormous amounts of exercise.

They were perfect.

Lisa Beckett, Training Specialist at the National Detector Dog Training Center in Orlando, says "They chose Jack Russells because of their really high prey drive. *Anything* that moves, they're after it. That worked well for that particular pest."

Handlers were trained to guide the dogs the same way drug-sniffing or bomb-sniffing dogs are guided; the person leads the dog along the car or cargo, pointing out places where the dog should sniff. When they locate a snake, the JRTs go nuts, jumping up and down, barking, or vigorously wagging their tails to let the handler know the location. "In recent years, the detector dog program has transitioned through aggressive alerts—biting—to passive response—sitting—to an active response protocol—scratching."

To find out if they were effective, Richard Engeman designed a test. He placed a Brown Tree Snake in a PVC tube with air holes drilled into it. Then he hid the snakes in cargo, asking the dock or airport workers not to let the dog handler know. He hid himself and watched as the teams worked.

Engeman is a statistician who keeps careful records of his work. He found that JRTs found the hidden snakes 70 percent of the time in 1997. They found them 61 percent of the time in 1998 and 64 percent in 1999, the years he carried out the tests. That figure sounded low to me, but Engeman was happy with it.[2]

"Remember, I'm carrying this plastic tube into the warehouse and hiding it in a box, which is not the same as a wild snake slithering in, leaving a scent trail all the way. The snakes' scent would be all over the box. But the only way scent gets spread from my PVC tubes is through these little air holes, which don't allow much. The dogs are finding these snakes from a tiny amount of scent. In a natural snake search, the percentage would be much higher." Dr. Engeman's many papers about his research were very positive about the ability of the dogs to provide a successful "last line of defense" against the snakes.

Fifteen Jack Russell teams now work all the shipping areas of Guam. On the Hawaiian Islands, other Jack Russells were used to check over the same cargo again, making sure the snakes didn't land.

"The Jack Russells don't care about getting nipped by a snake," Lisa Beckett told me. "They keep going back at the snake. They don't stop. A little bit on the nose doesn't bother them at all."

The prospect of these awful predators getting onto bird-filled

2 "Sustained Evaluation of the Effectiveness of Detector Dogs for Locating Brown Tree Snakes in Cargo Outbound from Guam." Engeman, Richard M., Daniel S. Vice, Darryl York, and Kenneth S. Gruver. International Journal of International Biodeterioration & Biodegradation, no.49, 2002.

Hawaii seemed extremely depressing to me. But Dr. Engeman said he's not worried. "The dogs provide a very effective barrier," he said. "With the trapping and spotlighting and then the dogs, snakes are not getting through." The Wildlife Services program on Guam trapped over 17,600 snakes from 1994 to 1998, but fewer in recent years. In fact, the number of snakes being found by the dogs has been going down because the effective trapping methods are keeping them out of cargo.

"We found a big increase in discoveries by detector dogs in the ten weeks following Supertyphoon Paka." That storm was one of the most powerful ever recorded in the world, and it knocked out many of the traps and other tree snake control technologies. But it didn't stop the dogs. "The detector dogs were able to resume duties the day following the storm," Rick Engeman said.

The Brown Tree Snake threat is taken so seriously that if one is sighted near cargo, an emergency-trapping plan goes into effect immediately. There are intense visual searches, traps are set all around, and a temporary barrier is built in the area of the sighting. Jack Russells are brought in to hunt even more aggressively in high-risk ship and air traffic areas for products leaving Guam. Hawaii APHIS inspectors are notified and begin the same intense precautions there.

DNA testing underway at the Wildlife Service Research Center is trying to determine if the population of Brown Tree Snakes on Guam could have evolved from just one pregnant female. At least eight Brown tree snakes have been found in Hawaii since 1981. It's unnerving to imagine that just one pregnant female could mean the end of birds on Hawaii. Native forest birds would go extinct, and the tourist industry would probably suffer from negative publicity. In keeping all snakes out of cargo, the dogs are providing an important service to man.

My nephew, Jake, has a Jack Russell Terrier that spends his days bouncing around the house. I told his father, my brother Drew, about the important work of the JRTs on Guam. "I've got one they could have," he said immediately. "If they need another Jack Russell, just let me know." Curiously, that comment was repeated again and again by the owners of Jack Russell Terriers, and even more often by their family members. "I've got one to send them" or "Are they accepting volunteers?" or even "When is the next flight to Guam?"

WHEN HEROES FALL

ON A WARM SPRING DAY in suburban New York, tall pine trees swayed gently in the breeze from their setting near the top of a steep hill. Below them lay a field richly carpeted with green grass and dotted with pink dogwoods spreading their blossomed branches like giant umbrellas under the sun. Tall viburnum bushes thronged near the sidewalk, their fullness blocking much of the traffic noise from the quiet of the cemetery.

Small songbirds in yellow and blue whistled as they flitted from tree to tree, landing so expertly on each that they surely were long-term residents here. I'm no birdwatcher, but what struck me was that the birds were watching *me*. Not like in a creepy Alfred Hitchcock movie, but in a friendly sort of way. As I moved from spot to spot through the cemetery, the singing birds were always with me, and the loveliness of their song was comforting, an orchestral gift from nature to ease a mourner's pain.

The birds were helpful, and they seemed to know it.

This cemetery was a new discovery for me, but the Hartsdale exit off Route 287 was one I'd passed a hundred times before, whizzing by between the Tappan Zee Bridge and White Plains, en route to my friend Marilyn's house in Connecticut and her kennel of English Toy Spaniels. Only today, when I read, "Next exit, Hartsdale," did it click in my brain that this must be the site of the famous Hartsdale Pet Cemetery. There was a War Dog Memorial statue here I'd always wanted to see. I pulled off at the exit and dialed the cemetery office for directions.

It should be easy to find, because it's practically in the center of Hartsdale, a hamlet of Westchester County. "Just one hundred yards north of the Dairydel, where Hartsdale Avenue meets Central Park Avenue," the friendly voice on the phone told me. But following his directions proved difficult, because they were based on landmarks I didn't recognize. "Right across from the church," the man said. There was no church in sight; then I figured out that the lunchtime drivers parking cars and hurrying across to a brick building were actually going to noon mass. The Church of the Sacred Heart bore an uncanny resemblance to an ordinary office building. Across the street from it, I saw only a wall of green, viburnum fifteen feet high, and planted so close to each other that they were more effective than a fence in preventing the curious from peeking in. A wrought iron arch over the entrance proclaimed, "Hartsdale Canine Cemetery." This was the place.

Entering through that iron arch brought the visitor into another world. The cemetery where my mother is buried always struck me as an eerie, foreboding place, a place to wear black and keep your eyes lowered as you go about the serious business of grief. This burial ground was peaceful and calm and welcoming, and the beauty of the steep green hillside, with grey, silvery headstones and fresh plantings of small pink and white and yellow azaleas, was somehow a reminder that all creatures end up here, not only you and those you love.

Once inside, it's pleasant to stroll the cemetery's quiet two acres. A stream burbles by. I stopped to watch it for a few moments. There is something tranquil about water flowing naturally like that, as if your worries are streaming away with it. There was a lovely feeling of being alone here, but I was not. A Mexican gardener, hoe resting on his shoulder, ambled by, twitching his mustache in my direction. He was dressed in the uniform of janitors and gardeners everywhere, green pants, green cap, tan shirt with the cemetery's name stitched in red over his heart.

As I began to ascend the steep stone stairs, a woman standing near the summit nodded in my direction and moved away. I followed her gaze; she was apparently waiting for the manager, who at this moment was showing a plot near the stream to a potential customer.

At the top of the stairs was the statue I'd come to see. He stood proudly on top of a five foot high slab of marble, a life-size German Shepherd, lean and strong and fit as a good war dog, like a good soldier, should be. His eyes and ears were alert in bronze. Lying by his side was a World War I helmet and canteen, stamped, U.S. A huge American flag flew above. His alert posture made me think he was standing guard, protecting all the Poodles and Schnauzers and Cocker Spaniels from whatever alien invader happened by. I moved closer to read the inscription.

DEDICATED TO THE MEMORY OF
THE WAR DOG
ERECTED BY PUBLIC CONTRIBUTION
BY DOG LOVERS, TO MAN'S MOST
FAITHFUL FRIEND, FOR THE VALIANT
SERVICES RENDERED IN THE WORLD WAR
1914–1918

At his feet, the plot was brimming with fresh, lively multicolored pansies of pink and purple and yellow and white. Water droplets rolled gently from the petals; the gardener had just been by with a hose. Fundraising for this memorial had been spearheaded by class upon class of American schoolchildren who heard the stories of the seven thousand canines who bravely helped their soldier owners during what they called back then, "the Great War." It was erected in 1923, after the sum of $2,500 had been raised, an enormous amount of money at the time. Robert Caterson, a sculptor and architect who worked on many parts of Grand Central Station, sculpted it. He used ten tons of fine quality granite from his own Vermont quarry.

Representatives of every nation that fought in the Great War attended the 1923 unveiling. During eighty-two years of service, it began to look its age, so in 2005, it was completely refurbished, this time with donations from the pet owners who buried their own beloved pets here. Now, a ceremony is held every June to honor all American war dogs. Wreaths are laid on the graves of the fallen heroes and speeches are made about their bravery. A veteran told me a representative of the military from the Pentagon always comes, but never wears a uniform in order not to offend the relatives of human soldiers who were killed in war.

Moving to the right, a much smaller headstone proclaims:

DEDICATED TO
THE CANINES AND THEIR TRAINERS
WHO SO NOBLY SERVED AS PART OF THE
FEDERAL EMERGENCY MANAGEMENT AGENCY
TASK FORCE
URBAN SEARCH AND RESUCE MISSION
IN OKLAHOMA CITY IN APRIL 1995

That brought back sharp memories of scenes I'd watched on TV. The Alfred P. Murrah Federal Building, its front ripped open, police and medical personnel and handlers with search and rescue dogs stumbling across its split and fallen cinder blocks; the desperate search for kindergarten age children who'd been in America's Kids Day Care Center on the second floor; a Golden Retriever barking at a jutting slab of concrete, signaling to his handler that an injured person was buried below. It was the kind of terrible terrorist event in which dogs provide necessary and unfailing assistance. One hundred and sixty-eight people died, including nineteen children, the deadliest act of domestic terrorism to take place in this country up to that date. Eight hundred were injured, many trapped in the rubble.

Moving to the right, I read another headstone.

IN MEMORY OF THE HEROIC CANINE
SIRIUS
AND ALL THOSE WHO LOST THEIR LIVES
AS A RESULT OF THE
TERRORIST ATTACK ON
THE WORLD TRADE CENTER ON
SEPTEMBER 11, 2001

This was the terrorist event from which no one in my generation will ever recover. I remembered this dog, Sirius, a yellow Labrador Retriever trained in explosive detection. His daily job was to search vehicles and cargo entering the underground garage of the World Trade Center for any sign of bombs, like the one that had damaged the towers back in 1993 and caused six deaths and one thousand injuries. His handler, Officer David Lim, had left him in his crate in the basement office of the Port Authority that morning of September 11, 2001. Officer Lim remembered that when he heard the blast, he said to Sirius, "Sounds like one got by us." Unbeknownst to him, the blast Lim heard was not a bomb, but the sound of American Airlines Flight 11 crashing into the eighty-fifth floor of Tower Two at 8:50 a.m.

He ran to the lobby of Tower One to see if he could help people stumbling down flights of stairs, first putting Sirius safely into his crate. At the Memorial Service, Lim remembered, "I told him, 'I'll be back to get you.'" He could not keep that promise. Lim was buried in the collapse for five hours himself before being rescued. Workers were not able to reach Lim's basement office until four months later.

On January 22, 2002, Lim was notified that Sirius' crate had been found. He rushed to Ground Zero to be there for the recovery of his dog. The rescuers only comfort was the news that Sirius would have died instantly. He would not have suffered.

Sirius was given full police honors that day. He was treated with the same respect firemen and police give to one of their own. His yellow body was lifted gently onto a stretcher and covered with an American flag. All work at the site came to a halt. Earthmovers and cranes were silenced, and their operators stood by, hats off, hands over their hearts. Eight New York Police Department Officers lifted the stretcher and carried it up through the rubble, as lines of uniformed police stood by, saluting as Sirius's body was carried to a police truck. A fifth grade class in Illinois was so moved that they raised money for a beautiful oak Memorial Flag box in which Officer Lim keeps the flag that was used that day.

More than one hundred police canines and their handlers attended Sirius's Memorial Service.[1] Officer Lim said, "We were very close; no matter where I went, he went. Whatever I asked him to do, he did. He never complained. Sometimes we'd be working for long hours, searching hundreds of cars or trucks, and he'd just look at me like, *What do you want me to do now?*'"

In the Memorial Program listing the details of Sirius' life and death, the writer expressed a sentiment felt by those who

---

[1] April 24, 2002, at Liberty State Park in New Jersey, where the view is of the lower Manhattan Financial District in which the Towers collapsed.

glimpsed the team on the job, "*Seeing them brought a sense of security and a smile to the faces of thousands of staff and visitors alike.*"[2]

The FBI Special Agent who had been in charge of searching for evidence and personal belongings at the Fresh Kills landfill on Staten Island presented Officer Lim with Sirius's metal water bowl, which had been pulled from Lim's car. It had been inscribed with Sirius' shield number and a saying, "*I gave my life so that you may save others.*" Officer Lim's calm gave way to tears at that point.

Sirius was the only police dog to die in the collapse of the World Trade Center on September 11. He was the only police dog killed in the Port Authority's eighty-year history. The British, a nation of dog lovers, awarded the Victoria Cross posthumously to Sirius at the British Embassy in Manhattan.[3]

I'd have my dog buried here, I decided; if I lived nearby, close enough to visit. The concrete steps in front of the war dog memorial were a cool and shady spot to sit. The cemetery provided all the rest and pleasure of the country orchard it once was. Two huge fir trees stood guard a short distance from me. A row of eight pink dogwood trees danced prettily in the breeze. Pink and white blossoms swayed in front of dozens of private headstones.

A sandal-shod woman with long dark hair descended the steps and paused to stand next to me in what felt like a comforting silence.

"It's a sad thing," she said, then continued her slow downward climb.

It's not just sad, it's heartbreaking. Certainly all cemeteries are full of the gravestones of the beloved, and there are occasional

---

[2] Sirius is not buried at Hartsdale. He was cremated and his ashes remain with Officer Lim.

[3] Americans have been ambivalent about giving state awards to dogs. Military dogs earned Purple Crosses and recognition of valor from World War I up to the Vietnam War. Then all the medals were retracted with a statement issued from the Pentagon that awarding medals to dogs detracted from their value to humans.

inscriptions such as "Husband and Father" or "Beloved Wife and Mother" so the living can declare a tiny bit of their affection for the dead.

But with dogs, as in life, the humans take the emotion to the extreme.

TEDDY & OTTIE
THEY GIVE NOTHING BUT
LOVE & AFFECTION
JULIA W. HOWARD

HERE SLEEP OUR BELOVED LITTLE SCHNAUZERS
1965–1979 BABY
1979–1995 JESSICA
THEY GAVE A LIFETIME OF LOVE, FAITH,
FRIENDSHIP, COMPANIONSHIP AND DEVOTION
OUR LOVE WILL NEVER FORGET THEM
WITH BROKEN HEARTS
RENEE & TIBOR ADORJAN

IN MEMORY OF
MAN'S BEST FRIEND
A DOG, A TOY BULL
LANNEY
JULY 24, 1936–MARCH 13, 1945

ARISTOCRAT,
GONE TO ETERNAL REST
DEARLY LOVED IN LIFE
DEEPLY MOURNED IN DEATH

And an extra sentiment at the very bottom—

IN GOD'S CARE.
1936–1948 BUNNY
THE SUNSHINE OF OUR LIVES
MOORE

1947–1961 SUSIE
ALWAYS IN MY HEART
MOORE

SNOOPY
HOME FOREVER
2-7-82–12-18-95

A friendly man in tan corduroy pants and a green jacket stopped to say hi. When I returned the greeting, he sat down beside me. I noticed he was carrying a folder embossed with the cemetery's name under his arm, and correctly guessed he was here to see about burying his dog.

"How did you find out about this place?" I asked.

He smiled and removed his glasses. "I used to live in Yonkers. A friend told me about it. It's famous." He stretched his legs and crossed his tennis shoes. "Did you know there's a lion buried here?"

I did not.

"In the 1920s, a Barnum & Bailey lion had a cub and it died. A visiting princess felt sorry for it and paid to have it buried here."[4]

"Where's the stone?"

---

[4] In 1910, Hungarian Princess Lwoff Parlaghy purchased the lion cub from Ringling Brothers Circus, and kept him as a pet at her residence in the Plaza Hotel in New York. "Goldfleck" died in 1912.

"I don't know the exact location. But they have a map up there." He gestured towards a white cottage. "Did you know people are buried here?"

I didn't know that, either.

"About eighty people. You can't bring a coffin. You have to get cremated first. There's always room for more ashes." We contemplated the stones silently.

"I wouldn't want to be buried here," he said. "Too much noise. You wouldn't get any rest, with all the meowing and barking."

We both admit we parked in the Dunkin Donuts parking lot next door. "They probably don't mind," he predicts, standing to leave. "They probably sell a lot of coffee that way."

Chips is buried here, a part-shepherd, part-collie, part-sled dog who stood guard at the Roosevelt-Churchill conference at Casablanca. Later, in combat, he attacked a pillbox and captured an enemy machine-gun crew. He held the gunner pinned to the floor by the throat until his handler arrived. Four other Germans had their hands raised above their heads in terror.

Koehler rests here in peace, a German Shepherd whose German family sent him to work with the Red Cross at the beginning of World War I. His tail was shot off in battle, but he never hesitated to serve bravely with the medics. After the war, his family sent him to the United States with an American friend, where he lived happily until the age of twelve, with good food and without the deprivations of postwar Germany.

Joachim was a tiny puppy when an American lawyer serving in the military found him in Vietnam. They relieved each other's loneliness. Each gave the other a sense of belonging. The new owner taught Joachim to drink beer and enjoy nights on the town. One evening, despite the fact that he had been hitting the brew, he sounded an alert moments before a sniper attack, for which he was credited with saving many lives. He retired to his owner's home in Scarsdale, New York, where he lived peacefully until a speeding car ran him down.

Also buried at Hartsdale is "Boots," a German Shepherd who starred in a long since forgotten propaganda movie, "Boots and Saddles." By showing the loyalty, devotion, and bravery of a war dog, Boots helped to raise over $9 million in war bonds for World War II from the dog-loving public.

The simple cottage at the top of the hill serves as both an office for the cemetery directors and a retreat for saddened owners. From the director, I learned that the cemetery was created in 1896, when a prominent New York City veterinarian, Dr. Samuel Johnson, offered his apple orchard to a friend to bury his beloved dog. After that first dog, Dr. Johnson welcomed others, but a pet cemetery was not in demand at that time. When the War Dog Memorial was put in place in 1923, there were two thousand graves at Hartsdale. Today, a century later, there are seventy thousand pets here. Most of them were beloved private citizens. But the shade of the War Dog Memorial is a good spot to begin to think of all the military war dogs who have died recently, in Afghanistan and Iraq, while serving their country.

Marine Cpl. Brendan N. Poelaert and his military working dog, Flapoor, deployed to Fallujah in November 2006, and immediately began helping troops take back the city from armed rebels. One day, their job was to help secure a building that had been the enemy's main command center. Flapoor went in eagerly, sniffing his way through room after room. Poelaert was about to give the all clear signal when he saw Flapoor freeze and lift his head, working a tendril of air through his nostrils. Flapoor looked pointedly at Poelaert and led him to a door to the building's cellar.

Specialists were called in, and found an improvised explosive device hidden behind a cache of weapons, set to go off the moment it was disturbed. It could have collapsed the entire building. If Flapoor had not discovered it, that building would have fallen on the heads of twenty Marines, likely killing many of them.

Two months later, in Ramadi, Flapoor was not so lucky. Three dog teams were providing crowd control for about three hundred people jostling to get in a police academy, eager to be hired for new jobs. Sgt Jesse Maldonaldo and his MWD went to the front of the line, Sgt. Adam Cann and his MWD Bruno took a position in the middle of the crowd, Sgt. Poelart and Flapoor were patrolling in the rear. A few minutes later, a terrible explosion shook the street. A suicide bomber wearing a vest packed with ball bearings and explosives detonated the device while standing next to Cann. The explosive ripped through the crowd, killing dozens. Poelaert thought he'd lost his arm, but was even more upset at the site of Flapoor, lying still in the street, his eyes open, not moving. Blood poured from his chest.

"I did what you do for any Marine," Poelaert said. "I called for the medics to come help a wounded soldier."

Poelart said as he looked through the crowd, he saw Cann's MWD, Bruno, dragging himself over to Cann. "He was badly injured, but he lay across Adam's body, like he was protecting him from anything else," he recalled. A friend back at Pendleton also recalled, "As Adam lay there Bruno laid next to him and put his head on Adam's chest."

Other dog handlers at the camp remembered that Adam's dog Bruno was not the ideal canine candidate for a MWD. He was too submissive. He had a reputation as a sissy. He wasn't tough. The friend recalled, "We would often tease Adam about his 'pet.'" At a point where many might have given up and asked for a new dog, Adam increased Bruno's training. By encouraging every small step in the right direction, he turned Bruno into a tough, aggressive, reliable MWD. The photo on his Web site shows Adam restraining a roaring Bruno, who has reared up on his hind legs and bared his teeth at the photographer.

They were deployed to Iraq. Immediately up their return, Adam volunteered for another deployment. He had a reputation as a hard worker. His friend Mike wrote on his blog, "He volunteered for every mission and patrol he could. In fact, he wasn't even supposed to be there that day. He had just come off some missions in the city when he got back and saw that two other dog teams, Sgt. Jesse Maldonaldo and Cpl. Brendan Poelart, were about to go out on another one. They had told him he didn't have to go but Adam refused and insisted he go with them."

Medics reached Cann quickly, but there had been no barrier between him and the bomber. Sgt. Cann was dead. He was the first K-9 handler to die in service since Vietnam.

Poelaert had multiple shrapnel wounds in his left arm. Bruno and Flapoor were injured. "Flapoor tried to come to me, but he just lay on the ground and stared," Poelaert said. "Medics wanted to treat me, but I was more concerned with getting the dogs to a veterinarian."

Despite his injuries, Poelaert refused to be moved to Al Asad for treatment without Flapoor at his side. It took several surgeries to restore the use of his left arm. Flapoor eventually recovered from his punctured lung and shrapnel wounds. The partners went through physical therapy under the California sun at Camp Pendleton, with a regimen familiar to athletes: icing, heating, stretching, and motion exercises. Flapoor quickly got back to his usual self in most ways: fast, friendly, and eager-to-please. "He hits like a ton of bricks and loves biting," Poelaert said. "You can tell he is missing it. We are both ready to get better and get back to work." But Poelart says he still suffers from a sort of canine post-traumatic stress disorder. "He's really jumpy around loud noises now."

In April, 2008, a newly-built K-9 training facility at USMC Logistics Base in Barstow, California, was dedicated to Sergeant Adam Leigh Cann. His family flew in from Florida to be at the ceremony. His father Leigh said sadly, "He sure did make us proud." Bruno was flown in from Camp Pendleton to be at the service. Inexplicably, a photo from the event shows him barking wildly as the honor guard with the American flag and the Marine Corps flag march by. The dog next to him is silent. It's as if Bruno knows why he's there, and is calling to his dead handler.

Cpl. Poelart and Flapoor were summoned to Baghdad to deploy in the surge to make the city neighborhoods safe, another assignment, another chance to face danger, another possibility of being killed.

When Marine Corporal Dustin Jerome Lee was five years old, his best playmate was his mother's Search and Rescue dog. Rachel Lee trained other dogs, too, for Search and Rescue work, teaching them to follow a scent and to alert the humans when they found the trail of a missing person. Dusty liked to rub his clothes against his mother's dog's nose, then run and hide until the dog found him. So it made sense that when he turned eighteen and enlisted in the Marines, he became a military war dog handler. Lee was assigned an older, experienced German Shepherd named Doenja, who helped him learn the intricacies of handling a bomb dog. When he was ready to be deployed, he was assigned a younger dog, Lex, a German Shepherd from Camp Lejeune. The two became fast friends. Lex and Lee were deployed together to Anbar Province in Iraq. But Dustin never forgot about Doenja. He kept in touch with trainers, worried about her health. She was eleven years old. When she began to lose her hearing and sight and was forced to retire, he was granted permission to adopt her, and sent her home to live with his family in Mississippi. The Lee family was happy to welcome their son's first dog to their home.

In Iraq, the work was hard. They spent their days inspecting insurgents' homes and hiding places. Lex gave Lee an alert every time he sniffed the faintest odor of an explosive, and Corporal Lee halted the patrol before it could be triggered and kill men.

But there was time to fool around and play, too. Lee had his mom send him a pointy red hat so he could play Santa Claus, and he put one on his dog, as well. A friend snapped a photo and e-mailed it to Rachel Lee, which gave the family a good laugh.

In March 2007, Lee and Lex were leading a patrol in Fallujah when insurgents targeted Dustin and Lex with a rocket propelled grenade. This time, they hit their target. The grenade landed inches from Dustin's feet, inflicting deadly wounds. He lay on the ground, wounded and bleeding. Lex was hit, too, but instead of running away, he lay down by his partner's side and refused to move. John Burnam, veteran and author of books about MWDs, and also the founder of the National War Dogs Monument project in Washington, D.C., described on a blog the thoughts that would have gone through Lex's head, "I feel sharp pains in my side and back. I'm bleeding but deal with it and concentrate on comforting my partner and protecting him from further harm" (Retirelex. blogspot.com). Marines had to pull the dog away so medics could treat him. Dusty died from his injuries. He had spent only twenty years on earth.

His body was shipped home to Quitman, Mississippi, to a hero's funeral.

Burnam described Lex's thoughts, "No one can measure the love and unconditional loyalty I have for Dusty. I'd sacrifice my own life for him...I just wish I could have stopped that RPG or pushed Dusty away from that powerful blast. It all happened in a blink of an eye and I didn't see it coming until it was too late. Now I sit alone in my kennel-run waiting for the day Dusty shows up."

At the family's request, Lex was flown to Mississippi from Camp Lejeune for his partner's funeral, where he sat in a place of honor at the front of the church, occasionally sniffing the air, prepared to alert if he smelled danger.

After the funeral, Lee's parents were devastated when Lex was ordered back to work. He was sent to Albany, Georgia, to be used to train young war dogs. The family was heartbroken. So friends launched a campaign to bring the German Shepherd home.

"He was my son's partner," said Lee's father, Jerome. "He was the last one to see my son alive."

Lee's family tried for months to adopt Lex, the dog their son had loved so much. Lex had nearly died, too, losing part of his tail and leaving shrapnel lodged dangerously close to the nerves in his spine. Lex was eight years old, but because he was still able to work, military regulations said that he could not be retired.

A letter from Terry Lynch, founder of Project K-9, was typical of many sent to Colonel Christian N. Haliday, commander of the Marine Logistics Base, "Given the type of injury suffered by Lex and the fact that he has shrapnel that was not removed, this will likely contribute to an arthritic condition as the dog grows older. Any additional usage of this canine as a working dog could aggravate his condition and result in great pain and suffering as the dog ages. Therefore it is the humane and proper action to retire the dog NOW and not continue to use this dog" (Retirelex. blogspot.com.).

An e-mail and Internet campaign was launched, but did not meet with success until they were joined by a congressman not from Lee's home state of Mississippi, but many states away, in North Carolina, U.S. Representative Walter Jones's congressional district includes Camp Lejeune, Marine Corps Air Station Cherry Point, and Marine Corps Air Station New River, so he was familiar with MWDs and their handlers. John Burnam called him about the plight of Lex and the Lee family.

"When I was presented with this story, it brought tears to my eyes," Jones said. With his access to military chiefs, he was able to take their case straight to the Marine Corps' top general.

The orders came through just in time for Lex to have a merry Christmas. On December 21, 2007, the Lee family and many others wiped away tears at a special retirement ceremony. Lex was brought out of the kennel facility on a leash, which was then handed over to Dustin's father. The Patriot Guard riders escorted the family back to Quitman, a 350-mile journey that took six hours.

"We knew that's what Dustin would have wanted out of this," said Jerome Lee. "He knew that we would take care of Lex and love him, just like our own."

Defense Department officials said Lex was the first dog in military history to receive early retirement. Two months later, on February 16th, 2008, the Lee family drove east once again, this time to the Air Armament Museum on Eglin Air Force Base in Florida for a special ceremony. Lex was given a commemorative Purple Heart, for wounds sustained in battle. A medal suspended on a purple ribbon was slipped over his neck.

"To look into Lex's eyes is like seeing Dustin's spirit with him," said Dusty's mother, Rachel. "Every day, he brings happiness back to our family. Through him, we are still able to love our son. Having Lex with us now is the reason I can continue to have faith in this cause. He gives me strength."

Another K-9 soldier's death was a personal shock to me. I'd been in contact with a military working dog handler named Kory Wiens in the summer of 2007, asking for an interview about his bomb sniffing dog, Cooper.

"I call him my son," he wrote back. "He is enjoying our deployment. He thinks Iraq is not bad as long as I'm here. I think the same about him."

He was easy to find because many news articles were written about him and Cooper in 2007. He was easygoing and charismatic. He had answers to reporters' questions which were both charming and sincere. He had a bright outlook on life that was contagious. If you wanted to interview a canine handler, the Army was quick to offer Corporal Kory Wiens.

Another day he wrote, "This may sound funny but we are having a grrreat time in Iraq!!! Hard to belive huh? Well I have Cooper with me so everything is alright."

After a week in which I couldn't get him to reply to any e-mails, I picked up the newspaper to read that Kory and his dog had been killed. They were on dismounted patrol in the Iraqi community of Muhammad Sath, south of Baghdad. Kory and Cooper were in the lead, along with Pfc. Bruce Salazar. An Improvised Explosive Device blasted them to pieces. All three were killed.

It's hard to explain how crushed you can feel over the death of a person you never met.

The U.S. military released few details. That's par for the course in situations like this. They say it's for security reasons. They don't want to give the enemy any useful information about what type of explosive killed the soldiers, or exactly where they were or what they were doing. But from covering war in the Middle East, I know that explosions like this tend to be extremely high velocity, which means they are over in an instant. People nearby hear a great roar and see a cloud of dust and smoke but by the time they register the event in their brains, it's over. There's none of the drama of fire and noise that causes audiences in movie theaters everywhere to gasp and drop their popcorn. Before you can say, "What happened?" the victims are already dead. Moviegoers perceive the slow velocity explosions as more powerful but it's actually the opposite. Explosions with high brisance are more deadly, but unsuitable for filming. The blast is over so quickly it can be missed while the film is moving from one frame to the next. The bang of a C-4 cutter charge is downright disappointing to hear. That's what happened to Kory and Cooper and Salazar. One minute, they were alive and well, the next moment, they were gone.

They were members of the Ninety-fourth Mine Dog Detachment, Fifth Engineer Battalion, and First Engineer Brigade, from Fort Leonard Wood, Missouri. A team like his was among the key tools being used to combat the efforts of Iraqi insurgents to blow up American troops. They were deployed together to Iraq in January, so they'd been there seven months. Kory, who rarely complained about anything, couldn't help but mention in his e-mails that he found FLW boring, which may be part of the reason for his enthusiasm for being in Iraq.

Cooper was a specialized search dog trained to detect TNT, C-4, detonation cords, smokeless powder, and mortars. The Mine Dog Detachment was in demand more than any other unit in their battalion. They were the unit most often deployed from Fort Leonard Wood. The Oregon National Guard put out a press release stating that Kory and Cooper's work before their deaths had saved countless lives by taking explosives and IED manufacturing materials off the streets of Iraq.

The military believes that much of the munitions for constructing IEDs in Iraq have come from large Iraqi military ordnance deposits looted by insurgents, or from stockpiles scattered in secret locations throughout that country before the war.

They didn't report who the suicide attackers who killed Kory and Cooper were, but the largest groups of such aggressors in Iraq are Sunni Iraqis, followed by foreign fighters who are members of sects like Al Qaeda, and usually hail from Saudi Arabia, Syria, and Kuwait. The Pentagon has found that insurgents build and deploy IEDs by using networks that have formed the sinews of commerce for centuries, connecting the many factions that have survived alongside each other since humans first formed tribes.

High demand for IEDs with which to kill Americans has led to the formation of a new group of professionals; skilled explosive experts make good money by hiring themselves out to other insurgent groups. They advertise their skills on Arabic Web sites on the Internet, and are temporarily contracted on a per-job basis. A typical IED terrorist cell consists of a financier, bomb maker, emplacer, triggerman, spotter, and often a cameraman who records videos of exploding U.S. vehicles and dead Americans. These are distributed via the Internet to win new supporters. Small crowds watch the videos in private homes in a party-like atmosphere, laughing and applauding as the soldiers die.[5]

So far, dogs like Cooper have proved the best defense against IEDs.. The commander of Kory's headquarters unit, Colonel Mike Iverson, said casualties among dog handler teams are extremely rare. The double deaths of Kory and Cooper were the first of both handler and dog since the 1970s, in Vietnam.[6] Deaths of specialized search dogs are extremely rare because of their high rate of success in finding explosive devices. And the training at Lackland Air Force Base, where Kory and Cooper spent twenty-two weeks, continues to advance, meaning that the dogs are getting better.

Colonel Iverson told reporters to focus not on their lost lives, but on the number of lives *saved* by their work. "The casualties that have been avoided among civilians and military in Afghanistan and Iraq is immense," he said. "These canine team detachments bring a unique capability that we have not really seen used in the military since Vietnam. The demand for these teams is very high." It is no wonder because, as he also said, the dog teams have discovered "well over one hundred thousand pounds of munitions, weapons, IEDs, caches, and mines."

"They are a combat multiplier in high demand," Iverson said.

---

[5] Peter Bergen, "The Taliban, Regrouped and Rearmed," The Washington Post, September 10, 2006, B4

[6] Military Dog Handlers Killed in Action:
Sgt. Adam L. Cann, USMC, January 5, 2006
T.Sgt. Jason Norton, USAF, January 22, 2006
Cpl. Dustin J. Lee, USMC, March 21, 2007
Cpl. Kory D. Wiens, U.S. Army, July 6, 2007
Military Working Dogs Killed In Action:
MWD Marco, USAF, January 20, 2007
MWD Cooper, U.S. Army, July 6, 2007
MWD Arras, USAF, September 25, 2007

"Corporal Wiens' unit was trained to a very high standard. It is just a phenomenal program. There is zero room for error. It is either 100 percent or nothing. If they are not at 100 percent, they simply do not go."

The relationship between Kory and Cooper was very close. "It was as close a relationship as you can imagine," he said, pausing, perhaps to consider his own words. "They were inseparable."

There is a huge need for non-canine ways of combating IEDs, and some are already in place, but they are so new that their effectiveness has not yet been established. An instrument called ICE, the IED Countermeasures Equipment, and the Warlock, use low-power radio frequency energy to block the signals of radio controlled detonators such as cell phones, satellite phones, and long-range cordless telephones. The JIN, Joint IED Neutralizer, and the NIRF, Neutralizing Improvised Explosive Devices with Radio Frequency, produce a high-frequency field that can neutralize IED electronics at a distance. A system code-named PING is now being utilized and shows great promise. It sends out electromagnetic waves to penetrate the walls of buildings to detect IEDs, and can be carried with the unit in their Humvee.

None of those things are yet in wide enough use to prevent the blast that killed Kory and Cooper.

Kory was born September 6, 1986, in Albany, Oregon. He was the middle son of three boys, born between Kevin and Kyle. He had one older sister, Lindsay. He was named after his grandfather who was a canine handler during the Korean War.

Here are some of the things Kory told me about himself: he was a member of the Boy Scouts of America, Pack 38 in Independence, Oregon. He was a wrestler and quarterback of the football team at West Albany High School. He worked as a fast-food restaurant manager. He graduated in 2005 and enlisted to gain experience for pursuing a career in law enforcement. He received an Army Achievement Medal for going above and beyond the Army's standards. He liked to customize his vehicles, especially his beloved, supercharged, two-door, hardtop 1972 Dodge Dart Swinger. He had a full life and much to look forward to.

One of his best friends at Fort Leonard Wood was a veterinary technician, Specialist Shem Umana. He said Kory had sought him out as a friend in order to quiz him about health care for Cooper. "Kory felt as long as he's with his dog, he's OK, he's the happiest guy. As long as Cooper was right there by his side, he felt he could accomplish anything."

Kory's company commander, Captain Danielle Roche, said, "Other handlers would put their dogs up in the kennel; Kory never did. He and Cooper were always together, always playing, training, doing everything and anything together."

A crowd gathered early Monday morning, July 16, 2007, at the Corvallis Municipal Airport to welcome their native son and his dog home. They stood quietly in Oregon's typical July weather; warm, a bit cloudy, but the sun as intense as it ever gets this far from the equator. Along the perimeter fence, a long procession of motorcycles, the Patriot Guard Riders, waited with engines off, their riders carrying large American flags. The Patriot Guard's mission is to prevent any sort of disruption at the service of an American fallen hero. Today, their only duty was to honor. No one in northwest Oregon wanted to interrupt this sad ending.

On the tarmac, sixty friends and family members settled into small groups, joined by police, firemen, airport workers, and various members of the public. Each held a small American flag. All eyes lifted when the small, white, chartered Dassault Falcon jet came into view. It came to a stop before the silent crowd. The Patriot Guard stood at attention, flags raised.

The honor guard of seven soldiers in formal uniform lined up by twos on the tarmac. One soldier stood at attention at the back. The cargo door swung up, and a small, blond-colored wood box and American flag, folded into a triangle with the white stars and blue field showing, was passed to them. In slow cadence, the soldiers moved to a maroon Chevy Suburban from the Dallas Mortuary Tribute Center, and placed the box and flag inside.

Patrol cars, cars loaded with family, friends, and the Patriot Guard linked into a procession that headed north toward Highway 34 for the forty minute drive to Kory's hometown, Dallas. Today, the route took somewhat longer, with a detour past Kory's alma mater, West Albany High School, where the flag was set at half-staff. A sign in front read In memory of Cpl. Kory Wiens, 1986-2007, and Cooper. Faculty, employees, Principal Susie Osborn and another military guard watched the procession. The motorcade continued to Tallmadge Middle School in Independence, and then on to the Dallas Mortuary Tribute Center.

At 10 a.m. Wednesday, most of the same crowd assembled at Faith Evangelical Free Church, "A Friendly Church with a Faithful Message." After the service, there was another procession, to the Salt Creek Cemetery, where a military honor guard saluted as the hero was laid to rest. The family felt that Kory would not have wanted to be separated from his canine partner. Cooper's ashes were buried with him.

All that was left behind of this twenty-year-old boy now was his page on MySpace, on which he'd written, "About me: My name is Kory Wiens, I like to work on trucks and cars. Im from Albany Oregon. I live in Missoure because Im in the Army. Stuck in Fort Leonard Wood with nothing to do. I love my dog that I have here, he is the best thing in Ft. Leonard Wood. My job is to play with him all day! The other good thing about this place is that I can go 4x4 when ever I want! Well not in FLW anymore!!! Now Im in Iraq!!!!! Hopefulley I will be In Oregon in September! Well if you want to know anything about me then just message me."

He'd returned to Oregon early; it was July.

If the writer of these words sounds bitter about his death, I am.

LEAVE NO MAN
BEHIND

"**YOU CAN ONLY** call me, 'H,'" the voice on the phone said. "I can't give you many details. I can't tell you exactly where this happened or anybody's name. You still want to hear the story?"

"Of course." This situation had come up many times before; soldiers told me they'd been ordered not to speak about a particular mission. The military wanted to keep details of a particular skirmish confidential. The standard explanation was that information was withheld for "security reasons." No one wants to compromise the security of any American soldier, and I wasn't trying to break news stories. I was writing a book about dogs. So I never pushed. But I often wondered if the withholding had to do with secret equipment and undercover spies, or was really a case of keeping an embarrassing incident out of the press. When the blanket of military silence falls over an event, there's no way to know.

The message I'd put out on the Internet had drawn few responses. "Looking for stories of brave MWDs," I wrote. When I'd circulated a similar message last year for my book *Paws & Effect: The Healing Power of Dogs*, e-mails and calls had poured in from people eager to talk about their healing dogs. Not this time. Later, a few handlers I got to know told me they'd seen my message and even joked about it. "Hey, Johnson, why don't you tell about nearly dropping Wolf out of the chopper?"

"The only way that's a story is if they're playing it on *Saturday Night Live*," another handler grumbled.

There were a lot of reasons the handlers didn't respond. A sort of comradely consensus that war dog stories belonged only to war dog handlers. Fear of being accused of being boastful. Or, possibly because the working dog handlers were in general poor writers, they didn't like typing out long messages. It was hard to drag up a name, and extremely difficult to track the person down and actually hook up with them on a telephone. I'd spent days, and weeks, and months chasing handlers that way. So the answer to my caller was no, I didn't mind not having the details. I'd settle for a good story.

"I'm flying TRAP with a CH-46," H said. Translation: I'm part of a helicopter crew making Tactical Recovery of Aircraft and Personnel using the Boeing Sea Knight tandem rotor cargo chopper. (I didn't want to interrupt him; I looked it up later.)

He spoke with disgust about the dust in Iraq; it was summer there and very dry, and the landing and taking off of choppers was the perfect way to stir it up. "I'm going nuts from dust," H said. "It gets on everything, all the equipment, into the weapons, your underwear, covers the chow. Sometimes I can even feel it on my teeth."

Other than that, he said, morale in his group was high. They were deployed out of California, but didn't miss home just yet. The air base in California meant endless training and drills; in Iraq, you were doing what you had trained for. "Some people enlist and never get a war," H said. It sounded like something the drill instructor told him.

"And you're a dog handler?" I prompted.

"No, no," he said quickly. "This is a story about a dog handler."

Okay.

They flew missions every night, H said. He couldn't say where. "You probably wouldn't even know the name of the place," he told me.

That was doubtful. I'm addicted to the news from Iraq the way my sports-loving friend Kaiser is addicted to the Giants. I can name every military base and major battle as quickly as he can recite the Giant's win-loss history and the name of every offensive tackle, tight end, and wide receiver.

"We were on an ASR[1] into a town where there'd been a lot of fighting, and all we knew was we were going to pick up these Marines. There were one dead, one injured, and four others. We were running late because our first stage hydraulic pump had dumped out on us. There was no hydraulic pressure getting to the main rotor and tail rotor servos.[2] There was no backup crew. This was a busy night and everybody was out. They were expecting another phrog[3] and they were going to send both of us out after these Marines.

"So we were getting anxious while the mechanics worked on it. Our pilot, we call 'Boss,' is a lot older and mean." This probably meant he was thirty. "He was mad as hell about being

---

[1] Assault Support Request.

[2] An automatic device that can sense errors and make adjustments to correct the performance of a mechanism. The cruise control on your car is a servo.

[3] Nickname for the CH-46 Boeing Sea Knight helicopter.

stuck when Marines out there needed us. He walked up and down cursing out the mechanics. It wasn't their fault. Finally we get underway.

"We get to the LZ[4] after midnight. There are no lights and we can only see with NVGs.[5] And nobody's there. Here we rushed like hell to get over here, and looks like they humped out or else somebody else picked them up. The pilot is on the radio trying to figure out what's going on. He's even more mad now."

All you could tell was that there'd been a big battle there, H said. Concrete sidewalks and walls were smashed from rocket-propelled grenade and mortar hits. There were dark lumps of ash in the street that used to be cars. All the buildings closest to them had suffered lots of shrapnel. He said, "We fly like this every night and we're usually not afraid. But this place… we wanted to get the hell out of there."

Just then, he heard the pilot say, "You sent me out here for a *dog?*" and at the same time, here came four Marines. Two were carrying a small body bag. One was limping, and alongside him was a German Shepherd, who also seemed to be limping.

The pilot hadn't seen them yet. He turned around and yelled to his crew, "They sent us out here for a goddam *dog.*" Then he saw the group, about twenty meters away, and shut up.

It was the way they were carrying the body that stuck in H's mind. He said he'd picked up a lot of body bags in his three months in Iraq, enough not to be squeamish or reflective about it. You did the job and got them out of there. He didn't really find the right words to describe what he saw, but I think what he was witnessing was the outward form of affection. He said

[4] Landing Zone.

[5] Night Vision Goggles.

they were carrying the bag very gently, and as they came in, he noticed that all four heads were downcast. No one made eye contact. They didn't even speak. Even the German Shepherd looked depressed.

By now, he'd figured out that the small body was that of a dog. He and the other gunner jumped out and tried to take the body bag from them and load it, the way they had dozens of times before. But the Marines waved them off. One handed him a Molle pack. Then all four of them lifted the dead dog onto the chopper, even though it would have been easy for just one man to do it. "It was like a ceremony," H said. "You wished you weren't even there. I had to look away."

The Marines loaded and he and the tail gunner buckled them in. The injured dog lay at their feet.

H said the marines they pick up from battle zones are often filled with relief and want to talk and joke around. Or sometimes they're tired and fall asleep. But not these Marines. It was over an hour back to base, and all four sat with their heads bent. It made it look like the back of the phrog was a church, or some kind of sacred place. The pilot kept looking back, but did not say a word. Normally he might have cussed them out and told them they were assholes. But he too was silent.

They landed and a vehicle was waiting to take the dogs to the kennels. "Some boxkicker jumps on board and goes to grab the body bag," H said. "I yelled at him to leave it alone. I wanted to move the dog myself. I went to pick it up and somebody else came up by my shoulder. It was Boss."

Boss had never offered to do something as lowly as unpack the bird. But he lifted the bag reverently, and the two men carried it out past the rotor arc to the waiting vehicle. Two of the combat Marines took it from them and gently put it inside.

In a spontaneous moment of insight, Boss and H saluted. One of the dog handlers said, "Thank you," and everybody went back to work.

Boss snapped, "I hope you treated that Marine with honor and respect."

H said, "Yes, sir, we did." They both knew he was referring to the dog. The MWD had gone from "that goddam dog" to a full-fledged Marine in less than an hour, based just on Boss's observation about how the other Marines felt about their fallen partner.

H says he thinks about that silent flight a lot. To him, it was a perfect metaphor for his loyalty to the service. It gave him faith, he said, "that when the Marines say, 'We leave no man behind,' we mean it. That dog was as much a Marine as any of us. And that handler... he'd lost his dog, his friend, his partner. The dog handlers have a close relationship with those dogs. They spend more time with them than they do with their wives."

H says he believes Boss came to be proud of belonging to an organization that would send out a chopper for a fallen Marine, even though that Marine was a dog. He's as aware as they all are of the work the dogs do, how they signal the presence of IEDs and other explosives and prevent more Marines from getting killed. He figures it is honorable work, and deserves respect.

"Got to go now," H said, coming quickly to the end of the story. He was uncomfortable with all he had told me. He wasn't sure if he'd violated some code of silence, or took my position that a story like that deserved a wider audience.

Here are the names of some of the K-9s currently at work in Iraq: Rico, Tasja, Eddy, Ben, Tako, Exa, Don, Fido, Ajax, Jacco, Rody, Charque, another Ben, Oran, Crock, Allen, Eesau, Fannie, Jag, Arno, Jaso, Petya, Diego, Cir, Riki, Valya, Rexo, Cezar, Natz,

Jecky, Alex, Iwan, Beny, Blacky, Danny, Rocky, Uli, Leo, Albert, Brit, Rico, Sonja, Jecky, Zimbal, Polo, Cezar, Torro, Zimbal, and Amber.

The Marine Corps' motto is also a description of their dogs: "*Semper Fidelis.*" It means *always faithful.*

Come home safe. We're waiting for you.

SEARCH AND RESCUE: SO THAT OTHERS MAY LIVE

THE CANOPY of tall trees filtered sunlight into shades of pale green and cooled the forest floor beneath my back. When I shifted position, rough leaves crackled beneath my shoulders, and little ferns danced along the outline of my legs. I tried not to move, because I was supposed to be hiding. I didn't want to alert the search dog by making any sound. An unconscious person wouldn't be able to do that. The dog was supposed to track victims with his nose.

Little songbirds darted through the branches of this Jockey Hollow State Park, brown chested martins and blue-headed vireos and my favorite, barn swallows. A barn swallow is identifiable by its tailfeathers, which take the shape of a pitchfork. My grandfather taught me that at his farm in Robbinsville, New Jersey, when I was five years old. Then I heard the dog.

He was crashing through low branches, leaping dead logs, and I could sense his enthusiasm as he plowed his way toward me. He came within thirty feet of where I lay, in the sheltering roots of an elderly scarlet oak. He passed me without a pause.

Now what? Jump up and let the handler know he'd failed to find me? Or wait and give him another chance? Lulled by the quiet forest, I decided there was no need to rush. I'd lie here in a pleasant reverie and see what happened.

After a few minutes, I heard two voices approaching on the trail. "Behind that tree," said Donna Hruniak, training director of New Jersey Rescue & Recovery K-9 Unit. She was pointing out where she'd directed me to hide. "He was too far downwind," said Denise Grimm, president of the unit, and the one handling Maverick, the German Shepherd who was supposed to find me. I peeked out at the two women. Donna took a container of baby powder from a fanny pack and sprinkled it in the air. The women watched as it dispersed in a southerly direction, then decided to take the dog south of me, where the wind would bring him my scent.

Maverick started to weave back and forth, more deliberately this time, and suddenly his head jerked up. I tightened my grip on the two tennis balls. When he found me and barked, these balls would be his reward. He circled the tree and stopped and looked down, his hot breath across my face. He seemed to be thinking. Then he barked.

Denise ran up and ordered, "Throw the ball!" It bounced across the ground and Maverick chased it eagerly. For about ten minutes, we played with him, tossing the balls and yanking on the plastic ropes attached to them for a game of tug of war, telling him what a good, brilliant, first-rate, superb search dog he was. We rambled back to the parking lot to meet up with other members of the group. Maverick kept coming back and poking me with his nose. I think he wanted me to get lost so he could find me again.

"It's fun but it's serious," said Denise. "You get to spend a lot of time outdoors with your dog. This is hard work which requires a lot of your own time and money."

Eric Martin, president of the New Jersey Search & Rescue Council, said, "Canine handlers spend ten thousand to fifty thousand dollars to get a fully operational dog. Once they do, there's an incredible bond between them." Denise and Maverick train at least twice a week. This group meets twice a month, but all six women belong to other SAR units, which train on alternate weekends, like the Palisades Search and Rescue Dog Organization, the Ramapo Rescue Dog Association, West Jersey K-9 SAR, and the big kahuna of Search and Rescue, New Jersey Task Force One.

Denise told me, "Very few handlers wind up on a disaster team doing 9/11 type work—most do local wilderness searches for lost kids, people with Alzheimer's, hunters, hikers, people missing from nursing homes, suicidal folks, things like that."

In order to join an SAR team, you need certificates in First Aid and CPR and skill in compass navigation, search methodology, and radio communications. Physical fitness is important; real searches go on for hours without a break. Two things set state and federal task forces apart; they usually respond to urban emergencies rather than wilderness ones. The terrorist attack on the World Trade Center towers is the most dramatic example, but there is also the bombing of the federal building in Oklahoma City in 1995, Hurricane Katrina in New Orleans in 2005, and tornadoes, mudslides, and earthquakes wherever they occur around the world.

Secondly, the requirements for joining a Task Force are rigorous. Potential members must crawl through a twenty-foot-long culvert, and upon reaching the end, crawl the length backwards; ascend a thirty-five-foot extension ladder; carry a fifty-pound box two hundred feet without putting it down; remove a forty-eight-pound hydraulic rescue tool from the lift gate of a truck, set it on the ground, and put it back, ten times in two minutes; walk an elevated, twelve-foot-long, four-by-four beam without stepping off. Once a member, your dog must be recertified in the work every year to guarantee that he's truly qualified.

Volunteers travel constantly to take the most up-to-date courses. From a quick Internet search, these courses were coming up: Basic Land Cadaver Search Techniques for K-9s, offered in Nineveh, Indiana. SAR Dog Training, Tracking, First Responder, Disaster K-9,

Cadaver, Disaster Recovery, Water Search Communications and Disaster Management, in Stroudsburg, Pennsylvania. International Detector Dogs Congress in Barcelona, Spain. Trailing, Air Scent, Cadaver, Water Cadaver, Equine SAR, Chiropractic for the Working Dog, and NIMS Crime Scene Preservation, in Potosi, Missouri.

How often you get called out has a lot to do with how highly the local police, rescue squads, park officers, and fire personnel think of you. So teams try to obtain certification from the National Association of Search and Rescue (NASAR), which is meticulous in its testing but brings consistency to squads throughout the country.

A more recent development in SAR is enthusiasm for finding dead bodies. "A dog trained in cadaver search will go right past live bodies," Denise says. "You try to train for one or the other. Some dogs can do both. But a dog that has been imprinted on one type of scent is more accurate than a cross-trained dog."

Denise has hidden a plastic jar that contains a human hipbone in another part of the woods, and now it's Donna's turn to train her dog, Sabre, in HRD (Human Remains Detection). Sabre flies down a park trail, his nose stretched up in the air. I think it's a strange way to search, until he hits his find—Denise lodged the hipbone in a high branch, which meant the scent cone would descend over a large area and become more intense as the dog lifted his head towards it. Now it's Sabre's turn to romp and play, his reward for his find.

HRD dogs find buried bodies, pieces of bone, blood evidence, and residual scents in the wilderness and at collapsed buildings, fire-gutted structures, burned vehicles, and crime scenes. They search for any evidence with human scent on it, which could be decomposing flesh or body fluids. These scents might be on an article, the actual body, in the ground, or residual to it. Dogs who can find dead bodies can be called by the police to find forensic evidence at a crime scene. Since there are crimes every day, a cadaver dog may have more opportunities to be called than a wilderness search dog, who is only called when someone is lost.

"People don't get lost as often as they used to anymore," Denise says. "They have GPS and cellphones. They call and say, 'Mommy, come pick me up!' And, more police departments have dogs. They use their own resource." The successful integration of detector dogs into all aspects of society has left individual dogs and handlers with less to do. "We get on average one search a month for lost persons. But it varies. Three weeks ago, we got three calls in one day."

A volunteer group in California, Canine Specialized Search Team, works with the Santa Clara Coroner's Office to sniff out forensic evidence. The whole country is swept up in an epidemic of enthusiasm for forensics, based on reality crime shows like *Cops* and dramas like *CSI: Crime Scene Investigation* and *Law & Order*. One of the CSST members, Adela Morris, is a consultant on *CSI*.

SAR volunteer groups often contain some military veterans, some police, and many firemen. But far more of the volunteers in K-9 SAR are people who were working with their dogs in other areas, like tracking competitions, hunting trials, agility matches, dock diving, and schutzhund, a dog sport developed in Germany to test dogs' fitness for police work. Denise discovered SAR when "somebody mentioned 'search and rescue' at an obedience class. I'd always done things with my dogs. I liked training them. I wanted to get involved. My first mentor told me, 'If you want to train the dog, stay with obedience. This is not about the dog; it's about both of you. This is a team effort.'"

SAR team members truly enjoy getting their dogs mission ready. An additional benefit is that the work they do is of great service to the community. Blessed are they whose passionate interest intersects a true human need.

Denise's dog in 1997 was a Rottweiler named Phoenix, who had structural problems that required surgery. "I went to a weekend with the Pennsylvania Search and Rescue Council and they said, 'Why don't you try HRD with her? It's less demanding.' She became my first cadaver dog."

Phoenix quickly obtained her national cadaver dog certification. "I was training five days a week. I had a job that was very flexible, so I had the time." Denise is a research scientist who was working on medication to cure arteriosclerosis.

The next thing she tried was training Phoenix to find bodies underwater. Movies from Hollywood always let the hero escape the hounds by splashing through a creek or swimming across a river. But the idea that dogs can't detect smells through water is false. It was probably thought up by a human scriptwriter who realized that he couldn't smell through water, therefore, how would a dog be able to do it? But water is a good conductor of scent. "The scent molecules work their way up through the water molecules, sort of like smoke in a chimney," one handler told me.

Phoenix and Denise were called to a lake in Pennsylvania where a fourteen-year-old Asian boy had disappeared. "He'd been walking in the water close to the shore, but he came to a place where a ledge dropped off and he couldn't swim. There were witnesses who knew where the boy had gone down. We had three dogs there are the time. They split us up into different areas. I went out in the most high probability area.

"This was my first search. I was completely green. I'd never been out on a search before. We got in a boat, and at one spot, Phoenix started pawing. I thought she was barking at a buoy. I told her to leave it alone. Then, I thought she was focused on ducks. I got her to leave them alone. We made a couple of passes through the area. At the same spot, she got excited and started grabbing at the bumper. I figured out some landmarks on the shoreline and the distance to where we were. Because what you want to do is delineate an area for a diver. A whole lake is hard to search.

If you can get down to one hundred foot by one hundred foot, that helps. The divers went out the next morning. They found the body exactly where she alerted. To pinpoint it like that, I thought it was one in a million. But she ended up having six water finds. Once we got there, she never wanted to take a break. She wanted to stay on the search."

As Denise drove home from work on the terrible afternoon of Tuesday, September 11, 2001, the day of the terrorist attack on the World Trade Center, she got a call from Bruce Barton of Rescue International, asking if she could bring Phoenix in that night to search the pile. "I was surprised because FEMA was taking control, and we weren't members of that. But Bruce said he had a contact who specifically requested cadaver dogs." She told him that Phoenix's legs were not up to climbing the rubble, which rose several stories high. "She can't handle that." Many SAR dogs from all over the country combed through the pile at Ground Zero. But there were no live finds to be made. There were no injured from the collapse of the towers. Only the dead.

Two days later, Denise was directed to Fresh Kills landfill on Staten Island. "It was hush-hush. They told us to keep it quiet so the media didn't get hold of it. They only wanted certain dogs. Phoenix was one of them."

Denise worried about going to Fresh Kills. It is one of the largest refuse dumps in the world. The site takes up 4.6 square miles on Staten Island. Twenty barges, each carrying 650 tons of garbage, arrived at it every day up until March 2001, when it was closed. The top was already taller than the Statue of Liberty.

Denise and Phoenix were cleared onto the site and an FBI agent was assigned to oversee their work. "I remember when we first pulled in, the smell of jet fuel and death was overwhelming. How could you train for something like this? The guys with earthmovers would take a shovel full from huge piles and spread it out, and FBI, NYPD, and CIA would go through it with little rakes on their hands and knees. If they found something, they would call the dog over.

"My trained indication was bark, but there were human remains everywhere. She would have been barking all the time. All she did was paw at the area or make eye contact with me. A lot of times you had to pull out a bone with a shirt wrapped around it. Or blood in a shoe. It varied but when we got there, she was indicating six or seven times an hour.

"Then, you called over the support person who put it in a bucket and labeled it with your number, 'Dog Team 6,' because the FBI was very strict on accuracy. The dogs had to be 60 percent accurate. The support person would take it to the examiners, and they would log it in. They would check to make sure it was human. A lot of dogs were indicating on food or ribs or something from the Windows on the World restaurant. If you kept bringing that in, that was the end of you. You were not invited to come back. The dogs weren't necessarily wrong, if they alerted on a piece of bread and a body had been lying next to it; the bread would have absorbed the smell. No one told me our accuracy rate. But we were always asked to come back."

In all, sixty dog teams worked Fresh Kills. Denise was glad she could drive fifty minutes and be home. "You were wiped out by the end of the day. I never went back two days in a row. I went every other day. It was demanding emotionally and physically."

The work went on for four months. Phoenix was eager to get to the site each day. "She had an incredible work ethic. She never got tired. I believe the largest find I had was an arm with a wedding ring still on the finger. Mostly it was very small stuff, just bits of bone. I would always have to peel clothing away to see what was there. You couldn't tell. You knew it was fabric, but you couldn't tell where the fabric ended and the body began."

Because of the hard work of cadaver dogs at Fresh Kills, many families were able to bury their loved ones. NASA officials called dog teams in 2003 when the space shuttle *Columbia* exploded before landing. Canines found human remains across a wide swath of Texas. California dogs searched for the body of Laci Peterson after she went missing in December, 2002. Her husband Scott was eventually found guilty of her murder. Dogs led law enforcement officials to forensic evidence that helped convict him. Now, dogs are entering the field of archeology, because handlers discovered they are able to pick up the smell of ancient bodies. Eva Cecil, owner of a Border Collie named Nessie, says, "The age of human skeletal remains does not seem to be a factor in the trained canine's ability to detect scent." Nessie proved that by finding a mass grave in Europe from 1860, where Napoleon and his French army had battled Prussians. She found skeletal remains dated to 450 A.D. at a site in Prague. In 2005, in Montana, she located the unmarked grave of Lolo, a fur trapper from the mid 1800s, along the Lewis and Clark Trail.

In every situation, through every tragedy, dogs have brought a sense of purpose and a touch of grace to our lives. Even in the most desperate situations, they bring out the kind and generous sides of our natures. We have the ability to reach out and help another member of our clan, but because we're busy, or tired, or expecting payment, we don't always do it. But dogs do. This is where the idea that dogs can protect and defend man has landed. Red Cross medics used them to find war wounded, military working dog handlers use them to find explosives, police use them to find criminals, and now, one of the widest uses of detector dogs is by volunteers who use them to find lost hikers and drowning victims.

Dogs have spent years teaching us the meaning of unconditional love. Now, they are teaching us the true, selfless spirit of volunteerism. We have a lot to learn.

FOR MORE INFORMATION

STUBBY
National Museum of American History
Smithsonian Institution
14th St. at Constitution Ave. NW
Washington, D.C.
Phone: (202) 633-1000 (voice/tape), (202) 633-5285 (TTY)
Web site: http://americanhistory.si.edu
info@si.edu

RETIRED MILITARY WORKING DOGS
People interested in adopting a military dog at the end of its service
    career may contact Lackland Air Force Base at 1-800-531-1066

UNITED STATES WAR DOGS ASSOCIATION, INC.
Ron Aiello, President
1313 Mt. Holly Road
Burlington, N.J. 08016
Phone: 609-747-9340
E-mail: ronaiello@uswardogs.org or canines@uswardogs.org
Web site: www.uswardogs.org

SPACE COAST WAR DOG ASSOCIATION
PO Box 254315
Patrick AFB, FL 32925
E-mail: admin@scwda.org
Web site: www.scwda.org

VIETNAM DOG HANDLERS ASSOCIATION
Web site: www.vdhaonline.org

U.S. CUSTOMS AND BORDER PROTECTION
1300 Pennsylvania Avenue, N.W.
Washington, D.C. 20229
Web site: www.cbp.gov/

U.S. DEPARTMENT OF AGRICULTURE, ANIMAL AND PLANT HEALTH INSPECTION SERVICE
For a list of food products which cannot be imported to the United
States: www.aphis.usda.gov

STATE FARM ARSON DOG PROGRAM
PR/Marketing Unit, B-4
State Farm Insurance Companies
One State Farm Plaza
Bloomington, IL 61710-0001
Phone: 309-766-2259 or 309-766-8866
Fax: 309-766-2259
E-mail: dawn.fones.cv9s@statefarm.com

ATF CANINE TRAINING AND OPERATIONS SUPPORT BRANCH
122 Cavalry Drive
Front Royal, Va. 22630
Phone: 540-622-6560

HARTSDALE PET CEMETERY

75 North Central Park Avenue

Hartsdale, N.Y. 10530

Phone: (914) 949-2583 or (800) 375-5234

Fax: (914) 949-2872

E-mail: info@petcem.com

U.S. ARMY QUARTERMASTER MUSEUM

Building 5218, A Avenue and 22nd Street

Fort Lee, Virginia

(804) 734-4203

www.qmmuseum.lee.army.mil

N.J. RESCUE AND RECOVERY, K-9 UNIT

Denise Grimm / Donna Hruniak

(732) 742-4050

www.njrescue-recoveryk9.org

N.J. TASK FORCE ONE

NJ-TF1 provides advanced technical search and rescue capabilities to
victims trapped or entombed in structurally collapsed buildings

www.state.nj.us/njoem/taskforce1/contact_info.html

SEARCH AND RESCUE COUNCIL
OF NEW JERSEY

P.O. Box 397

Fanwood, NJ 07023

www.sarcnj.org

info@sarcnj.org

BIBLIOGRAPHY

BOOKS

American Rescue Dog Association. *Search and Rescue Dogs: Training the K-9 Hero.* Howell Book House, 1991.

Amin, Hussein. *The Sad Muslim's Guide.* Cairo: Madboly Library, 1987.

Bauer, Nona Kilgore. *Dog Heroes of September 11th: A Tribute to America's Search and Rescue Dogs.* N.J.: Kennel Club Books, 2006.

Behan, John M. *Dogs of War.* New York: Scribner's, 1946.

The Brown Treesnake Control Committee. *The Brown Treesnake Control Plan.* Honolulu: U.S. Fish and Wildlife Service, Aquatic Nuisance Species Task Force. Honolulu, 1996.

Burnam, John C. *Dog Tags of Courage: Combat Infantrymen and War Dog Heroes in Vietnam.* 1st Books Library, 2006.

Burnam, John C. *Dog Tags of Courage: The Turmoil of War and the Rewards of Companionship.* Fort Bragg, GA: Lost Coast Press, 2000.

Cummins, Bryan D. *Colonel Richardson's Airedales.* Calgary, Alberta: Detselig Enterprises, 2003.

Downey, Fairfax. *Dogs for Defense.* New York: McDonald Press, 1955.

Grow, Malcolm C. *Surgeon Grow: An American in Russian Fighting.* New York: Frederick A. Stokes, 1918.

Jaffe, Eric. *And No Birds Sing: A True Ecological Thriller Set in a Tropical Paradise.* Newy York: Simon & Schuster, 1994.

Kelly, Kevin Sean. *The Diary of a Wilderness Mantracker.* 1st Books Library, 2004.

Kelly, Kevin Sean. *It Takes One to Catch One.* 1st Books Library, 2002.

Lemish, Michael. *War Dogs: A History of Loyalty and Heroism.* Dulles, Va.: Brassey's, 1999.

Martin, Edward C. *Dr. Johnson's Apple Orchard: The Story of America's First Pet Cemetery.* Hartsdale Canine Cemetery, 1997.

Morgan, Paul B. *K-9 Soldiers: Vietnam and After.* Central Point, Ore.: Hellgate, 1999.

Plutarch. *Vita Alexander* 61.3

Richardson, Lieut.Colonel E.H. *Forty Years with Dogs.* Philadelphia: David McKay Company, circa 1920s.

Rogers, Robert F. *Destiny's Landfall: A History of Guam.* Honolulu: University of Hawaii Press. 1995.

Sanderson, Jeannette. *War Dog Heroes: True Stories of Dog Courage in Wartime.* New York: Scholastic, Inc., 1997.

Snovak, Angela Eaton. *Guide to Search and Rescue Dogs.* Hauppauge, N.Y.: Barron's Educational Series, 2004.

Thurston, Elizabeth. *The Lost History of the Canine Race.* New York: Avon, 1997.

Wynne, William A. *Yorkie Doodle Dandy: Or, the Other Woman Was a Real Dog.* Ohio: Wynnesome Press, 1996.

Young, Rick. *Combat Police: U.S. Army Military Police in Vietnam.* 1st Books Library, 2002.

ARTICLES

Alexander, Tiffani. "A Firefighter's Best Friend: Arson Dogs." *Fire & Arson Investigator,* Online. Firehouse.com, August 8, 2003.

Cross, Elysa. "Mediterranean Fruit Flies Attempt to Sneak in—Again." *Customs and Border Protection Today Magazine,* October–November 2004.

Donohue, Pete. "Dogged Determination: MTA's K-9 Unit Sniffs Out Danger." *New York Daily News,* August 13, 2006.

Donohue, Pete. "Recruiting Foreign Dogs: Seek Terror Helpers Abroad."

New York Daily News, August 20, 2006.

Donn, Jeff. "When Dogs Go to War, They Get Care Worthy of Soldiers."
Associated Press, August 12, 2007.

Engeman, Richard M., Daniel S. Vice, Darryl York, and Kenneth S.
Gruver. "Sustained Evaluation of the Effectiveness of Detector Dogs
for Locating Brown Tree Snakes in Cargo Outbound from Guam."
International Biodeterioraation and Biodegradation, no. 49, 2002.

Fitzgerald, W. G. "The Dogs of War." Outlook Magazine, 1907.

Fones, Dawn. "Arson Dog Program Continues to Sniff Out Fraudulent
Fire Claims." Fire & Arson Investigator, January 2002.

Fritts, T.H., and D. Leasman-Tanner. "The Brown Treesnake on Guam:
How the Arrival of One Invasive Species Damaged the Ecology,
Commerce, Electrical Systems, and Human Health on Guam." www.
fort.usgs.gov/resources/education/bts/bts_home.asp, 2001.

Miles, Donna. "Military Working Dogs Protect Forces, Bases During
Terror War." American Forces Press Service, September 2, 2004.

"The Price of Freedom: Americans at War: Stubby." Armed Forces History,
Division of History of Technology, National Museum of American History Catalog,
Washington, D.C.

Reynolds, Jon K. "The Dogs of Georgetown." Georgetown Magazine,
September–October 1983.

Richardson, Major E. Hautonville. "War Dogs." Army and Navy Gazette,
October 18,1902.

St. George, Donna. "Wounded Sergeant Fights for a 'Best Friend.'"
Washington Post, November 20, 2005.

Snead, Cpl. Micah. "Marine and Devil Dog Survive IED Attack, Recover
Together." Jet Stream, Marine Corps Air Station Beaufort South Carolina,
February 10, 2006.

"Stubby of A.E.F. Enters Valhalla." New York Times, April 4, 1926.

Thomas, Colonel Thomas P. "Stubby the War Dog," Connecticut Military, nd.

Vice, Daniel S. and Richard M. Engeman. "Brown Tree Snake Discoveries
During Detector Dog Inspections Following Supertyphoon Paka."
USDA National Wildlife Research Center Staff Publications, University of

Nebraska, nd.

Willett, Anslee. "Explosive Critically Injures Peterson Sergeant in Baghdad." *Colorado Springs Gazette*, December 26, 2005.

"A Woman and Her Best Friend, Reunited; Yes, There Will Be a Dog in the First Lady's Box at the State of the Union." MSNBC.com, February 8, 2006.

WEB SITES

www.blogs.orlandosentinel.com/features_lifestyle_animal/2007/08/dogs-of-war.html#more

www.britannica.blog.com "Alexander and the Thrilla in Guagmela." Michael Feldman, April 2007

www.ct.gov/military, Connecticut Military Department, State of Connecticut

www.fsik9.com, Forensic & Scientific Investigations, David Latimer

www.k9fitness.blogspot.com, K-9 fitness, the animals who affect our lives, and the things that affect our animals' lives

www.qmfound.com, Quartermaster Foundation's Web site

www.si.com/history, National Museum of American History, part of the Smithsonian Instituion

www.smokywardog.com/Yorkie Doodle Dandy

www.soc.mil, Official Web site of the United States Army Special Forces Command

www.uswardogs.org, United States War Dogs Association, Inc.

www.vdhaonline.org, Vietnam Dog Handlers Association

VIDEO

Reid, Chip. *Injured Soldier and her War Dog*. NBC News, December 6, 2005.

War Dogs: America's Forgotten Heroes: The Untold Story of Dogs in Combat. GRB Entertainment. PBS, May 1999.